Adam's Fallacy

ADAM'S FALLACY

A GUIDE TO ECONOMIC THEOLOGY

Duncan K. Foley

THE BELKNAP PRESS OF
HARVARD UNIVERSITY PRE   **3 1336 07466 5747**
Cambridge, Massachusetts / London, England / 2006

ISBN-13: 978-0-674-02309-3
ISBN-10: 0-674-02309-9

The Cataloging-in-Publication data is available from the Library of Congress.

}

FOR MY COLLEAGUES

Acknowledgments

Michael Aronson of Harvard University Press, the editor with whom I have worked happily for more than twenty years, initially suggested my writing this book. His encouragement, support, and suggestions have been invaluable to me. I'd also like to thank Suzanne de Brunhoff, Nicholas Foley, Gerard M. Foley, Thomas R. Michl, Rosemary Waltzer, and Martin Weitzman, who read various draft versions of the manuscript and made many suggestions to improve it. Every page of this book has benefited from Mary Ellen Geer's copy editing. Sylvia Hewlett originated the course, "Theoretical Foundations of Political Economy," which prompted me to study these texts and write the lectures from which this book grew. Students who have taken courses based on this material at Barnard College, Columbia University, and Lang, the New School for Liberal Arts, have contributed greatly to my understanding through their questions, discussions, and papers.

Contents

Preface

People ask me from time to time to recommend a good book on economics for educated but nonspecialist readers. I tend to be stumped by this question. There are innumerable fat introductory textbooks, crammed (now) with graphics and pop-up boxes, which trudge through the standard Economics 101 curriculum but in my view are unreadable as books. I usually wind up pointing to the classic book *The Worldly Philosophers* by my late colleague at the New School for Social Research, Robert Heilbroner. It might be a better idea to leave this problem in Heilbroner's capable hands, but the book you hold is an attempt to explain the core ideas of economics from my own point of view. Obedient to the dictum that each equation in an economics book loses half the readership, I have relegated both equations and graphs to an appendix which the reader is positively invited, if not instructed, to skip over, unless uncontrollable curiosity takes over.

For many years I taught a course, "Theoretical Foundations of Political Economy," at Barnard College of Columbia University. The subject matter of this course had evolved in discussions in the Economics Department drawing from Sylvia Hewlett's original ideas, and in my version the students were asked to read original excerpts from Adam Smith, Thomas Malthus, David Ricardo, Karl Marx, William Stanley Jevons, Carl Menger, John Bates Clark, and John Maynard Keynes. This course filled a gap for most students, who came out of it understanding economics not just as a collection of graphs and facts, but as a coherent dialogue; the course provided a kind of map on which students could locate the landmarks of economic language and ideas. After a while I put my lectures into written form, and they became the core of the present book. I later taught a version of this course at Lang, the New School for Liberal Arts, broadening it to include works by Thorstein Veblen, Friedrich von Hayek, and Joseph Schumpeter. The reactions of my students convinced me that these were worthwhile and compelling additions to the original reading list.

This is not, however, a book on the history of economic thought proper. It uses a historical perspective as a happy way to organize a complex set of ideas into a coherent and understandable story. It reflects much reading and teaching of particular texts in the history of economic thought, but I am far from an expert or a deep scholar of this extensive and demanding subject. In places I have ventured beyond the texts of the authors in question and pursued my own imaginative reconstruction of debates behind the debates, and the sometimes unconscious ground from which political economic knowledge arose. This is my own take on economics, and exploits the great figures in the history of political economy shamelessly for my own ends. Be warned.

Three questions are bound to be asked, given the title of this book. First of all, what do I mean by "Adam's Fallacy"? Adam Smith says many things in *The Wealth of Nations* that are not fallacious. For example, it is undoubtedly true that self-interest is a powerful motivating force for human beings (though far from being the only one). It is also true that harnessing the pursuit of self-interest through competitive capitalist markets can be (though it is not invariably) a powerful mechanism for fostering progressive technical change and producing material wealth. It would be far from correct to claim that all pursuit of self-interest through competitive markets is morally bad. By "Adam's Fallacy" I mean something a little more subtle than these much-debated claims. For me the fallacy lies in the idea that it is possible to separate an economic sphere of life, in which the pursuit of self-interest is guided by objective laws to a socially beneficent outcome, from the rest of social life, in which the pursuit of self-interest is morally problematic and has to be weighed against other ends. This separation of an economic sphere, with its presumed specific principles of organization, from the much messier, less determinate, and morally more problematic issues of politics, social conflict, and values, is the foundation of political economy and economics as an intellectual discipline. Thus to my mind Adam's Fallacy is the kernel of political economy and economics. A full understanding of the arguments of the great economists requires seeing them in the context of this dubious division. In fact, as I hope this book will demonstrate, political economy and economics is at its heart an attempt to come to terms with this dualistic view of social life.

Second, is it true that Adam Smith committed this fallacy? A better qualified scholar of Adam Smith could make this case textually on the basis of *The Wealth of Nations* more persuasively than I can, starting from Smith's discussion of self-love as a powerful motivator of human action (Book I, chapter 2), continuing with his characterization of frugal wealth-owners as public benefactors (Book II, chapter 3), and culminating in his famous invocation of the "invisible hand" (Book IV, chapter 2). But I would argue that it is more to the point that everyone who reads *The Wealth of Nations* comes away believing that Smith presents the world through the lens of what I have called his fallacy. Smith is too clever and too wily to present the fallacy in its barest form; his political economic world of self-regulating competitive self-interest actually depends crucially on innumerable value-laden political contingencies and institutions. Smith's qualifications of the principle of laissez-faire, for example, wind up presenting a reasonably balanced view of the interaction of politics and the economy. But the premise of Smith's book is that it makes sense to start with the examination of purely economic principles that arise from the interaction of self-interested individuals in the context of competitive markets for privately owned commodities. As I try to show in this book, his successors' investigations and discoveries are already inherent in Smith's conception of the political economic problem.

Third, is the "Fallacy" as I conceive of it indeed a fallacy? Here I think the thesis of my book is bound to be controversial. Contemporary economics, which has grown into a major intellectual industry, is the direct successor of Adam Smith, and has deeply embedded within it the idea of a division between specifically economic and broader social and political spheres. The teaching of economics consistently reinforces the world-view I call Adam's Fallacy, sometimes explicitly in its treatment of the philosophical foundation of presumed economic laws and principles, and even more pervasively in implicit presumptions built into its models and theorems. Economists often describe this aspect of their work as teaching students to "think like economists." In this respect my book is a brief for a prosecution case. Thinking like an economist comes hard to many people, and I personally am grateful for that fact. I hope this book will show that the economic way of thinking is just as value-laden as any other way of thinking about society, and can foster dangerous mistakes of judgment.

I call this book a "guide to economic theology" to underline what seems to me the fundamental point that at its most abstract and interesting level, economics is a speculative philosophical discourse, not a deductive or inductive science. I have used the idea of Adam's Fallacy as an organizing point of view for similar reasons. The most important feature of Adam Smith's work is not what it tells us concretely about how the economy works (although it tells us a great deal about that), but its discussion of how we should feel about capitalist economic life and what attitude it might be reasonable for us to take toward the complicated and contradictory experience it affords us. These are discussions above all of faith and belief, not of fact, and hence theological. (Or ideological, but this favorite term of Marxist social sciences carries so much polemical baggage by now that I shy away from it.)

I think this is an interesting story. I find that I have spent (or misspent) a substantial part of my life contemplating it, teaching it, discussing it, and reflecting on it. I don't have conclusive answers to the questions I raise here, but I think they are important and inescapable. May the Invisible Hand guide you to the truth.

Adam's Fallacy

1 / Adam's Vision

The publication of Adam Smith's *The Wealth of Nations* in 1776 marks a turning point in political economy. Before Smith, political economy addressed problems of public policy and particularly public finance, seeking to advise sovereign governments how to manipulate and channel the wealth-creating power of markets to their direct advantage. Smith widened the perspective to embrace the much larger questions of how society can function productively, and the relation between economic institutions like the market and individuals' lives. In taking this step Smith consolidated, even if he did not initiate, a way of looking at modern society as made up of two spheres: an economic sphere of individual initiative and interaction, governed by impersonal laws that assure a beneficent outcome of the pursuit of self-interest; and the rest of social life, including political, religious, and moral interactions which require the conscious balancing of self-interest with social considerations. This division is the foundation of the liberal economic world-view that in one form or another has shaped political economy and economics as intellectual disciplines.

Adam Smith was a student and then a professor of moral philosophy at the University of Glasgow; his interests moved from moral philosophy proper to the sphere of political economy. He was part of the circle of the Scottish Enlightenment, a hotbed of liberal and progressive thinking in mid-eighteenth-century Europe. After the publication of *The Theory of Moral Sentiments* in 1759, the support of a patron allowed Smith to retire from active university teaching to travel and meet leading foreign political economists as part of his work on *An Inquiry into the Nature and Causes of the Wealth of Nations*.

Adam Smith was not the first political economist, nor indeed the first proponent of the ideas on economic life and policy that made him and his book famous and influential. Nor were his ideas about political economy remarkable for their technical discoveries, despite the tendency of modern economists to adopt him as a patron saint. Smith was a moral philosopher, and the secret of his powerful hold on our imagination lies in his accomplishing two intertwined purposes in his writing. He manages to put forward a clear vision of how capitalist society might develop, a vision that withstands the criticism of hindsight better than that of most of his contemporaries and successors. But he also addresses more directly than anyone else the central anxiety that besets capitalism—the question of how to be a good person and live a good and moral life within the antagonistic, impersonal, and self-regarding social relations that capitalism imposes. Smith asserts the apparently self-contradictory notion that capitalism transforms selfishness into its opposite: regard and service for others. Thus by being selfish within the rules of capitalist property relations, Smith promises, we are actually being good to our fellow human beings. With this amazing argument, Smith proposes to absolve us of the moral ambiguity and pain that haunt capitalist reality.

This is Adam's Fallacy. For many people it works as a rationalization for tolerance or active support of the fundamental institutions of capitalism, private property, and the market. But it is an argument that is logically fallacious (like a lot of Smith's purported arguments), and in the end it is unsatisfactory both morally and psychologically.

The moral fallacy of Smith's position is that it urges us to accept direct and concrete evil in order that indirect and abstract good may come of it. The logical fallacy is that neither Smith nor any of his successors has been able to demonstrate rigorously and robustly how private selfishness turns into public altruism. The psychological failing of Smith's rationalization is that it requires a strategy of wholesale denial of the real consequences of capitalist development, particularly the systematic imposition of costs on those least able to bear them, and the implacable reproduction of inequalities that divide people from one another in society.

Adam's Fallacy is all the more seductive and dangerous because Smith delivered it to the world wrapped in a cloud of sensible, often insightful, observations on the operation of capitalism. These observations address the grand themes of political economy: technical progress, the distribution of income, economic development through the accumulation of capital, and population growth. In the end there is no way, despite the efforts of Smith's successors in political economy, to sort out the economic good sense in his writing from the philosophical confusion, to separate a scientific core of truth in Smith's arguments from his moral philosophy. Political economy and economics since Smith have continued, as we will see, to combine the two lines of thought. Thus Adam's Fallacy is not just Smith's dubious moral argument, but the way of looking at capitalist economic life and relations that stems from it. Even a critic of capitalism like Karl Marx succumbs in the end to this aspect of Adam's Fallacy.

I believe that the only honest way to learn what political economy and economics have to say is to keep this problem of the intertwining of moral and scientific arguments in mind. If you are going to learn economics, you are going to learn economic theology along the way.

The Division of Labor

Adam Smith starts his discussion of the sources of the wealth of nations with the concept of the division of labor. Smith means by this the breaking down of useful production into a series of separate tasks, each of which can be accomplished separately from the others.

For Smith the primary effect of the division of labor is to increase labor productivity, the average amount of useful output available per hour or day of labor. Labor productivity is measured fundamentally as a ratio of the output of some particular good—pins, wheat, houses, cars, education—to the amount of labor required to produce it. Thus the basic measure of labor productivity in a firm or country or the whole world takes the form of statistics on the amount of wheat produced divided by the total number of labor hours devoted to producing wheat, or the number of automobiles produced divided by the total number of labor hours devoted to producing automobiles.

Since labor productivity and its rate of increase differ in sectors producing different products, we often want to take an average, or index, of labor productivity over a whole economy. Economists do this by adding up the value of the output of all sectors at actual market prices (the Gross Domestic Product, or GDP) and dividing by an index of prices relative to some base year to calculate real GDP (adjusted for price inflation).[1] Labor productivity can then be estimated by dividing the real GDP of an economy by its total labor input measured in hours or days of work or the number of employed workers.

Thus Smith argues that an important factor in determining labor productivity is the degree of division of labor, and that increases in the division of labor can lead to major increases in labor productivity, both in individual sectors and for an economy as a whole.

Advantages of the Division of Labor

Smith proposes three ways in which the division of labor increases labor productivity: the increase in dexterity of the workers, the reduction in time lost passing from one task to another, and the invention of machinery specialized to particular tasks.

The dexterity of individual workers is supposed to increase because the worker spends all her time on one task, and can become extremely skilled at it. Anyone observing the difference between the speed with which a professional specialist can perform a task and the speed of a novice is struck by this effect. On the other hand, excessive specialization can also lead to boredom, fatigue, and alienation from the task, which can lower a worker's output.

The reduction in time lost moving from task to task is of limited importance, since these gains can be realized by workers who move from one task to another relatively infrequently, so that the setup costs are spread out over long runs of effort. For example, a pin maker might spend one whole day cutting pins from wire and the next day sharpening them, thus avoiding time lost while moving from one task to another within the same work shift.

---

1. Defining an index of this type requires specifying the weights to be given to changes in prices in different sectors. One widely used index is the GDP deflator, which compares the value of output in the base year in current prices to its value in base year prices.

The use of machinery, on the other hand, appears to have almost no limits in increasing the division of labor. Tools and machines can be specialized to maximize the worker's effectiveness at each aspect of a productive task. In metalworking, for example, a worker might become quite skilled at shaping gears and cams with specialized files and jigs, but a greater impulse to productivity comes from the introduction of lathes and other specialized cutting tools; an even greater increment from the employment of dies and stamping machines adapted to producing particular shapes; and still greater advantages from the use of computerized control of the machine tools.

The division of labor can thus give rise to the emergence of wholly new specialized tasks, and makes possible the production of completely novel outputs. Instead of wiring circuitry with soldering irons, for example, modern electronics workers etch integrated circuits onto silicon chips. The emergence of a market for self-contained electronic circuits with particular functions can give rise to entirely new methods of production and, eventually, to new products.

It should be noted that for Adam Smith, much of what we think of as technological change—the emergence of new products and new methods for producing existing products—is at its root an aspect of the division of labor, and hence is a predictable consequence of the ongoing process of economic development. Modern economics jargon refers to this as "endogenous technical progress."

Detail and Social Division of Labor

Though Smith's famous example of the pin factory suggests that the division of labor takes place in the individual factory or site of production, his larger discussion makes clear that the division of labor also takes place at the level of the whole economy or society. The detail division of labor is the process by which production at a certain site is divided up into specialized tasks, along the lines of the pin factory. The social division of labor is the process by which different aspects of a complex production process can be separated into different points of production, which may be located in different firms, or even different geographic regions.

Again, if we think of the production of modern electronic devices, we can see the social division of labor at work. A computer or calculator is often designed using an already existing integrated circuit chip as its core. Thus the computer manufacturer in effect farms out the manufacture of the chip to a completely different firm. The stages of chip manufacture, as well, may be spread all over the world, with the logical chip design located in, say, Texas, the physical chip design and creation of the templates for etching in Massachusetts, the actual etching and creation of the chip in Taiwan, and the attachment of pins and connectors to the printed circuit in the Philippines.

The social division of labor can be supported either by decentralized trade or by social planning mechanisms, or, more frequently, by a combination of both. The construction of the railroads in the United States in the nineteenth century was in part a spontaneous response to market forces, but was also fostered by a strong and effective national transportation policy, including the provision of substantial subsidies in the form of land grants to railroad builders. The market fostered the development of the railroads because they allowed for a much more refined social division of labor (for example, concentrating wheat production in one area of the country, and dairy and fruit production in other areas), but it was the federal government's policies that shaped the broad outlines of this national economic pattern. Japan's spectacular economic development since 1960 has been the result of a mixture of social planning of the division of labor through the Ministry of Industry and Trade (MITI), and the market-mediated efforts of individual firms.

[a] Smith tends to emphasize the market and market exchange as the primary method by which the division of labor is regulated and promoted. In his account human beings have a natural tendency to

"truck and barter," that is, to trade with each other, which simultaneously permits the division of labor (since producers can meet their actual consumption needs by exchanging what they produce on the market) and encourages the division of labor (since producers who specialize produce more to exchange on the market). Smith leaves unresolved the chicken-and-egg question of whether it is ultimately the human propensity to truck and barter that leads to the division of labor, or the division of labor that compels people to exchange.

Division of Labor and Extent of the Market

Having established the idea that the increasing division of labor promotes labor productivity, Smith argues that the division of labor itself is largely determined by the extent of the market. In modern language we would refer to increasing returns to scale—the tendency for the costs of production to decline with the overall scale of production. This is an extremely important and pervasive theme in political economy. In many lines of production, it is possible to lower unit costs by building large production facilities with the capacity to produce very large amounts of the output. The high fixed costs of the facility are eventually paid for by the lower variable costs and higher profits achieved for each unit of output. A good example is the mass production of automobiles undertaken in the early twentieth century by Henry Ford. Ford's assembly-line methods of production allowed him to produce cars at a fraction of the cost of the individually hand-made automobiles produced by his competitors, but he could recover the cost of his factories only by selling a very large number of units.

The scale of production in an industry depends on the size of the market, that is, the number of units of output the industry can sell. This in turn depends on the number of consumers, the income and demand patterns of the consumers, and the number of producers sharing the market. The number of potential consumers of an industry's product can be increased by population growth and by improvements in transportation technology which make the product available to a larger number of people.

The income and demand patterns of the consumers also have an important influence on the size of the potential market for output. As wages, profits, and rents for land and other natural resources increase in the course of economic development, the same number of consumers can support larger productive facilities because they buy more goods and services of all kinds. In addition, economic development leads to a shift in demand patterns, away from locally-produced and toward mass-produced goods. Just why this happens is not immediately obvious, but it has occurred over and over again in the course of economic development. These shifts also foster the increase in the extent of the market.

The size of productive facilities, and as a result the degree of division of labor that can be achieved, also depends on how many firms share the market. If there are a thousand small firms of approximately equal size sharing a market, the average scale of production facilities of each one is going to be much smaller than if there were only five or ten firms in the industry. This is one of the main motivations for mergers and acquisitions, which allow a large number of small firms to coalesce into a small number of big firms with bigger productive facilities and lower costs. This phenomenon constantly recurs in capitalist development, with waves of consolidation in one sector after another. The restructuring of the banking industry in the United States is an example. In most countries, retail banking is concentrated in fewer than ten very large banks that operate branches everywhere. In the United States up until the late twentieth century, federal and state regulations that limited interstate banking and branching within states protected the continued existence of more than 10,000 commercial banks, many of them quite small. Because economies of scale in banking are significant, there is substantial market pressure to consolidate this industry into a smaller number of bigger banks. Federal and state legislation gradually changed to permit this consolidation. Similar shakeouts take place from time to time in other industries, such as computers, retail discount stores, automobile production, and transportation.

The Virtuous Spiral of Economic Development

The links between the division of labor and the extent of the market create a system of positive feedbacks, in which increases in the division of labor lower costs, raise real incomes, and extend the market, thus leading back to more increases in the division of labor. This process creates a self-reinforcing positive spiral of economic development. For Smith, this positive feedback process is the deep secret of the wealth of nations. Those nations which can foster the spontaneous creation of the virtuous spiral, and whose policies allow it to proceed without running into legislative or institutional limitations, will prosper and grow economically.

Smith is aware that it is not always easy to create the conditions for the virtuous spiral of economic development to take hold, and that positive feedback processes are sometimes difficult to manage because of their inherent instability. Nonetheless, Smith puts his faith in the ultimate benefits to be gained from harnessing the virtuous spiral to increase standards of living and enhance the wealth of (in his day) the sovereign.

"Say's Law"

The increasing division of labor with its consequent rise in labor productivity has at least one immediate negative effect: a reduction in the demand for labor in the industries undergoing rapid rises in productivity. The reason for this is that the increases in the productivity of labor may run ahead of the widening of the market. Even though more units of the product are being produced and sold, if labor productivity is rising even faster, fewer workers will be required to produce the output, and unemployment can result.

Smith acknowledges this effect of the increasing division of labor, but argues, on the basis of reasoning that later came to be known as "Say's Law," that in the aggregate there cannot be a chronic excess supply of labor. The argument is that the workers unemployed by technological change in one industry can eventually find jobs in other industries. The reasoning of Say's Law is based on the idea that the source of demand for commodities over the economy as a whole is just the willingness of workers and the owners of capital and land to make their resources available for production. In real life, this potential demand can become effective only if money is available to finance the start-up of production with the unemployed resources. Smith and his successors who reason on the basis of Say's Law are assuming that the financial system of the economy is flexible enough to allow all potentially productive resources to be employed. Thus Say's Law is based on a belief in the efficiency of the financial institutions of a capitalist economy.

This is Adam's Fallacy in action. The immediate effect of increases in labor productivity is to impose costs (unemployment) on a group (workers) who are in a weak position to protect themselves from these costs. Ordinary moral reasoning would regard this as a bad thing. Smith offers the hope that *some* of these displaced workers will eventually find alternative jobs (though some others may not), and that lower prices of products will benefit consumers of products. Thus the direct, concrete evil of unemployment is instrumental to achieving the indirect, abstract good of lower prices.

Say's Law comes up again and again in this story, and it will help to keep two points in mind. Over long periods of time, it appears that something like Say's Law does operate: at least there is no long-term drift toward constantly increasing unemployment as a result of technological change and rising labor productivity. On the other hand, over shorter periods, the absorption of technologically unemployed workers into new jobs can be quite slow, creating real social, economic, and political problems. The stubbornly high unemployment rates in many Western European countries over the last three decades of the twentieth century are an example. Thus one important issue about Say's Law is what time scale we are looking at, and what we believe is the analytical connection between economic events on a short and a long time scale.

The Theory of Value

Theories of value and distribution inevitably arise when we analyze the operation of exchange-based economic systems like capitalism. Theories of value have the aim of explaining why commodities have value and what determines the relative value of different commodities. Theories of distribution focus on the division of the value of commodities among the different components of income: wages, profits, and rents.

Nominal and Real Price

Smith distinguishes what he calls the nominal price of a commodity (the amount of money for which it exchanges) from the real price of the commodity, the amount of labor required to produce it. In Smith's view the labor expended in the production of the commodity (and thus embodied in it) is the ultimate real social price paid for it—in other words, in this line of thinking labor is the only scarce productive resource.

The fundamental insight for Smith in the labor theory of value is that the ultimate source of wealth for human societies is labor productivity. Earlier political economists tended to be misled by appearances into seeking the sources of wealth in agricultural rents or in the accumulation of money. Smith correctly swept away those cobwebs to focus on the actual organization of human labor time and the determinants of labor productivity as the ultimate sources of wealth.

Smith is not entirely clear, however, about the labor price of a commodity, since there are two possible meanings one can give to this. One is the amount of labor embodied in the production of the commodity. But once we have money prices of commodities and labor sells for a wage, we might also understand the labor price of the commodity to mean the amount of labor the commodity could exchange for by selling it for its price and using the money to hire labor—that is, the labor commanded by the commodity. There is a difference between labor embodied and labor commanded because wages in capitalist societies comprise only a fraction of the price of the commodity, since some of the value contained in the commodity becomes profit and rent. Thus in general, a commodity can command more labor than it embodies.[2]

If money is a produced commodity like gold, as it was in Smith's time, then there is a direct relation between nominal price and real price established by the real price of gold.[3] The basic vision of

---

2. An example may help to make this point clear. Suppose that 1 year's labor and 20 bushels of seed corn can produce 120 bushels of harvested corn. The *net product* of the year's labor is 100 bushels of corn (since of the 120 bushels harvested, 20 just go to replace the seed corn used up). Under these circumstances the labor embodied in 100 bushels of corn is 1 year. But suppose that the real wage of agricultural workers is 50 bushels of corn, with the other 50 bushels taking the form of profit and rent. Then 100 bushels of corn could command 2 years of labor. Smith shifts back and forth between the labor-embodied and labor-commanded conception of the real price of commodities.

3. For example, if 10 hours of labor are required to produce a table, 20 hours of labor are required to produce an ounce of gold, and 5 hours of labor are required to produce a bushel of wheat, 1/2 ounce of gold or 2 bushels of wheat will exchange for a table. If an ounce of gold is equal to $20 (as was the case in the United States from 1791 to 1933), we would find the price of a table to be $10 and the price of a bushel of wheat to be $5.

Smith's labor theory of value is that labor is expended to produce commodities which are then sold for money. The nominal price of a commodity, in this view, can vary because it takes more or less labor to produce the commodity, or because it takes more or less labor to produce gold, or because the relationship between gold and money changes as a result of state policy. The first case arises when there is a fall or rise in the cost of producing a commodity. For example, as computer technology develops the cost of computing capacity in money falls. The second case is not so easy to perceive. If gold becomes easier to produce (because of the discovery of new, cheaper mines) or harder to produce (because of the exhaustion of existing mines), then the value of gold relative to other commodities must fall or rise. This process is not focused on any one commodity market, in contrast to the computer case, but is a pervasive pressure on all other commodity prices to accommodate themselves to the changing costs of producing gold. The last case involves devaluation or debasement of a national currency when the government changes the amount of gold for which it exchanges its money. In 1933, for example, the United States devalued the dollar in relation to gold by changing the price at which the Treasury would buy and sell gold for dollars from $20 an ounce to $35 an ounce. In order to keep the gold price of commodities unchanged, the money prices of commodities have to rise after a devaluation.

Market Price and Natural Price

In discussing the theory of value Smith makes a distinction, which is extremely important for later political economy, between the market price and natural price of commodities. The market price is just the amount of money for which the commodity changes hands at any particular moment; it rises and falls because of shortages and gluts, changes of taste and supply, and speculation. But Smith believes there are important forces that tend to push the market price back toward a certain level, which he calls the *natural price* of the commodity. Since there are always disruptions in any market, he does not expect the market price to converge smoothly to the natural price and then stay there, but instead believes it will fluctuate or (adopting an image from Newtonian planetary physics) "gravitate" around the natural price.

Smith argues that the theory of value concerns the determination of the natural price, and that forces of "supply and demand" are responsible for the fluctuations of market price around the natural price. This is rather different from modern price theory, which views supply and demand as the proximate determinants of market price.

Smith's Labor Theory of Value

Smith starts off his discussion of the theory of value by positing a labor theory of value in which the relative prices of commodities depend primarily on the relative amount of labor required to produce them. This is consistent with his argument that labor is the real price of commodities.

Smith's discussion of the labor theory of value raises many different ideas and issues that have prompted an unending stream of books and articles ever since. Smith himself does not by any means resolve all of these issues, and may not even have been aware of some of them. The situation is further complicated by the fact that Smith abandons the labor theory of value in the middle of his argument without explaining why, and shifts over to another theory, the "adding-up" theory of value.

Smith explains the labor theory of value with the parable of the "producers" of deer and beaver in a hunting economy that has no settled agriculture or industry. He argues that the hunters of deer and beaver would exchange deer for beaver at a ratio corresponding to the ratio of the average labor time it takes them to hunt and kill each animal. If it costs one day's labor to hunt a deer and two days' labor to hunt a beaver, for instance, the exchange will be two deer for one beaver.

There are two different reasons why this exchange ratio might hold, and Smith's opinion about them is not very explicit. First, the exchange might be in this ratio because both parties view this as a "fair" price, in that they both subjectively value the expenditure of labor as the ultimate real cost of a good. Second, competition might force the exchange ratio to be the ratio of labor times because anybody in this society can shift his effort from deer hunting to beaver hunting. If a beaver hunter holds out for a higher price of beaver in terms of deer than the relative labor time—say, demanding three deer for his beaver—then the deer hunters will refuse to trade with him, since they can go out and hunt their own beaver. Because it would cost them three days' labor to kill three deer and exchange them for one beaver, and only two days' labor to hunt the beaver themselves, they will prefer to shift over to beaver hunting. Of course these two arguments tend to merge into each other, though the second requires the additional hypothesis that anyone can shift costlessly between the two types of production.

If we project this parable into a society with settled agriculture and industry, it suggests that relative commodity prices will tend to reflect the relative labor time it takes to produce the commodities. As in the example in note 3, if a table requires 10 hours of labor to produce and a bushel of wheat requires 5 hours, the table will exchange for 2 bushels of wheat. But as we move from the hunters in the primeval forest to production in a capitalist society, there are important institutional changes that might influence relative prices. The hunters in the primeval forest did not have to pay any rent to hunt, and they owned their own weapons, traps, and snares. But in a modern capitalist society the worker typically does not own her own means of production, and landowners have appropriated the productive land and will charge a rent on it. Thus a shift from producing tables to producing wheat is not simply a question of shifting the labor resources around, but a question of shifting capital goods and land as well. This calls into question the argument that the ability of labor to shift from one line of production to another will ensure that commodities can be exchanged in proportion to the labor required to produce them.

Value-Added Accounting

Instead of pursuing these subtleties to a conclusion, Smith turns his attention to value-added accounting, which explains how the price of any commodity can be resolved into wages, profits, and rent. The basic insight of value-added accounting starts from the income statement (also called the profit-and-loss statement) of a commodity-producing firm. The firm calculates its profit over a year by subtracting from its sales revenue the cost of the commodities it has produced and sold. The revenue from the sale of commodities is divided into four categories: the cost of inputs and raw materials purchased from other firms on the market; the wages paid to labor; the rent paid to landowners; and the profits remaining to the owners of the firm. On the other hand, the value added by the productive effort undertaken in the firm is the difference between its sales revenue and the cost of purchased inputs: the firm has added this amount to the value of the purchased inputs. A cloth-making firm, for example, buys yarn as an input, and works it up into cloth. The cloth has a higher value than the yarn, and the difference is the value added by the firm's productive activity. Furthermore, the cost of purchased inputs in turn is resolved into the wages, profit, and rent of the supplier firm, together with its cost of purchased inputs. Over a whole economy, the cost of purchased inputs can be entirely resolved into wages, rents, and profits. Thus Smith thinks of the price of the commodity as equaling the sum of wages, rents, and profit received by the workers, landowners, and capitalists who participated in its production.

Capitalist firms care about the "bottom line"—profit—not about how much of their costs are wages and how much are purchased inputs. As a result, capitalist firms have no particular interest in value added. There is no advantage to the individual firm in increasing its value added (unless by doing so it also increases its profit). Economists, on the other hand, are quite interested in the value added by a whole economy, since it is a good measure of the economy's economic production. The Gross Domestic Product or GDP of an economy is basically a measure of its value added.[4]

There are two ways to think about value-added accounting. On one hand, we could view the whole price as being given by the labor time required to produce commodities, so that one of the income shares (profit) would be determined as whatever is left over once the others (wages and rent) have been paid. This way of thinking leads to the labor theory of value pursued by David Ricardo and Karl Marx. On the other hand, we could view the price of commodities as being determined by wages, rent, and profit. Smith seems to abandon the labor theory of value in midstream and shifts over to this second way of looking at the prices of commodities, developing what has come to be called an adding-up theory of value.

Smith's adding-up theory proposes to determine the natural price of the commodity by adding up the labor required to produce it multiplied by the natural wage, the land required to produce it multiplied by the natural rent, and the capital required to produce it multiplied by the natural profit rate. This conception organizes the

---

4. The difference is that GDP includes the depreciation of the fixed capital used up in production, while theoretical value added counts depreciation as part of the cost of purchased inputs.

remainder of Book I of *The Wealth of Nations.* Smith addresses in order the theory of the wage, the theory of the profit rate, and the theory of rent. Smith's discussion of the components of value added—wages, profit, and rent—provides a lot of interesting insights, which have been the foundation of important later work in economics, but it does not, in the end, give the promised systematic account of the determinants of the natural levels of wages, profits, and rents.

Competition and Gravitation

The decomposition of price into wages, rent, and profit is the basis of Smith's (and the other classical economists') theory of why market price will tend to gravitate around natural price. If the market price of a commodity is above its natural price, then one or more of the income components must also be above its natural level. For example, if furniture is selling at market prices above the natural price, either wages or profits (or both) in the furniture industry are likely to be above their natural levels. These excess returns to labor and capital will tend to attract labor and capital from other sectors into the furniture industry, increasing the output of furniture and driving down the price. This is a negative feedback process: the hypothetical starting point, a price higher than the natural price, sets in motion forces that tend to eliminate the excess.

If market price in a sector lies below the natural price, Smith argues symmetrically that returns to labor and capital in that sector will be depressed below their natural levels, with the result that labor and capital will tend to leave the sector, reducing the output and raising the price (and raising wages and profits for those workers and capitalists who stay in the industry).

The classical economists viewed this gravitation of market price around natural price as a never-ending fluctuation. Market price chases natural price but can never catch it, except perhaps for a fleeting moment, because other factors, such as technology and patterns of demand, will always be changing and as a result disturbing the relation between market price and natural price in one direction or the other.

Contemporary economics, on the other hand, focuses more theoretical attention on the ideal imaginary state of equilibrium, where market price and natural price coincide and there are no residual forces tending to push the market price in one direction or the other. It is not always clear what the theoretical rationale for this focus is, but one position that many economists take is that the forces of negative feedback keep the economy close to the equilibrium state at all times, so that an understanding of the equilibrium state of the economy is a good approximation to its actual state. Other economists criticize this position on the grounds that what we care about is precisely the forces in play at any moment that are bringing about change in prices and incomes, and these forces are ignored in a purely equilibrium analysis.

Wages

Smith, like the other classical political economists, recognized that wages have the social function of allowing workers (including the poorest members of society) to reproduce themselves. Classical political economy sees population reproduction and growth largely as the consequence rather than the cause of economic development. In order for wages to perform this function, they have to be high enough to allow workers to buy a subsistence standard of living. Smith thought that wages could not fall for very long under this level.

At the time Smith was writing most urban workers had relatively recently moved from the countryside to the city, and they still had close family and community contacts in rural areas. In these circumstances, one response workers will have to wages falling below the customary subsistence level is to leave the urban labor market and move back, at least temporarily, to rural communities.

While Smith thought that customary levels of subsistence put a floor under the level of wages, he argued that, in fact, wages in progressive and developing capitalist economies are normally above the subsistence level. The reason for this is that as capital accumulates it normally requires more labor, which must be attracted from the countryside by higher wages. The process of increasing division of labor through the accumulation of capital, according to Smith, tends to raise wages above the subsistence level, so that workers to some degree share in the fruits of technological progress and the increasing productivity of labor. (We will see that other classical political economists had rather different views on the operation of the capitalist labor market.)

Smith associates high wages and a high worker standard of living with a growing capital stock, rather than just with a large capital stock, and associates depressed wages and low worker standards of living with a declining capital stock, rather than a small capital stock. Thus he would expect a country with a prosperous and rapidly growing economy to exhibit high and rising wages, even if its actual capital stock is smaller than that of another country that is not growing so rapidly.

Smith believed that employers have a structural advantage over workers in the wage bargaining process (at least under the British laws of his time). Workers' "combinations" (that is, unions) were illegal under eighteenth-century British law, but there were no comparable restrictions on the tacit or open combination of employers to depress wages.

These observations are penetrating and have stood the test of time, but unfortunately they do not amount to an actual theory of the natural level of wages, which Smith needs in order to complete his adding-up theory of value. Smith's theory of wages addresses the *dynamics* of wage levels, that is, the forces tending to raise or lower wages, more directly than the forces that determine the actual level of wages in a country at a particular time. In order to accomplish his project of explaining the wage part of the value of commodities on the basis of a natural level of wages, Smith would have to tell us what forces determine the natural level of wages, which in the end he does not manage to do.

Profits

Capitalist production is organized around the pursuit of profit. Once the firm has paid for its raw materials and other purchased inputs (including tools and facilities for production) and has paid its workers (and, if relevant, rent to landowners), the money left over from sales revenue is profit. Since large firms with large sales will tend to have more absolute profits than smaller firms, profitability is measured in two ways: the *profit margin* is profit as a percentage of sales revenue, and measures what proportion of the total price of the commodity represents profit; the *profit rate* expresses profit as a percentage of the capital invested in production. Capital invested is the value of the factories and machinery the firm owns and its average inventories of inputs. The profit rate is economically the more significant measure. A prospective investor is concerned with how rapidly her wealth will increase as a result of investing in a firm, which is determined by the profit rate, and does not really care what the profit margin is.

Adam Smith makes several important observations on profit rates and their evolution over time, though he does not actually put forward a theory of the natural rate of profit.

Competition tends to equalize profit rates　Smith puts great emphasis on the tendency for competition among capitalists to equalize profit rates between different industries. His argument for this is a key element in his support for laissez-faire policies, and is also an important foundation of the concept of competitive equilibrium in later economic theory.

The idea is that if profit rates in one industry are higher than the average for the economy (Smith seems to identify this average profit rate with the natural profit rate), capitalists will tend to shift their capital toward that industry. As a result labor will move as well, and the output of the industry will rise, which tends to reduce prices and profit rates there. Symmetrically, capital will tend to leave industries where profit rates are lower than the average, leading to higher prices and thus to higher profit rates for the capitalists who remain. In this way competition provides a negative feedback that tends to make profit rates in all sectors equal. This is a key part of Smith's view of the capitalist economy as a self-regulating system that requires no external governance, a concept that underpins his support of laissez-faire economic policies.

While Smith saw a tendency for competition among capitalists to equalize profit rates, it is doubtful that he thought profit rates in any real economy would ever be completely equalized. The reason is that changes in demand, technology, and foreign competition will always be changing the relative profitability of the various sectors of the economy. The movement of capital to seek profit rate equalization is a central part of the metabolism of the capitalist economy, but it will never reach its goal of completely eliminating differences in the rate of profit across sectors.

The process of competition, however, does support the emergence of an *average* rate of profit as a key regulating element in a capitalist economy. While no firm or sector may actually achieve the exact average rate of profit, owners of capital will be aware of this average level and will use it as a benchmark in deciding where to put their capital and what investment projects to fund.

The average rate of profit is an example of an "emergent" property of a complex system like a capitalist economy. It is the result of innumerable decisions made by many capitalists, but is not directly traceable to any one of them. In turn, the average rate of profit plays a central role in shaping the decisions of individual capitalists, who use it as a benchmark against which to measure the profitability of production and investment plans.

The profit rate and the interest rate   Smith thought that interest rates paid on money loans to capitalists were a good approximate indication of the profit rate in a given country at a given time. In a rough and average sense this is probably true, but there are many circumstances in which profit and interest rates can move in opposite directions. Certainly capitalists cannot afford to pay interest rates above their profit rates for very long (though they may do so temporarily in order to stay in business for the long haul), and competition among capitalists for funds generally will tend to pull interest rates above zero.

The profit rate falls with accumulation   Smith argues that profit rates (like real wages) will vary from place to place and over time, so that it is impossible to settle on one level of the profit rate as normal or appropriate. In this connection Smith raises a major theme of economics and political economy in asserting that profit rates tend to fall with the accumulation of capital (which he calls "stock"). Smith's discussion of the fall in the rate of profit with accumulation moves between several different levels. Clearly if we think of any particular sector of the economy, there will be a tendency for the rate of profit in that sector to fall as more capital moves into it, other factors being equal, since more capital means more production and more competition, which will tend to lower the price in the sector.

But Smith also argues that the rate of profit in the economy as a whole will tend to decline with the accumulation of capital in all sectors. He isn't so clear about why he thinks this will happen. This decline might be due to rising real wages if population does not expand as rapidly as capital, a theory that neoclassical economists embraced in the twentieth century. It might also be due to rising rents if agricultural productivity does not rise in proportion to accumulation, a theory that Ricardo develops, though Smith tends to be optimistic about the availability of imported food and new techniques of agriculture. Almost all schools of economic thought have adopted some version of the thesis that profit rates tend to fall with accumulation, and the investigation of this idea has been one of the most fruitful lines of thought in developing the ideas of political economy.

Smith's discussion of profitability has many important insights that are the source of later economic theories and models. But in the end he does not put forward an unambiguous theory of the natural rate of profit or its determinants in a given economy at a given time.

Variability of Wages and Profit Rates

Smith argues for competition among workers and among capitalists as a pervasive force that tends to equalize wages and profit rates in the economy. But he also points to factors that lead to long-lasting differences in wages and profit rates between different "employments" of both labor and capital.

Some jobs are simply pleasanter than others to do. Other things being equal, Smith argues that the pleasanter jobs will have lower wages. Novelists, composers, and painters, for example, will on average have lower incomes from those employments than clerical workers, since the production of art is more interesting than accounting.

Every line of employment involves some expenses in learning the skills and information required to do the tasks effectively. Smith thought that employments that had high costs of training would have correspondingly higher wages.

Some sectors of the economy experience a relatively steady demand and others a highly variable demand. Smith thought that wages in the variable-demand sectors would be higher, to compensate workers there for the uncertainty and inconvenience of fluctuating employment opportunities. The construction trades are an example of this in the modern economy, since construction is highly sensitive to the business cycle and construction employment varies a lot over time. The wages of construction workers also tend to be higher than the wages of comparably skilled workers in other sectors. Curiously enough, Smith limits this effect to wages and does not include profit rates. This is because he thinks, on the basis of eighteenth-century experience, that most capital is circulating capital that can be quickly moved from one employment to another in response to changes in demand. In the modern economy, a much bigger proportion of capital is fixed capital which cannot be moved very rapidly from sector to sector. As a result, profit rates in sectors with volatile demand also show a tendency to be higher than profit rates in stable-demand sectors.

Some employments, in Smith's view, put a high premium on the moral character of the workers. He gives the example of doctors and goldsmiths (the latter were the forerunners of deposit bankers), whose wages he thought were high because of the scarcity in the population of the trustworthy moral characteristics required in those lines of work.

Some lines of work are inherently riskier than others. It is harder to predict the success of a lawyer, for example, than of a shoemaker, according to Smith, and as a result successful lawyers will have higher incomes than successful shoemakers. This effect likewise is important in the entertainment and sports sectors, where the success of individual aspirants is highly variable.

Rent

Finally, Smith turns his attention to the last component of value added, *rent* on land and other scarce resources. Smith views rent as a monopoly price. The owner of a particularly fertile piece of land, or a river that can generate hydropower, or an oil well or iron mine, can exclude producers from making use of the productive power of her assets. As a result she is in a position to *bargain* for a share of the profits in production, which takes the form of rent. For Smith, then, the basis of rent is *monopoly*. The landowner can command a rent insofar as there are not other equally good alternatives available to potential producers.

This theory (which is the basis of Ricardo's and later analyses of rent) implies that rent is an *effect* of the price of the commodity produced on the rented land. If the price of corn rises, so will the rents paid to landowners whose land is particularly well-suited to producing corn. If the price of corn falls, so will the rents on corn-producing land, because potential producers will not anticipate as large excess profits from producing on the landowner's land.

The further implication of Smith's analysis of rent is that there is no "natural" level of rent that can help to explain the natural price of commodities, because rent itself is determined by price, not the other way around.

The Theory of Value Revisited

Smith's organization of Book I of *The Wealth of Nations* around the idea of natural price and the decomposition of value added into wages, profits, and rents is a brilliant pedagogical device. It gives us a coherent picture of the whole economy in the microcosm of the value added of the individual commodity, and leads to an easily grasped survey of the theory of value and distribution.

But logically Smith's discussion is incomplete as an account of the adding-up theory of natural price. In the first place, he does not deliver the theories of natural wages and the natural level of the profit rate that are required to make the adding-up theory complete. Instead, he offers an insightful account of the way in which competition among workers and capitalists will tend to equalize wages and profit rates (taking account of other factors such as risk) and will lead to the emergence of average wage levels and profit rates in the economy against which sectoral differences will be tested. But he is unable to specify exactly what will determine the level of these economy-wide averages.

The problem with the adding-up theory of value becomes particularly acute in the case of rent, which Smith analyzes, quite convincingly, as a residual *determined by the level of prices*. But if this account of rent is correct, the adding-up theory, which tries to explain the level of prices by the natural level of rents, is unacceptable because it depends on circular reasoning. In order to know the level of prices, according to the theory, we have to know the natural level of rents; but the theory of rent tells us that it is the level of prices that determines the level of rent, so we are left without a firm determination of either rents or prices.

As Ricardo argued later, the labor theory of value is not subject to this criticism of circularity. The labor theory of value gives an independent determination of the whole average price of commodities— the labor time required to produce them—which depends on the technology and state of development of the economy. Only if the whole is determined, Ricardo argues, is it possible to reason rigorously about its division into the parts of wages, profit, and rents.

Capital Accumulation

After his discussion of the theory of value and distribution, Smith turns in Book II of *The Wealth of Nations* to a direct consideration of the sources of private and national wealth. The central concept here is *accumulation,* the process by which a part of the value newly produced in each year is reinvested to increase the stock of assets.

Measuring Stock: Private and National Balance Sheets

The first step in understanding the accumulation of assets is to measure them in a conceptually coherent framework. Smith's treatment of capital assets (which he calls stock) is quite close to the modern conception of the asset side of the balance sheet. One aspect of Smith's discussion that shows striking foresight is his proposal to use the same balance sheet concepts to measure the wealth of private individuals and that of the society (or nation) as a whole.

Smith divides the assets of private households (which would include firms, since in his day most firms were individual proprietorships) into three categories: a consumption fund consisting of the stocks of goods held for consumption, including inventories of foodstuffs, furniture, houses, private transportation vehicles, and so on; a circulating capital fund, which the firm uses to buy inputs to production that are rapidly consumed, such as raw cotton for a spinning factory, or nails and lumber for a builder; and a fixed capital fund consisting of long-lived assets such as improvements to land, productive buildings, and equipment that lasts through many cycles of production.

The circulating capital fund at any one moment consists partly of money and partly of inventories of goods, because as the items in inventory are used up in production and the output sold, their value returns to the form of money, and usually remains in the form of money for some time before the inventory is replenished by new purchases. Both the money and the goods circulate from the point of view of the individual firm, since it is constantly turning money into goods and goods into money in the process of doing business.

Smith uses the same division to conceptualize the assets of society as a whole. He asks us to imagine a social consumption fund, consisting of all the houses, private vehicles, furniture, appliances, and inventories of food and other perishables held by all the households in the country. This fund provides for the consumption needs of the population, and it has to be replenished as it is used up. The social circulating capital is the aggregated stocks of inventories of raw materials, partly finished goods, and finished goods awaiting sale held by all the productive enterprises of the society. The social fixed capital is the aggregated stock of machines, buildings, improvements to land like dams, and roads, as well as the acquired useful abilities of the population, which modern economists call human capital.

There is some doubt as to whether money, which forms part of the circulating capital of the household and the firm, should be viewed as circulating or fixed capital at the level of the society as a whole. The reason is that the stock of money, though it circulates among households and firms, mostly stays put within the nation as a whole, and depreciates relatively slowly. Thus the stock of money (gold coins) appears from a social point of view to be more like an element of fixed capital.

Productive and Unproductive Labor

Smith's vision of accumulation starts from the idea that the consumption fund of the society serves primarily to employ labor. The larger the consumption fund of society, the more labor it can employ, and therefore the more it can produce.

In Smith's way of thinking, the central question of accumulation has to do with how labor is employed. He distinguishes between productive labor, that is, workers who produce a vendible, tangible product that can be added to the stock of the country, and unproductive labor, which consumes part of the consumption fund but produces no tangible output to add to stock as a result of the labor. For example, the same owner of capital may pay wages to workers in a factory, who spin raw cotton into thread, and to servants on his estate, who keep up the house, groom the horses, and stand behind the guests' chairs at dinner. The factory workers are productive labor in Smith's view because they labor to add to the stock of cotton thread, which is part of the total assets of society. These total assets grow as a result of their labor. The household servants are unproductive labor in Smith's framework, not because they do not work, but because their work produces nothing to add to the stock of society's assets. Smith puts this in another, slightly different way by pointing out that the owner of capital increases his capital by employing factory work-ers, since he recovers their wages and even makes a profit on the sale of their output, but decreases his capital by employing household servants, whose wages do not return to him in the form of money.

Looking at the matter from a social point of view, Smith argues that many high-status occupations are in fact unproductive labor. He says that the King and the army represent unproductive labor from the social point of view, since their efforts, however desirable and even necessary they may be from a social point of view, represent a net drain on the stocks of society because the King and his soldiers do not produce a vendible, tangible product that can add to the so-cial stock. Lawyers and judges also fall into the unproductive cate-gory (as do opera singers and doctors) for the same reason.

Private and Public Benefits of Accumulation

With an eye to the substantial fortunes that many of his readers looked to inherit, and in the grand Scottish tradition of parsimony, Smith praised saving and accumulation at the expense of consump-tion, and recommended the employment of productive rather than unproductive labor. Not content with holding out the joys of in-creasing wealth for the accumulator, Smith went so far as to charac-terize savers as *public benefactors.*

There is no doubt that those who accumulate wealth make them-selves better off in material terms (without getting into the difficult philosophical questions of the relation between wealth and happi-ness). But it is not so clear why Smith thinks that private accumula-tion has benefits to the public at large. You might think that the cap-italist, by accumulating wealth, does public good by providing more jobs for workers; but as we have seen, Smith does not envision chronic underemployment of labor, and he believes that over long periods the population adjusts to the demand for labor. Under these assumptions, it is hard to see how the accumulation of private wealth does anything more than increase the number of workers at the same standard of living.

If Smith believes that a large population is a good thing in itself—for example, because it is a source of military power for the sovereign (as it was in the eighteenth century)—then that would explain why he thinks the accumulation of private wealth is a public advantage. But modern individualistic welfare economics argues vigorously that there can be no welfare of the society as a whole that is not the welfare of some individual.

Smith may also have in the back of his mind the issue of the division of labor and the extent of the market, though he is not very explicit about this. If there are large unexploited increasing returns in production, then the increase in population and production from private accumulation will have the side effect of increasing the productivity of labor and potentially raising the whole society's standard of living. In this perspective the private investor is a public benefactor because society as a whole always invests too little to take advantage of the increasing returns to scale that are possible. In modern economics jargon, investment has a *positive externality* in this case because the increase in the nation's capital raises everyone's productivity and wealth above and beyond the levels anticipated when individuals make a decision to invest.

This part of Smith's argument is important because it is here where we might expect to find the crucial support for Adam's Fallacy, the claim that selfish behavior is somehow transmuted by capitalist social relations into public benefaction. There is a sketch of such an argument in the connection Smith makes between the private accumulation of capital and the exploitation of the division of labor to raise average labor productivity. But he offers no explanation for how society at large will actually receive the increases in standard of living that the widening division of labor makes possible. Since workers and capitalists still meet as antagonists in the market, there is no reason for capitalists to share the increases in labor productivity with workers as higher wages. In the absence of this link in the argument, Adam's Fallacy remains uncorrected. The selfish pursuit of gain by capitalists may create the *potential* for broad social benefits through the accumulation of capital and the widening division of labor. But society as a whole can only achieve these potential gains by going beyond capital accumulation to distribute the resulting wealth.

The Invisible Hand and the State

The National Balance Sheet and Economic Policy

Smith approaches the problem of economic policy through a consideration of the national balance sheet. In outline, the national balance sheet looks like this:

National balance sheet

Assets	Liabilities
Gold	Debts owed to other nations
Consumption fund	
Circulating capital	
Fixed capital	*National Net Worth = Assets − Liabilities*

The mercantilist writers of the late seventeenth and early eighteenth century tended to focus entirely on the quantity of gold in a country, and shaped their policy recommendations in order to maximize the amount of gold. For example, the mercantilists favored restrictions on imports, to prevent gold from leaving the country, and subsidies to exports, since exports brought gold into the country.

Smith criticizes the mercantilists on the ground that the real measure of national wealth is the national net worth, not just the gold stock. In focusing their attention purely on the gold stock, the mercantilists make two serious errors, according to Smith. First, mercantilists support measures that increase the gold stock but diminish the national net worth. For example, policies that induce citizens to sell assets to foreigners for gold below their market prices might increase the gold stock, but will decrease the national net worth because the real value of the gold gained is smaller than the value of the assets given up. But this is precisely what an export subsidy scheme amounts to, in Smith's view: the subsidy induces citizens to sell assets (commodities produced within the country) to foreigners at a loss, that is, effectively at prices lower than the world market price. Similarly, a tariff on imports prevents citizens from exchanging gold for commodities that might be worth more than the gold given up.

Second, Smith argues that the mercantilists are misguided in their claim that the economic strength of a nation is determined by its stock of gold, rather than by its national net worth. Smith maintains that what matters to a country is the real development of its productive resources—people, land, and capital—rather than its cash money holdings. A country with a large and well-developed productive base will in the end have more resources to pursue its policy goals through diplomatic and military means. Smith, in fact, believes that the nation is best off with the smallest gold stock it can manage, because holding gold diverts capital from productive enterprises that turn a profit.

Smith's discussion of the national economic interest is in many ways the most influential aspect of his book, and it continues to be the basis of the modern consensus of political economy, at least in Anglo-Saxon countries. Nineteenth-century Britain became almost a laboratory model of Smith's political economic conception, as it developed the first and (at the time) the largest modern industrial economy on the basis of free trade and the policy of holding an extremely small reserve of gold.

The issues that Smith raises in his discussion of the national balance sheet remain timely and relevant today. The fallacies with which he charges the mercantilists continually crop up in political debate in one form or another. For example, during the last twenty years politicians of both parties in the United States have tended to focus their attention disproportionately on the federal deficit and stock of debt, neglecting the impact of their policies on the federal net worth (and its impact in turn on the national net worth). This has led to policies that are highly questionable economically, such as allowing the cutting of trees in federal forests at below market prices. As the trees are turned into money, the federal deficit appears lower, but the federal net worth may decline because the loss of the natural resource assets is larger than the gain to the deficit.

Smith's Case for Laissez-Faire

Smith generalizes these insights to build a powerful case for a particular philosophy of economic policy: laissez-faire, the French idiom for leaving things alone to take care of themselves. It is important to see exactly what Smith means by laissez-faire policy, and the distinct limits he envisions for it.

In keeping with his analysis of the national balance sheet and the accumulation process, Smith argues that national income is maximized when each unit of national capital seeks out the highest profit rate at world market prices. This will be the result of the self-interested decisions of capitalists as long as they are free to invest their capital as they see fit and the prices they face are world market prices. If part of the national capital is invested in a sector with a lower than average profit rate, then the whole profit income of the nation, and hence its whole national income, will be lower than if the capital were shifted to a higher-profit-rate sector.

When the government attempts to intervene to encourage or discourage the investment of capital in certain sectors, one of two things happens, according to Smith. It may be that the government policy is ineffective and doesn't actually change the allocation of capital, in which case the policy is harmless but also useless. On the other hand, if the policy works and actually changes the allocation of capital, from Smith's point of view it must result in lowering net national income at world prices. The reason is that national income at world prices would be maximized by allowing individual capitalists to seek the highest profit rate they can find; and if the government induces them to do anything different, this must result in lower overall profits and national income.

For example, if the government decides to protect capital and jobs in an industry threatened by foreign competition by putting tariffs or quotas on imports (as the U.S. government currently does in several sectors such as agricultural products and clothing), the effect is to induce U.S. capitalists to invest more of their capital in the protected industries than they would without the tariff. But the profit rate in these industries at world market prices is lower than the average profit rate, and as a result national income as a whole must decline. The tariff makes the profit rate in the protected industry *appear* to be equal to the average, but only by diverting funds from other sectors or consumers of the protected commodity; and the amount of income diverted must, according to Smith's reasoning, exceed the subsidy to the protected capital, so that overall the nation experiences a loss. Thus Smith concludes that the national interest, in the form of the national balance sheet, is best served by getting rid of tariffs, subsidies, and other forms of intervention in private-market allocation of capital.

This argument rests on several assumptions that Smith does not make completely explicit. First, he is implicitly assuming that the country cannot influence the world market prices of the commodities it produces. In modern economic jargon, he is thinking of a small country in a large world economy. If the country in question has so large a share of the world market that its policies can influence world prices, then intervention might be able to shift some of the world profit to the country, thus increasing its national income. Smith's laissez-faire reasoning would still apply at the level of the whole world economy, so that the income gained by one nation through its protective policies would be more than offset by the losses to other nations.

Second, as I have emphasized, Smith assumes that Say's Law is operating, so that there will be no long-term unemployment of labor or capital. If a nation reduces tariffs protecting some sector, that sector will generally shrink in size, disemploying some labor and capital. Say's Law reasoning makes the assumption that this unemployed labor and capital will find new employment in other sectors, thus allowing the nation to maximize its overall profit rate and national income.

Qualifications of Laissez-Faire

Smith makes several specific qualifications of his laissez-faire policy recommendations. First, he argues that defense or national security considerations may require a nation to protect and subsidize a sector that otherwise would not be profitable. The example he gives is the British Navigation Laws of the eighteenth century, a complex system of restrictions on trade aimed at securing strong merchant-shipping and ship-building sectors for Britain. Since Britain depended on its naval strength to defend itself against continental European powers, a pool of experienced seamen and ongoing ship-building facilities were an important national security asset. Smith endorses these navigation measures on this ground, despite his recognition that under laissez-faire British capital would not be able to appropriate the average profit rate in shipping and ship-building, and that these sectors would become much smaller.

This general concern continues to arise in contemporary political economic debates. The United States has subsidized its merchant marine for many years, for example, and the U.S. government tries to intervene in computer and nuclear power markets on the basis of national security concerns.

Another qualification to pure laissez-faire is the use of tariffs as bargaining chips or retaliatory measures in international negotiations. Here the idea is that it might be worth paying a short-term economic price in national income in order to induce another country to adopt better policies. The United States uses this kind of economic policy quite frequently, for example, in our linkage of trade privileges to other countries' domestic policies on human rights.

In line with his emphasis on increasing the division of labor, Smith sees a role for tariffs in fostering the growth of small firms in important sectors—the "infant industry" exception to laissez-faire. The idea here is that a nation may have the potential to make the average profit rate in a sector, but only if it can reach a certain scale of production. Without protection, small firms venturing into the sector will be destroyed by existing foreign competition. A tariff in such a case may permit the growth of a large enough domestic industry to compete internationally. The contemporary Asian "tigers," including Korea, Taiwan, and Singapore, have successfully encouraged infant industries through tariff restrictions, export subsidies, and low-interest loans.

Finally, Smith acknowledges that there may be significant short-term adjustment costs to implementing laissez-faire policies, because of the slowness with which capital and labor disemployed in sectors vulnerable to foreign competition will be reabsorbed into other parts of the economy. To cope with these short-term adjustment costs, he accepts the need for a gradual movement toward laissez-faire through the elimination of tariffs and subsidies.

The State and the Market

As we have seen, Smith has a lively and vivid appreciation of the spontaneous growth potential of the private economy through capital accumulation and the division of labor, but he also puts forward a sophisticated and complex view of the relation between the market and the state. While he recommends against the state intervening in particular markets for purely economic ends, Smith sees a need for the state to create a social and legal environment within which markets and enterprise can flourish. The state, for example, needs to establish and protect property rights and enforce contracts in order to create the legal substructure within which trade and production can grow. But inevitably the definition of property rights and contract responsibilities involves the state in concrete issues of resource allocation and investment planning. The reason is that in defining the limits of property rights (through environmental regulations, land-use zoning, regulation of monopoly, and the like), the state indirectly influences the directions in which the private division of labor will develop. For example, state restrictions on a landowner's right to use property to create a nuisance in a neighborhood or to pollute the environment inevitably change and direct economic activity.

There are many modern instances of these political economic issues. We are currently in the midst of a major reform of property rights in the electromagnetic spectrum (radio and television broadcasting frequencies). Many countries, including the United States, are moving to create transferable property rights in parts of the spectrum, and as a result are creating new markets and new economic possibilities, as well as new sources of wealth. But these reforms also inevitably have a major impact on the development of the broadcasting, telephone, and information transmission industries. A similar development of property rights in various kinds of environmental pollutants (sulfur emissions, greenhouse gas emissions) is in a more nascent stage on the international scene. The chronic debates and problems that we have concerning health and automobile insurance are also closely related to the establishment of property rights and responsibilities.

Thus Smith's vision of laissez-faire is not a one-sided encouragement of private enterprise and the market to the neglect of political and governmental institutions, but a balanced understanding of the interplay between market and state institutions in allowing the virtuous circle of economic development to proceed.

Smith's Theory of Money

In Smith's time most countries adopted a gold-standard system of money, in which the government establishes a legal relationship between the national money (dollars or pounds or francs) and a quantity of gold. As we have seen, in this type of system the money prices of commodities are regulated over the long run by the relative production costs of gold and commodities. The price level (or its rate of change, which we call *inflation*) under a gold standard is determined by the gradual change in relative production costs of gold and other commodities as technology changes.

The quantity of gold required to circulate the commodities in a country depends on the velocity of money, that is, how many transactions each gold coin can participate in over a year. The velocity of money can be measured as the ratio of the value of transactions in a year to the stock of gold money. On average, the velocity of money in transactions depends on the payment customs of a country, as well as the degree of development of its banking system.

Smith puts considerable weight on the fact that the stock of gold required to circulate commodities is a drain on the profit-making capital of the country. If the country could increase the velocity of money, it could divert some of the capital tied up in holding gold into profit-making investments, and thus increase its wealth. One way the velocity of money can be increased is through the wider use of banks, which centralize the gold reserves of many depositors. Since the demands of different depositors for gold are not exactly correlated, the bank can hold a lower gold reserve than the depositors would need if each held their own, and the velocity of money increases. Smith, like many Scots, is an enthusiastic supporter of banking, banknotes, and cash accounts, an early form of credit card that allowed depositors to hold lower average balances in managing their affairs. (There is an English saying that "the Scotch hate gold.")

Smith extends his laissez-faire recommendations to the banking system, proposing that banks should be allowed to issue whatever amount of deposits or banknotes they wish, as long as they are in a position to redeem deposits and notes with gold on demand. In his view, banking and credit share the self-regulating character of the market in general. If banks issue more banknotes than the public wants to hold, the public will redeem the notes for gold, and thus will regulate the total note issue to the appropriate size.

Smith was aware of certain pathologies that unregulated banking systems could encourage. These are all, in one way or another, connected with an unstable multiplication of credit. In Smith's time a great deal of trade was financed with bills of exchange, a receipt for goods in transit signed by the shipper, which other merchants and banks would accept as collateral for cash loans. In boom periods, some traders would issue bills beyond their actual inventories of goods in transit, which would allow an unstable growth of loans and credit in the economy as a whole. Such pyramids of credit are vulnerable to sudden crises, in which the failure of some of the issuers of bills to pay triggers off a chain reaction of other traders' failures. The credit system collapses temporarily, ruining many merchants and often interrupting trade and production, thus creating unemployment.

Smith argues that this kind of overtrading in bills of exchange can be avoided if banks strictly follow a policy of lending only on the basis of "real bills," that is, bills of exchange that are backed by actual goods sold and in transit to their purchasers. This "real bills" doctrine has played a key role in banking policy debates ever since.

Smith's monetary theory is interesting in part because it is not a quantity theory of money in the modern sense. The quantity of money theory of prices argues that it is the quantity of money, rather than the cost of production of gold, that determines the average price of commodities. The quantity theory is the dominant consensus theory in modern policy circles, and it underlies the monetarist policies of controlling money-supply growth that many central banks have adopted. Smith argues for a flexible, demand-determined money supply on the ground that, in a gold-standard system, the price level will be anchored by the production cost of gold relative to other commodities.

Smith's monetary views are also different from those of Keynes. While Keynes argues that the quantity of money determines the interest rate (rather than the price level directly, as the quantity theory predicts), Smith thinks the interest rate is largely determined by the rate of profit, not by the amount of money or credit created.

While both the Keynesian and quantity theories of money recommend interventionist monetary policies in which a central bank regulates the supply of money, either to influence interest rates or to stabilize the price level, Smith's monetary theory fits consistently with a laissez-faire policy of banking.

Adam's Fallacy Revisited

The Wealth of Nations is the product of Adam Smith's teaching of political economy at the University of Glasgow. Smith, as a teacher, was more concerned with introducing key ideas and insights of political economy to his students than with constructing a consistent framework for these ideas. At critical points in his argument, he plausibly changes the subject in such a way as to obscure the inconsistency of the various points he is making. A leading example is his inconsistent discussion of the theory of value, where he shifts in midstream from the explanation of the labor theory of value to the adding-up theory of value, and then again when in developing the adding-up theory of value he fails to provide explanations for the natural wage and profit rate, and contradicts his own point by arguing that rents are dependent on the value of products rather than the other way around.

A similar haze of inconsistency surrounds Smith's attempt to synthesize his moral views with his support of laissez-faire capitalism. This is the real heart of *The Wealth of Nations*. Other writers have been able to capture the inner logic of capitalist competition and accumulation as well as or better than Smith. But Smith stands out as a philosophical and moral defender of capitalist social relations through his ingenious, if tortured, claim that the ruthless pursuit of self-interest, which can lead people to do bad things to other people, is transmuted by capitalist social relations into a moral good. If only this claim could be made good, how much simpler the history of capitalism would have turned out to be! In his views about the capitalist project, Smith sheds his general good sense and moral authority without rigorously establishing the logical basis for his approbation.

A good example of this type of argument in Smith's hands is his famous observation that it is not from the love or goodwill of the butcher or baker that we get our dinner, but from our appeal to their self-interest through our paying for meat and bread. The common sense and realism of this remark are unchallengeable. That is indeed how capitalist society works and reproduces itself. But to support the claim that this pursuit of self-interest is a positive good, Smith would have to show that antagonistic market exchange relations are the only possible way to support the division of labor, and that we have no alternative to accepting the distributional inequities and moral violence that accompany private property relations as the means to securing our dinners. Smith comes no closer to making this argument stick than he does to reconciling the dependence of rent on the value of the commodity with the adding-up theory of value.

Smith's inconsistencies betray a tension between his economic theology and his good sense. As a theologian of capitalist social relations, he is willing to remove traditional moral constraints on the pursuit of self-interest through the accumulation of capital. The enormous (and very real) increase in labor productivity, with its potential improvement in human conditions of life latent in capitalist economic development, is too great a temptation for Smith to forgo. But another side of his character recognizes the damage that this license to pursue self-interest can do to society as well. Smith deals with these contrary insights by balancing his glittering vision of a virtuous spiral of economic development with the idea that economics can be contained within a larger political and social framework. Laissez-faire, yes, but the Navigation Acts, too. Free trade modified by the infant-industry exception. Unregulated banking, as long as banks strictly follow a "real bills" policy.

By the time Smith wrote his great book, the fundamental conditions for the explosive emergence of industrial capitalism were all in place in European and especially in British society. Even if Smith had written a very different book, emphasizing the caution needed to handle these explosive social forces and counseling a renewal of traditional moral sentiments to balance the seductions of the market, he could not have altered the actual course of events very much. *The Wealth of Nations* as it does exist leaves these unresolved issues on the table for Smith's successors to grapple with.

2/ Gloomy Science

dam Smith's upbeat assessment of the prospects for capitalism intervened in a long-standing political conflict between the declining landed aristocracy which had controlled British political life for generations and a new class of industrializing capitalists. Smith's strong defense of property rights appealed to both sides of this divide, but his laissez-faire prescriptions for national economic policy threatened many of the entrenched special interests of the day.

Second Thoughts

Thomas Malthus and David Ricardo were the two outstanding successors to Smith in developing and qualifying his analysis of the historical prognosis for capitalism. Their work raised the specter of limits to capitalist growth arising from overpopulation and consequent upward pressure on the prices of food and raw materials. Malthus expressed major doubts about the wisdom and viability of unbridled capitalist development on a number of fronts. Ricardo shared many of Malthus's worries, but had a stronger interest in clearing the way for capitalist accumulation through policy reform. Malthus explicitly raises doubts about Adam's Fallacy, questioning whether the path of laissez-faire capitalist development can be consistent with a moral (in his terms, Christian) society. Ricardo, however, seems to accept Adam's Fallacy as a rationale for pursuing unbridled capitalist accumulation.

Malthus and especially Ricardo worked hard to address the logical gaps in Smith's argument, supplying more rigorous analyses of population as well as theories of value and distribution.

Malthus and Population

Thomas Malthus was an English clergyman who had a strong interest in the life of the English poor and working class, and an equally strong interest in political economy and philosophy. His 1799 pamphlet, later revised as a book, *An Essay on the Principle of Population,* is widely regarded as a seminal contribution to demography, the systematic scientific study of population growth and its dynamics. Malthus's ideas have had immense political influence, and continue to be expressed in contemporary debates over population growth, population control measures, and the management of the finite resources of the earth.

Malthus corresponded and debated with Ricardo on political economic issues. Ricardo, as we shall see, adopted important parts of Malthus's theories in constructing his own system, but he strongly criticized Malthus for misunderstanding the principle of Say's Law. Karl Marx also took Malthus's work as a foil, vigorously criticizing his claim to have discovered universal laws of population, and arguing that Malthus's ideas are a classic expression of the ideological prejudices of the British ruling-class coalition of landowners and capitalists.

The Context of Malthus's *Essay*

By the late eighteenth century it had become apparent, especially in England, that the systematic application of engineering and science to productive technology would revolutionize the productivity of labor, and make possible previously undreamed-of levels of wealth creation. The implications of this development became the subject of an ongoing philosophical debate, which prefigures the politics of the nineteenth and twentieth centuries. The drama of the French Revolution, with its overturning of the centuries-old institutions of the *ancien régime,* fueled this debate and underlined the urgency of the issues at stake.

Some optimists, among them William Godwin, the husband of the early feminist Mary Wollstonecraft (and the father of Mary Shelley, the creator of Frankenstein's Monster), argued that the dawning new age would allow human beings to "perfect" society by eliminating the scourges of poverty, disease, war, and social conflict. The perfectibilist idea was that if the enormous surplus production inherent in the technological revolution were turned to social ends and distributed equally, it would provide the resources to bring everyone to a modest, comfortable standard of living, and to provide the social infrastructure of sanitation, housing, and transportation that would eliminate endemic disease and starvation. A key point in the perfectibilist position was the assertion that humankind was in control of its own destiny: people could decide what to do with the newly created social powers of production to solve human problems. We can see in this position the seeds of the socialist movements of the nineteenth and twentieth centuries, which were based on the attempt to realize this dream.

The perfectibilist position predictably met a strong ideological opposition from conservatives. The conservatives argued on several grounds that the hopes of the perfectibilists were illusory and that the pursuit of their ideas would be dangerous to the well-being of society. Some conservatives found the perfectibilist position objectionable on theological grounds, because it claimed too much responsibility and power for human beings at the expense of God. Other conservatives saw the perfectibilist emphasis on social control of the new technologies and their surplus product as a threat to class interests and to the political stability of the nation, which rested on class hierarchy. Conservatives argued that the ills of humanity which the perfectibilists aspired to eliminate by social action were in fact the consequence of "human nature," which could not be changed by technology or increased productivity of labor. In the eyes of these conservative critics, the perfectibilist proposals were fraudulent promises that could only serve the perfectibilists' ambitions for power.

These issues have dominated twentieth-century history and political economy. Many conservative attacks on socialist and communist movements are based on the claim that the "idealism" or "utopianism" of progressive philosophy will inevitably lead to totalitarian politics. These arguments play variations on themes that were already present in the debates around perfectibilism.

Malthus wrote his *Essay* as a critique of the perfectibilist position. He claimed to establish a mathematical proof of the impossibility of the realization of the perfectibilist program. Malthus was thus one of the first writers to introduce explicitly mathematical arguments and models into social science. It is worth noting the structure of Malthus's rhetoric: rather than appealing to theological or philosophical arguments directed at proving the undesirability or imprudence of the perfectibilist goals, he puts forth mathematical arguments against the feasibility of their ideas.

Malthus's Postulates and Their Implications

Malthus's demonstration of the impossibility of realizing Godwin's proposals takes the form of a logical argument resting on two postulates (somewhat analogous to the postulates of geometry), one concerning the dynamics of human populations, the other concerning the dynamics of food production.

Human Populations Tend to Grow Geometrically

Malthus's first postulate is that in the absence of any checks, that is, countervailing forces, human population tends, on account of the "passion between the sexes," to grow geometrically (or exponentially), that is, according to the mathematical pattern 1, 2, 4, 8, . . . Each woman tends to bear more than the two children that are required to replace herself and her mate, so that each generation will exceed the preceding one in total size. The power of procreation knows no natural limits, according to this postulate.

Agricultural Output Tends to Grow Arithmetically

Can this geometrically growing population feed itself? Malthus argues that it cannot, because the growth of food production, depending in his view on the cultivation of more land or the more intensive cultivation of existing land, cannot sustain more than an arithmetic pattern, 1, 2, 3, 4, . . . , based on addition rather than multiplication. In the first few stages of population growth, the arithmetic increase in food supplies can keep pace with the growth in population, especially if the natural rate of population growth is low. But geometric growth, no matter how low its rate, always overtakes and dwarfs any arithmetic series. In Malthus's examples the ratios are 1:1, 2:2, 4:3, 8:4, 16:5, . . . , so that population always overwhelms the food supply if the two postulates hold.

Checks to Population

The postulates themselves thus lead to a contradiction: they predict that eventually the population will outgrow its food supply by whatever factor you choose if you wait long enough. Since people cannot live on air, something must intervene, argues Malthus, to bring population into balance with the food supply. Malthus calls these equilibrating forces "checks." They are factors that tend to reduce population growth, by either lowering the birth rate or raising the death rate, so that it marches in step with his postulated law of arithmetic increase of food. Malthus classifies these factors (not always completely consistently, especially in the later revision of his book) into the categories of preventive checks and positive checks.

"Preventive checks" are practices that lower the birth rate and thus reduce the underlying tendency of the population to grow exponentially. If women delay marriage, so that the average age at marriage rises, they spend a smaller part of their fertile lifetimes at risk of conception, and therefore fertility rates fall. If a higher proportion of the women in a society choose not to marry and have children at all, the fertility rate and population growth rate will fall. Finally, if married couples abstain from sex, they will conceive fewer children and lower the fertility rate. Malthus clearly appreciates the potential of these preventive checks to control fertility, but does not believe that in practice they will be very effective.

Another possibility is the use of contraceptive devices or drugs. As far as we know, one or another form of contraception has been known and employed in all human societies. (These methods were of varying effectiveness, of course, as are contemporary methods.) Malthus is aware of this possibility, but he follows the Church of England of his time in adopting the position that sexual intercourse with contraception is against "natural law," and is therefore a "vice." Malthus views the wider use of contraceptive methods as a moral evil, and hence not an acceptable solution to the problem of controlling fertility.

If preventive checks do not reduce the fertility rate enough to bring population growth in line with the posited arithmetic growth of food output, Malthus argues that "positive checks"—starvation and disease—will raise the mortality rate to bring about the inevitable equilibrium. As population outstrips the food supply, some part of the society will become malnourished, and will die either directly from starvation or indirectly from diseases that are the result of their weakened condition.

Malthus's own experience with the British poor and working class indicated that the most sensitive components of the mortality rate were the death rates of the very young and the very old. Infants and the elderly are those most vulnerable in periods of want. As food becomes more expensive, mothers' nutrition declines, and as a result children are born underweight and vulnerable to infectious disease. Poorly nourished mothers might themselves survive, but their lactation is poor, and their babies often died as a result. Novels and biographies from the early nineteenth century underline how pervasive infant mortality was among all classes.

The Majority of Humanity Must Always Live in Misery

Malthus thus draws his conclusion (which led some of his contemporaries to call political economy the "dismal science") that the majority of humanity must of mathematical necessity live in great enough misery and poverty to stabilize the total population through a high mortality rate, especially among infants. The only theoretical loophole is the possibility that people might control their sexual passion and therefore fertility rates would be lower. Malthus thinks this would be a good thing, but does not seem to have high expectations that it will come to pass.

In Malthus's eyes, these considerations show the vanity and emptiness of the perfectibilist project to harness technology in order to ameliorate the human condition. Certainly technology might raise output per worker in industry and urban wages; but the higher standard of living supported by high wages will lead to an explosion of population, largely because of a decline in the rate of infant mortality. The resulting population growth will outstrip the growth of the food supply, and the real wage will fall as food prices rise, forcing the urban working class back to the margins of subsistence, where vice, neglect, and want once again will raise mortality rates, especially infant mortality, to restore equilibrium. Malthus thus invokes the whole prestige of mathematics in supporting this gloomy view of the human fate. He challenges Godwin and the other perfectibilists to show where the logic of his argument has gone wrong.

Charles Darwin was struck by the relevance of Malthus's arguments to the situation of species competing for survival. Indeed, Malthus's vision of human society was one of the important sources of Darwin's vision of natural selection as the basis of biological evolution.

Mathematical arguments, if they are correctly reasoned, can do no more than link a set of assumptions to a set of conclusions. The conclusions may follow logically from the assumptions, but they will apply to reality only to the extent that the assumptions themselves reflect the relevant aspects of the real world. Computer programmers refer to the "garbage in–garbage out" phenomenon: computers won't make arithmetic mistakes, but they will produce nonsensical output if their program or input data are defective. Similarly, economic theoretical reasoning can work out the consequences of systems of assumptions about economic life, but this type of argument in itself cannot validate these assumptions as good representations of the real social forces at work.

Demographic Equilibrium

Malthus's analysis of population was an important early instance of equilibrium reasoning, and it became a key element in Ricardo's influential model of capitalist development. Malthus's conception links the standard of living of workers, which he associates with the real wage, to mortality, fertility, and the size of the working population.

There are three key relationships in Malthus's reasoning. The first is the decline of mortality with a rising real wage, due especially to lower infant mortality. The second is a gradual rise of fertility with a rising real wage, due to earlier marriages and better maternal nutrition. The third, which is crucial to both Malthus's and Ricardo's conclusions, is a decline in the real wage with rising population due to rising food prices, since more food has to be produced on limited land. This is the assumption of diminishing returns—the working population rises with no increase in land to grow food.

At a very low real wage, mortality is high and fertility is low in Malthus's system, and as a result the working population will decline. The shrinking working population puts less pressure on agricultural land, so the real wage and the standard of living of workers will be rising. As the real wage rises, mortality declines and fertility increases until the working population stabilizes. This level of the real wage represents a demographic equilibrium in which deaths just balance births, and the working population is stable. If the working population were to rise above this level, the real wage would fall because of rising food prices, mortality would increase, fertility would decline, and the population would fall back to the equilibrium level. Thus the assumption that a rise in the working population will depress workers' standard of living makes Malthus's demographic equilibrium stable.

The level of the real wage at which deaths balance births *defines* the demographic equilibrium of Malthus's system, while the *stability* of that equilibrium depends on the assumption that a larger working population leads to a lower standard of living. (I give a graphic presentation of Malthus's analysis in the Appendix, pp. 237–240.)

Malthus's Critique of the Poor Laws

As in modern industrial capitalist societies, there was a fierce debate in Britain during the early years of the industrial revolution over welfare policy, which the British called the "Poor Laws." In Malthus's time the Poor Laws required each parish (a unit of local government) to support its own paupers at a minimum income level, through the provision of "workhouses" or "poorhouses," where the poor lived at parish expense. The inmates of workhouses had to labor at low-skilled jobs in order to repay some of the expense of their upkeep. (Charles Dickens's portrait of the misery and abuse to be found in workhouses and poorhouses contributed to the later rejection of this system in favor of direct money payments to poor families.) This system of relief was financed by local property taxes. Since each parish was responsible only for "its own" poor, many parishes tried to prevent poor families from moving in, to avoid their becoming a "charge" on the tax bill. As a result, it was very difficult for poor families to move around within Britain to take advantage of employment opportunities.

The Poor Law system was expensive and failed to reduce absolute rates of poverty and dependence. There were many proposals for the reform of the system. Malthus's position was that the Poor Laws encouraged (or perhaps even created) poverty. His argument grows out of his general analysis of population. The Poor Laws, according to Malthus, allow people to marry and have children without being able to provide for them. Since in his view the supply of food is relatively inelastic, this larger population will raise food prices and lower the wage of employed workers, leading to more poverty. Malthus thus sees the Poor Laws as raising fertility, leading to a lower equilibrium real wage and higher infant mortality.

Malthus's approach to the political economy of welfare has vigorous advocates in modern advanced industrial capitalist societies. During the debates on federal welfare policy in the United States in recent years, critics of the policy have used arguments very similar to Malthus's to claim that welfare actually creates poverty, or at least makes the problem worse. Malthus, like these critics, is less explicit about what he thinks will happen to the poor if the Poor Law system of support disappears.

Malthusian Logic

Like most highly influential social/political arguments, Malthus's is part logic and empirical science, and part ideological projection of particular moral values. Malthus is unusually explicit about at least some of the values that inform his argument—for example, his attitude regarding the morality of contraception. His argument also has implications about social justice and equality, and the causes (or blame) for the suffering caused by poverty. In Malthus's eyes, the structure of property rights and property ownership in society takes the form of unchangeable constraints, like natural physical laws, and the focus of possible change is directed at the behavior of poor and working-class people in the context of these constraints. One may doubt whether Malthus is actually addressing the poor and working class directly at all: perhaps his target is the discomfort that members of the middle and upper classes in Britain felt at the evident polarization of their society. One tendency of his argument is to fix the sources of poverty in the moral attitudes and behavior of the poor, and to discourage direct attempts to alleviate the suffering of poverty on the grounds that they make the whole situation worse through their indirect effects on the equilibrium wage.

On the one hand, Malthus says that human population tends to increase geometrically. But is this consistent with the rest of his analysis, especially his discussion of preventive checks? The preventive checks (which lower the fertility rate for every level of standard of living) raise the equilibrium level of the standard of living and reduce fertility below the theoretical maximum. Doesn't this imply that every human society has customs and practices that control fertility rates? What then happens to the postulate of inexorable geometric increase in population due to the "passion between the sexes"?

If (as Marx suggests in his criticism of Malthus) we amend Malthus's postulate to say that every society has its own law of population growth, which must correspond to its own productive powers and system of social distribution, what happens to Malthus's critique of the perfectibilists? Perhaps the prosperous utopia envisioned by Godwin and his associates will solve its population problem precisely by solving its production problem, and thus will achieve a stable population at a high standard of living with low fertility and mortality rates.

Population and Food since Malthus's Time

These logical considerations are not entirely abstract and theoretical: the history of industrialization and population growth has played out many of these themes and possibilities in the time after Malthus. In the usual frustrating way of history, these subsequent events do not unambiguously settle the debate between Malthus and Godwin on either side. Some of what has happened supports the perfectibilist vision, but experience has not completely dispelled the Malthusian shadow, either.

Population Growth, Economic Growth, and the Demographic Transition

As more and more nations and regions of the world have experienced industrialization and urbanization, some fairly clear patterns have begun to emerge that extend and modify Malthus's postulates. The basic scenario is the shift of population from a traditional, low-productivity, low-technology, rural, agricultural mode of production to a modern, high-productivity, high-technology, urban, industrial mode of production. This shift tends to take place more and more rapidly as time goes on. As it occurs, average standards of living rise rapidly as measured by income, education, health, or housing indexes. At the same time, some sectors of the population sink into the terrible misery of rural stagnation or urban congestion and decay.

Demographic statistics confirm over and over again Malthus's stylized mortality schedule. A rise in standards of living, leading to better average sanitation and nutrition, lowers mortality sharply, especially infant mortality, as Malthus predicted. The immediate result is a more or less explosive growth of population, also in line with Malthus's predictions. The growth of the population also permits the Smithian division of labor to increase as the basis of the increase in labor productivity that raises standards of living.

The history of fertility rates in the course of economic development, however, tells a more complicated story than Malthus, who expected a mild rise in fertility rates with increasing wages. What happens in country after country experiencing economic development is that at higher levels of the standard of living fertility begins to fall. Some of the factors behind this phenomenon are fairly well understood and are documented in the demographic literature. In traditional agricultural societies, children are seen largely as an economic asset, since their labor contributes to family income from a relatively early age, and the parents' main hope of support in their old age is a large number of children. In urban industrial societies, however, the decision to rear children becomes more like the decision to acquire other discretionary consumption goods, and children themselves become more expensive with rising costs of nutrition, health care, and education. The support of parents in old age shifts more to their savings invested in financial assets and to state pensions. Moreover, women's economic lives change in ways that make later childbearing and lower total fertility rates more attractive to them. As more women undertake high-productivity economic activity, they have to forgo more opportunities for pregnancy and childbirth. As a result, women delay childbearing and choose childbearing patterns that result in fewer births per mother. These effects are called the "demographic transition."

If fertility falls at high standards of living, there can be a demographic equilibrium at which deaths balance births at a high standard of living. Under Malthus's assumption that a larger working population leads to a lower standard of living, however, this second demographic equilibrium would be unstable. If the working population were to increase above the equilibrium, the standard of living would fall, according to the assumption of diminishing returns, and at a lower standard of living fertility would rise again, increasing the working population still more and pushing the society back to the Malthusian demographic equilibrium at a low standard of living.

On the other hand, if the standard of living were to *rise* with an increase in the working population, the high-standard-of-living demographic equilibrium would be stable. Adam Smith proposes a mechanism that would lead to a rise in standard of living with a larger working population in his analysis of the division of labor: the larger the total population, the more extensive is the division of labor, and hence the *higher* is labor productivity. Smith's theory puts increasing returns to the working population in place of Malthus's assumption of diminishing returns. We might call the high-standard-of-living demographic equilibrium that results from the demographic transition a "Smithian equilibrium," because it would be stabilized by forces that tend to raise the wage with an increase in population. If there is in turn a link between labor productivity and the level of workers' standards of living, which indeed seems to be the case in most countries over a long time horizon, then an increase in population will tend to raise the real wage and push the population back toward the Smithian equilibrium.

Thus the combination of Smith's division-of-labor effect and the demographic transition in fertility suggests quite a different scenario for the long-run fate of modern society. In this scenario, population at the world level stabilizes through a fall in fertility. The larger the absolute size of the equilibrium world population (at least up to a point), the higher will be world income and wealth. This not-so-gloomy scenario, however, tells us little about the *distribution* of income levels in a stabilized world population. We can see already a strong tendency for the world to divide into a group of richer countries with older populations and negative natural rates of increase (Europe, North America, Japan), and a group of poorer countries with younger populations and positive rates of natural increase (the rest of the world).

Thus Malthus's first postulate, that population grows inexorably at a geometric rate, has fared rather badly at the hands of history in the two hundred years since he wrote his *Essay*. It appears that population growth, both through fertility and mortality, is highly sensitive to the processes of economic development, and that people have adapted their reproductive behavior to changing economic circumstances in more subtle and sophisticated ways than Malthus anticipated.

Feeding the World

What about Malthus's second postulate, that the food supply can increase only arithmetically, and is thus doomed to fall short of the geometric growth potential of the population?

History has not been particularly kind to this postulate over the last two hundred years, either. On the whole, food supplies have grown somewhat more rapidly than human population, which is to say that food production has also sustained a geometric rate of increase. At the present time the world's population produces more than enough food to feed itself. However, the maldistribution of food as a result of the imbalances of economic development and political conflict and incompetence regularly leads to devastating regional famines, such as those in East Africa in the late 1980s and North Korea in the mid-1990s. This increase in food output is all the more remarkable because there has been a considerable rise in the costliness, if not the nutritional quality, of the world's diet, as more and more people eat higher and higher on the food chain.

How has this increase in food production been accomplished? The two most important factors have been the opening of new and more productive agricultural regions, on the one hand, and the application of advanced technology in the form of mechanization, pesticides and fertilizers, and genetic engineering of food crops and animals, on the other. These developments have transformed both labor and, to a lesser extent, land productivity in agriculture. Together they have defeated the forces of diminishing returns that Malthus apparently thought would dominate historical trends in food production.

But the specter of diminishing returns still haunts humanity. The technological advances that have allowed us to feed ourselves have also brought serious environmental problems and have depleted important resources. There is no guarantee that the future path of food production will continue the trends of the last two hundred years, though many experts in this area are cautiously optimistic that humanity can continue to feed itself even if the population were to increase fivefold from its current levels. We cannot be sure, however, that some ecological or resource catastrophe might not intervene to frustrate these projections.

8 to 30 Billion People

Demography continues to be an uncertain and controversial science. While a consensus view does currently exist concerning the broad outlines of world demographics, there is a great deal of controversy about many details, and some serious scholars challenge key elements of this consensus.

The consensus holds that the world as a whole is undergoing the demographic transition observed first in the early industrializing countries. Fertility rates are dropping in newly industrializing countries, as they did historically. In fact, if anything, fertility rates seem to be falling more rapidly in recently industrializing countries than they did in earlier industrializers. A look at the extended Malthusian model indicates that the predicted equilibrium size of the world population depends very sensitively on the exact shape of the fertility schedule, which is not known with a high degree of accuracy. Estimates of the time at which the world population might reach equilibrium vary from as soon as 2050 to as late as 2150, and estimates of the eventual size of the world population vary from 8 to 30 billion people. These are enormous uncertainties.

The consensus view on the stabilization of world population due to the demographic transition does not extend to a very detailed vision of the distribution of wealth and income in the stationary population. Distribution, which to a very great degree determines the amount of suffering and the minimum welfare of people, depends on even less predictable political and economic factors than fertility and mortality themselves.

Ricardo and the Limits to Growth

David Ricardo was a successful London stockbroker who took up political economy as a kind of hobby. He was a founder of the Political Economy Club in London, which came to exert a powerful influence on British economic policy through its efforts to educate Parliament in the principles of liberal, free-trade political economy. On several occasions Ricardo prepared testimony for various committees of Parliament, especially concerning monetary policy and free trade.

Ricardo had a profound influence on the development of British and world political economy. His unusual gift for analyzing complex economic interactions through simple and powerful abstractions established the paradigm for later economic reasoning and model-building. Ricardo's logic is subtle and powerful, but he never loses sight of the implications of his abstract analysis for the concrete complexity of the real world.

Ricardo's liberal political economy emphasized the laissez-faire aspects of Adam Smith's analysis, and firmly supported free trade. Like Malthus, with whom he carried on a fertile intellectual dialogue on political economy, Ricardo opposed attempts to alleviate poverty through Poor Laws or welfare programs. These policy prescriptions became almost a religion among the British political elite in the nineteenth century. Ricardo's analyses of rent and comparative advantage are the foundation of the contemporary neoclassical school of economics, and his discussion of the labor theory of value is the starting point of Karl Marx's critique of political economy and the capitalist system. The last half of the twentieth century has seen the emergence of a small but vigorous neo-Ricardian school of economics dedicated to completing the analytical framework that Ricardo created.

Ricardo's Labor Theory of Value

Ricardo begins his *Principles of Political Economy and Taxation,* first published in 1817, by saying that he agrees with everything Adam Smith has to say, except Smith's treatment of the theory of value and distribution. Since theories of value and distribution underlie all economic analysis, the exception Ricardo makes is perhaps more important than his general endorsement of Smith's ideas.

Ricardo criticizes Smith's adding-up theory of value on the grounds of circularity, particularly involving rent. He argues that the labor theory of value, properly understood, is the only logically sound foundation for political economic reasoning.

Ricardo focuses attention on what Smith called the natural price of commodities that are easily and widely produced. He explicitly excludes commodities whose value depends on their rareness or scarcity—like the paintings of dead old masters, or unique geological or archaeological specimens—from the labor theory of value. Ricardo's interest is in the determinants of the value of commodities that are being produced routinely all the time, like food grains (which he, following British usage, refers to generically as "corn") and textiles.

In Ricardo's view, the value of reproducible commodities is fundamentally determined by the amount of labor embodied in them. If it requires 20 hours of labor to produce a table and 1 hour of labor to produce a bushel of corn, then according to this labor theory of value the natural price of tables will be twenty times the natural price of a bushel of corn. If the price of tables gravitates around $40, the price of a bushel of corn will tend toward $2. One advantage of the labor theory of value is that it gives a precise and unambiguous answer to the question of what determines the relative value of commodities.

If gold or silver were also produced within a country, and if the national money were defined in terms of a certain amount of gold or silver, the same reasoning would establish the money prices of commodities as well. For example, if it took 10 hours of labor to produce an ounce of gold and the dollar were defined as 1/20 of an ounce of gold, the natural price of the table would indeed be $40 and the natural price of a bushel of corn, $2.

Ricardo is aware that there are different types and qualities of labor employed in an economy with a developed division of labor, depending on the skill level of the workers and the particular branch of production in which they work. He takes a rather commonsensical approach to this problem, arguing that it is possible at any particular moment to establish at least a rough equivalence between different types and qualities of labor across industries. In other words,

Ricardo assumes that there is a unit of standard labor to which all specific forms of labor can be reduced. An hour of a skilled computer programmer's time might represent five or six of these standard labor hours, for example. Ricardo does not worry very much about the technical methods that might be used to estimate this standard. The important issue for him is that once the standard is established, it is possible to reason on the basis of the labor theory of value using that standard.

Ricardo's Correction of Smith

One of Smith's versions of the labor theory of value equated the value of a commodity to the amount of labor it can command in exchange on the market rather than to the amount of labor it embodies. Ricardo criticizes this labor-commanded interpretation of the labor theory of value on the ground that it makes the value of commodities depend on the wage. If, given the assumptions made above about tables and corn, the wage is $1/hour, a table commands 40 hours of labor and a bushel of corn 2 hours of labor. If the wage for some reason were to rise to $2/hour, without any change in the production methods used to produce tables and corn, the value of the table in the commanded-labor sense would fall to 20 hours, and the value of a bushel of corn to 1 hour. In Ricardo's view this implication of the labor-commanded interpretation is a fatal defect, because he wants the labor theory of value to determine the value of the commodity *independently of variations in wages*. As we shall see, this feature of the labor-embodied interpretation plays a key role in Ricardo's reasoning.

Comparative Advantage and Trade

One important use that Ricardo made of his version of the labor theory of value was to develop the theory of comparative advantage as the basis of trade between countries. Ricardo considers an imaginary world economy in which two countries, "England" and "Portugal," produce two commodities, "wine" and "cloth." Ricardo assumes that in England it requires 100 hours of standard labor to produce a bolt of cloth and 120 hours of labor to produce a barrel of wine, while in Portugal it takes only 90 hours of standard labor to produce a bolt of cloth and 80 hours to produce a barrel of wine. In labor terms, Portugal has an absolute advantage in the production of both commodities, since it requires less labor to produce them in Portugal than in England.

Nonetheless, argues Ricardo, there is the possibility of mutually advantageous trade between England and Portugal, in which England exports cloth to Portugal in exchange for wine. The reason is that the opportunity cost of a barrel of wine in terms of cloth is 6/5 bolts of cloth per barrel of wine in England, and 8/9 bolts of cloth per barrel of wine in Portugal. Thus it is cheaper for Portugal to get cloth by producing wine and selling it to England to buy cloth than by producing cloth directly. This analysis shows that Ricardo believed that the labor theory of value holds *within* each country, but not *between* countries, presumably because capital and labor are not free to move from one country to another to bring about an equilibrium.

The theory of comparative advantage has been very influential but also extremely controversial. It is a major analytical support for the policy of world free trade which became the dogma of nineteenth-century Britain, and has been politically dominant in the United States since the Second World War. It has also been challenged in important ways. Ricardo is not very explicit about the source of comparative advantage. The example he chooses suggests that comparative advantage is rooted in geographic and climatological differences, that is, differences in the natural-resource endowments of different countries. But in the modern world a huge amount of trade takes place between countries that have very similar resource endowments, which suggests that the widening division of labor itself is a cause of comparative advantage.

If comparative advantage is an effect of the division of labor, it might be possible to influence the development of trade patterns dynamically through economic policy. It might, for example, be extremely disadvantageous for a country to adapt passively to emerging world patterns of comparative advantage, rather than seeking to develop its comparative advantage in certain directions.

The Quantity-of-Money Theory of Prices

Ricardo's example of trade between England and Portugal also presupposes an adjustment in the gold price of cloth and wine in both countries. Ricardo believes that the gold prices of their commodities can vary so as to maintain the comparative advantage equilibrium. In making this argument, Ricardo appeals to the idea that the gold prices of commodities in a country rise or fall with the quantity of gold in that country.

The gold prices of commodities together with the volume of commodities in a country being sold in a year determine the value of total circulation. The stock of gold money necessary to accomplish this circulation depends on the number of times each piece of gold can participate in a transaction in a year—the velocity of money. In a monetary economy, these two values have to be equal. (In modern economics this relation is called the "equation of exchange.")

The stock of gold required to circulate commodities depends directly on the value of the total circulation and inversely on the velocity of money. In Ricardo's quantity-of-money theory of prices, the equation of exchange determines the gold prices of commodities to be consistent with the quantity of gold circulating in the economy, the quantity of commodities circulated, and the velocity of money. If the quantity of gold increases, holding velocity and the quantity of commodities circulated constant, the gold prices of commodities will rise. Monetarist economists in the twentieth century adopted Ricardo's quantity-of-money theory of prices to argue that price inflation depends only on the quantity of money in a country, and can always be controlled by controlling the growth of the quantity of money. (In the Appendix, pp. 240–241, I write out the equation of exchange in mathematical terms.)

Ricardo used the quantity-of-money theory of prices to support his theory of comparative advantage. If England and Portugal allow free trade in cloth and wine, the gold prices of wine and cloth (corrected for transportation costs) will have to be the same in the two countries. If gold prices of both cloth and wine are initially lower in Portugal, gold will flow from England to Portugal and will raise gold prices of cloth in Portugal until English cloth is cheaper and can be sold there.

Ricardo regarded money as a "veil." Despite the fact that in the real world commodities are sold for money, Ricardo argues that the final effect is the exchange of commodities for commodities, just as in a system of barter without money. In a barter system the demand for one commodity is just the supply of some other commodity. If money is indeed a veil, Say's Law (see Chapter 1), which argues that the aggregate willingness to sell commodities for a whole economy creates an equal aggregate demand, will hold. Ricardo, like Adam Smith, concludes on the basis of Say's Law that the labor and capital which become unemployed because of competition from foreign imports will be absorbed into an expanding export sector. Say's Law is thus a key part of the laissez-faire argument for free trade.

The quantity-of-money theory of prices neatly closes Ricardo's argument for comparative advantage; however, it is inconsistent with Ricardo's labor theory of value. If Ricardo used the same reasoning to explain the value of gold as he used to explain the prices of corn and other commodities, he would have concluded that the gold prices of commodities were determined by the relative production cost of gold and commodities, not by the quantity of gold in circulation.

Competition and the Labor Theory of Value

Ricardo was aware of another difficulty with his interpretation of the labor theory of value, which is that it is potentially inconsistent with Smith's claim that competition among capitalist firms will equalize profit rates across industries. The problem is that according to the embodied-labor theory of value, full-time workers of standard quality in different industries will all add the same amount of value to the product. If wages are equal, which will tend to be the case if workers are free to move from one industry to another, then each standard full-time worker will also produce the same amount of profit. But workers in different industries may work with very different amounts of capital, measured by value. Since the profit rate is defined to be the ratio of the profit flow to the capital invested, under these circumstances profit rates will not be equal in different industries.[1]

When prices are proportional to embodied labor, but capital in-

---

1. A numerical example may help to clarify this point. Suppose one full-time worker can produce 1 ton of steel or 100 bushels of corn. Then according to the embodied-labor theory of value, the price of a ton of steel should be the same as the price of 100 bushels of corn. If the price of a bushel of corn is $2, then the price of a ton of steel should be $200, according to the theory. Suppose that the wage of a full-time worker is $100/year. Then both steel workers and agricultural workers produce $200/year in new value, of which $100/year goes to wages, leaving $100/year as profit. But suppose each worker in the steel industry is equipped with $2,000 worth of capital, and each worker in the corn industry is equipped with $500 worth of capital. Then the profit rate in the steel industry will be ($100/year/$2000) = 5%/year, while the profit rate in the corn industry will be ($100/year/$500) = 20%/year.

vested is not proportional to embodied labor, the embodied-labor theory of value predicts different long-run profit rates. Ricardo, however, basically accepts Smith's argument that competition tends to equalize profit rates across industries through the movement of capital from lower-profit-rate to higher-profit-rate industries.

It is possible to show mathematically that if profit rates are equalized, relative prices will change with wages, unless the capital invested per worker is the same in all industries. This is a further problem for Ricardo, because, as his criticism of Smith's commanded-labor theory of value shows, he thinks that a theory of value should determine the prices of commodities independently of movements in the wage rate.

Ricardo was aware of this logical difficulty, and had two ideas for dealing with it. In the *Principles*, he argues that equalization of profit rates will make price ratios deviate from embodied labor ratios, but not by very much, because differences in capital invested per worker are not very big in fact. George Stigler dismissively dubbed this the "93% labor theory of value." Curiously enough, there is evidence that even in modern economies the deviation between long-run supply price ratios and embodied labor ratios is not very big.

In any case, Ricardo proceeds to develop his larger theory on the basis of the embodied-labor theory of value. His conclusions will hold at least to the extent that variations in capital invested per worker across industries are small.

The invariable standard of value   Ricardo also considered another way to make the embodied-labor theory of value consistent with competitive profit rate equalization. Ricardo argues that if we could find *one* commodity which was always produced with the *average* amount of capital per worker, the value of that commodity would be unambiguously determined by the amount of labor required to produce it, and its value would be independent of the wage. He called this commodity the "invariable standard of value." (The value of the standard is "invariable" to changes in the wage, not to changes in technology.)

The advantage of the invariable standard of value is that Ricardo could analyze changes in its value due to technology and then modify the conclusions reached for other commodities depending on how much the capital invested per worker in producing them deviated from the average. Thus the conclusions reached on the basis of the embodied-labor theory of value could be rigorously extended to all commodities.

Unfortunately, Ricardo never found a commodity that could reliably serve as his invariable standard. When he died, an unfinished essay headed "The Invariable Standard of Value" was found on his desk. Despite considerable investment of intellectual resources in this problem in subsequent years, no procedure for finding an invariable standard of value that works in all economies has been found.

Accumulation and the Stationary State

Ricardo uses his embodied-labor theory of value as the foundation of an extraordinary analysis of the dynamics of capital accumulation. The idea is that the labor theory of value determines the whole value of the commodity (on average over the whole society), which then is divided up between wages, profits, and rent according to the theory of distribution. Ricardo then makes the simple and plausible assumption that workers spend all their wages as a class on wage goods to reproduce themselves, while landowners spend all their rents on luxury goods, but that capitalists save a large part of their profits as the source of saving and capital accumulation. Thus as long as the profit rate is positive, capital accumulation will increase the stock of capital, the demand for labor, and the population. This self-sustaining growth process will come to a halt only when the pressure of population on land raises food prices so high that profits become zero—the stationary state.

The Corn Model

Ricardo begins his analysis by considering the production of agricultural food grains, or corn. In the simplest case, the cultivation of corn requires land, labor, and capital in the form of stored-up corn to feed the agricultural workers until the next harvest. The land is owned by landowners who rent it out to capitalist tenant farmers, who in turn hire agricultural labor to work it.

Industrially produced commodities require capital and labor, but negligible amounts of land. Ricardo assumes that labor and capital are freely movable among different sectors of the economy, so that the wage rate and the profit rate in every industrial sector must settle in a long-run average sense at the same level as in agriculture. Thus a correct analysis of the determination of the wage and the profit rate in the agricultural sector will also determine the wage and the profit rate in the economy as a whole. This insight allows Ricardo to reduce the problem of his theory of distribution to understanding the determinants of wages and profits in agriculture.

The analysis of distribution can be carried out either in terms of money prices and wages or in terms of corn. When we use the money price system, we will assume that money is gold, and that gold is produced by a given amount of labor, so that the monetary unit is effectively a unit of labor time.

The Natural Wage

Ricardo adopts Malthus's analysis of population and wages, arguing that the dynamics of mortality and fertility determine an equilibrium level of the corn wage at which the population will be stable. This equilibrium corn wage becomes the natural wage for Ricardo.

He assumes it to be a given characteristic of an economy—though different countries may, because of differences in customs and culture, have different levels of the natural wage—and to change very slowly over time in any given country.

Abstracting from the costs of tools and seed, Ricardo assumes that the wages advanced to agricultural workers account for the lion's share of capital. The given level of the corn wage then also determines the amount of capital required to employ a worker. Workers and capital are applied together in fixed proportions to the land.

Like Malthus, Ricardo assumes that the overwhelming majority of the population of a country will be workers, in either agriculture or industry. There may be differences in wage levels due to differences in skill and cost of training in different sectors of the economy, and differences in cost of living in different geographic regions, but these can be averaged out as far as the analysis goes. The amount of capital available to be advanced as wages (the "wage fund") determines the number of workers, and this in turn determines the population of the country and the demand for food.

Rent

Ricardo then turns his attention to the situation of the landlord and the determinants of rent. The theory of rent is easiest to understand if we reason in terms of corn, though the same arguments can be expressed in terms of money in a straightforward way.

The land in a country is not all of equal fertility for growing corn. Some land has very good soil, easy access, and better local climate, and as a result it will produce a very large harvest of corn with a given application of labor. Other land is not quite so favored by nature, and yields somewhat less corn for the same application of labor. In fact, we could imagine ranking all the land in a country in order, from the most fertile to the least fertile, at any moment in time. It is convenient to measure the quantity of land by the amount of labor (or capital, since capital per worker is fixed in Ricardo's model) required to cultivate it. So let us imagine the whole land of a country divided up into plots that require one person-year of labor to cultivate. Some of these plots may be bigger in area than others, of course.

As the population grows, the more fertile plots of land will be cultivated before the less fertile. The number of plots of land cultivated determines the number of workers employed in agriculture. At any point in time, the least fertile plot of land cultivated is the agricultural margin. As less fertile plots of land are cultivated, the total agricultural output of the country increases, but each newly cultivated plot and worker adds a smaller amount to the total than the last. This additional output from the marginal plot is the "marginal product of labor" in agriculture. The assumption that agricultural output can be increased only by cultivating less fertile land is the principle of diminishing returns for agricultural employment, which we have seen is a key element in Malthus's demographic analysis. Agricultural output per worker declines as total population and agricultural employment increase because workers have to work on worse and worse land. This is inconsistent with Adam Smith's theory of the division of labor, which implies that output per worker will increase with a larger population, at least for a significant range of levels of population. Smith's theory implies increasing returns to population.

On any plot of land, the sum of profit and rent must be equal to the output of the land less the corn wage of the worker cultivating it. The output of the plot of land less the wage of the worker cultivating it is sometimes called the *surplus product,* since it is what is left over after the full costs of production, including the reproduction of the labor force, are deducted. What determines the division of this surplus product between profit and rent?

Ricardo considers the bargain that will be struck between the capitalist and the landowner. The capitalist is, by assumption, free to switch her capital to any other piece of land or to industrial production in search of a higher profit rate. If the landowner demands a rent so high that the capitalist would be left with less than the average profit rate, no capitalist will rent the land. On the other hand, if the capitalist tries to demand a rent so low that she makes more than the average profit rate on her capital, the landowner can easily find another capitalist who will pay somewhat more rent. Therefore, the rent must be set just high enough to make the profit rate on the plot of land equal to the profit rate on all the other cultivated plots and on industrial capitalist production. This is Ricardo's theory of rent. The rent is "differential" because it depends on the relative fertility of the landowner's plot to the marginal plot of land.

In theory, the marginal (lowest fertility) land in cultivation gets zero rent. This is an abstraction, of course, since in reality the landowner would demand a very low nominal rent to pay for the cost of making the rental contract. But in economic terms, the principle that marginal resources command no rents is a central analytical idea. From this point of view, it makes sense to consider a nominal rent as the equivalent of a zero rent.

The land beyond the margin could be used to grow corn, but its output is too small to provide a capitalist with the average profit rate once she has paid workers the natural wage, and therefore no capitalist will invest to cultivate it. If the profit rate were to fall, however, some of this land would become profitable and would come under cultivation.

Ricardo's theory of rent implies that as the population expands, bringing less fertile land into cultivation, the rent of the already-cultivated land will rise. The owner of the previously marginal plot, who could not bargain for more than a nominal rent, now finds it possible to raise the rent above zero. Furthermore, as the agricultural margin shifts outward, a larger and larger proportion of the total corn output goes to rent.

Ricardo's theory of rent is important because it gives us a correct insight into one of the basic mechanisms determining incomes in a market economy. Rent is obviously important in the pricing of all natural resources, such as mineral resources, hydropower, and petroleum reserves. Economic rents, however, arise whenever the owner of a resource is in a position to collect a higher price for its use than it costs her to employ it. The high incomes of movie and sports stars are economic rents in this sense, and thus subject to Ricardo's principles.

As we will see in Chapter 4, contemporary neoclassical value theory is based on the idea of applying Ricardo's theory of rent to *all* factors of production, including labor and capital.

Marginal Land and the Profit Rate

At any moment in time the population of a country is given and requires a certain amount of corn as food, given the natural wage. This determines the agricultural labor force, the capital invested in agriculture, the total amount of land brought into cultivation, and the margin of cultivation. Ricardo's extraordinary insight is that because the marginal land yields no rent, the surplus product on the marginal land determines the profit rate *in the whole economy*. Remember that Ricardo, like Smith, believes that competition will tend to equalize profit rates in different sectors of the economy. The profit rate of capital invested on marginal land will, then, tend to be equal to the profit rates on other land (as a result of differential rent) and equal to profit rates in all sectors of industrial production. Since the size of the population determines the marginal land in cultivation, the profit rate in the economy as a whole has to adapt.

This beautiful discovery closes Ricardo's system and gives it complete determinacy. In effect, it solves the problem of distribution. Malthus has already given a theory of the natural wage in his demographic analysis; Ricardo has given a rigorous form to Smith's theory of rent as a residual; all that remains is to determine the profit rate, which Ricardo has now accomplished.

We can summarize Ricardo's theory of distribution in the following terms. Malthus's laws of fertility and mortality establish the long-run natural real wage in a country. The population may expand or contract as a result of changes in the amount of capital available to employ workers, but the workers themselves find their standard of living always returning to the same level. Given the population of the country, the fertility of its land determines how much of the land has to be brought into cultivation to provide the necessary food, which in turn determines the fertility of the land on the agricultural margin. The surplus product of workers on the marginal land takes the form of profit, and determines the profit rate. All workers share basically the same standard of living, and all capitalists share the same rate of profit on their capital. The surplus product on land that is more fertile than the marginal land takes the form of rent.

Accumulation

Ricardo's next step is to put his theory of distribution into motion as a theory of capital accumulation.

Ricardo's theory of accumulation is based on assumptions about the consumption/saving behavior of the classes of workers, landlords, and capitalists. Ricardo thought that workers as a class consumed their wages in the process of reproducing themselves. This view, which is held by Smith, Malthus, and Marx in addition to Ricardo, may not be very far off the mark even for contemporary capitalist societies. Contemporary working-class households, of course, do save—for retirement, to finance their children's educations, and to tide themselves over spells of unemployment. But all these motives for saving are also motives for dissaving: the saving of households contemplating retirement is offset by the dissaving of retired households, for example. Because of these offsets, the net saving of workers' households may in fact be rather small or even zero. Since official statistics do not categorize households by class status in Ricardo's sense, it is difficult to be sure one way or the other. Neoclassical economists reject the class divisions that Ricardo and Smith took for granted, and attribute all private saving ultimately to "households," but this category includes both the wealthiest capitalists and the poorest workers.

Ricardo thought, or at least provisionally assumed, that landowners also spent all their rental income on consumption. Here he was reflecting the British social reality of his day. Large British landowners were generally aristocratic families who spent fortunes to maintain their political influence and power, but very little in improving their estates or, with a few notable exceptions, building factories or mills.

Thus for Ricardo pretty much all of the saving and capital accumulation in the society was attributable to capitalists. Indeed, Ricardo went further and assumed that capitalists saved practically all of their income. This may seem strange in light of the enormous homes and estates we associate with successful nineteenth-century capitalists, but in fact even these substantial expenditures absorbed only a tiny fraction of the total income available to them. Ricardo falls into line with the image of the abstemious capitalist, who works to make money without stint and hardly spends anything on himself.

If all profits are accumulated, in the next year there will be a larger demand for labor, and the population and agricultural labor force will increase, moving the agricultural margin to less fertile land. This is the basic dynamic of capital accumulation, according to Ricardo's thinking.

The effect of capital accumulation is to increase the population, food output, and agricultural labor force; to increase total rents; but to lower the rate of profit as the surplus on the marginal land declines because of diminishing returns. The total amount of profit may increase in the early stages of capital accumulation, because the amount of capital is rising faster than the profit rate is declining, but eventually the amount of profit has to decline as well. Over time, the profit rate and the amount of profit have to approach zero.

The Stationary State

This quite extraordinary conclusion of Ricardo's analysis has proved to be remarkably influential. Ricardo has a logically powerful argument that capital accumulation will eventually bring about its own demise—eventually the rate of profit will fall to zero and accumulation will cease. Ricardo called this the "stationary state."

Eventually the population of a society becomes so large that the marginal land is just fertile enough to pay the natural wage and yields no surplus product at all, and therefore no profit. There is, of course, a very large total surplus product, but in the stationary state it all takes the form of rent, which, according to Ricardo's assumptions, will be consumed, not accumulated. In the stationary state capital invested can be recovered, but without the increment of profit. There is a very large population living at the subsistence (or natural wage) standard of living, and regulated by the Malthusian mechanisms of high fertility and high mortality. The capitalists as a class have to struggle competitively as hard as they can simply to maintain their capitals intact; they find they have no profits to reinvest in order to expand production.

Ricardo's stationary state will arrive as long as there are diminishing returns to labor, whether or not landowners appropriate differences in productivity as rent. Unowned resources, such as the atmosphere and the oceans, may impose diminishing returns on a growing world population, even without rent, and choke off capital accumulation.

Looked at from another point of view, Ricardo's stationary state represents the imposition of resource limits to growth. At the stationary state the population has grown to its maximum level, given the capacity of limited land to provide food. The limits to growth in Ricardo's world come from diminishing returns to capital accumulation, and take the form of rising rents, which eat away profits. If we look at the system in terms of money and money prices, the profit rate is eaten away by inexorably rising money wages, which are required to allow workers to subsist in the face of constantly rising food prices. Our contemporary anxieties about resource and environmental limits to economic growth ultimately stem from the same belief in diminishing returns; we worry more, however, about the environmental catastrophes and costs that might bring economic growth to a halt than about rising rents.

Ricardo's analysis also gives us a rigorous answer to the puzzle raised by Smith's claim that the profit rate in the economy as a whole tends to fall with the accumulation of capital. The reason, according to Ricardo, is the diminishing returns to labor and capital resulting from the limited supply of agricultural land.

It would not help the stationary state if landlords accumulated. In fact, accumulation by landlords would drive the profit rate below zero, since the only use that could be made of their capital would be to cultivate land on which the surplus product was negative. (See the Appendix, pp. 241–244, for a graphic presentation of Ricardo's corn model.)

Foreign Trade and Technical Change

While Ricardo believes that the stationary state lies inevitably in the future of capitalist accumulation, he also thinks that in the short and medium run there are two forces that might delay the stationary state and allow capital accumulation to continue: foreign trade and technological progress.

Both foreign trade and technological progress increase the marginal productivity of labor and capital. Foreign trade has this effect because a world market in corn, for example, effectively brings all the potential agricultural land in the world into the agricultural competitive system. The number of available plots of land of any fertility increases dramatically, and the diminishing returns to accumulation are greatly slowed, if not halted altogether. The fall in the rate of profit due to rising rents slows down.

Ricardo and his followers used this argument very effectively in support of their free trade politics in nineteenth-century Britain. The climactic episode in the political struggle over trade policy came in the 1830s after Ricardo's death, when Parliament repealed the Corn Laws, the tariffs and quotas that prevented the free import of grain into Britain. This event marked the shift of effective political dominance in Britain from the landowning aristocracy to the rising capitalist class; the landowners' interest in high and stable food prices gave way to the capitalists' interest in low food prices and low wages.

Technical change that increases the output of agricultural land— say, through better fertilizers, or pesticides, or mechanical cultivation, or irrigation—also has the effect of raising the marginal products of capital and labor. Technical progress increases the amount of corn that can be produced on each plot of land. The effect, in Ricardo's eyes, is similar to the opening up of foreign trade. Technical change raises the rate of profit immediately, and allows for more capital accumulation and more population increase before the stationary state arrives.

Ricardo, like Malthus, thought that technical changes in agricultural production were possible, but he could not imagine a continuous, unending process of technical change driving economic growth. Individual inventions that raise productivity might sporadically raise the rate of profit and allow for an increase in population, but eventually, he believed, the inevitable forces of diminishing returns would set in again and the profit rate would start to fall. Ricardo is all in favor of technical progress—he thinks that capital accumulation is the fundamentally dynamic force in European society, and he dreads the arrival of the stationary state—but he has no hope that technical change can put off the stationary state forever.

History and Ricardo's Vision

How has history treated Ricardo's predictions? This is a difficult question to answer because of the gigantic sweep of Ricardo's vision, and the very long time it might take for the forces he analyzed to play themselves out.

In the nearly two hundred years since Ricardo wrote, the two off-setting forces he analyzed, foreign trade and technical change, have clearly played a dominant role in the world economy. The development of the American continents, Australia, and southern Africa, and the opening of South and East Asia to the world economy, have greatly enlarged the stage on which the drama of capital accumulation plays itself out, and have correspondingly slowed down the Ricardian fall in the rate of profit. It is not at all clear that humanity has exhausted the possibilities of increased utilization of agricultural land. The agricultural potential of Siberia is barely developed, for example. Much of the most fertile land in the world, in Asia, is still cultivated by extremely low-productivity methods. An optimist might fantasize that irrigating the Sahara Desert could have the same impact on world agricultural output as the irrigation of the Central Valley in California had on U.S. food production.

The process of technical change, which Ricardo saw as a welcome but unpredictable relief from the pressure of diminishing returns, has if anything gained momentum over the past two hundred years. One major technological revolution after another has emerged: steam power, electricity, synthetic chemistry, the internal combustion engine, telephony, radio, electronics and digital computers and all the rest.

But the historical experience of the last two hundred years is not sufficient to dispel all the anxieties so beautifully encoded in Ricardo's model. How do we know that diminishing returns in the form of environmental decay or collapse or the exhaustion of natural resources won't eventually wear down our ingenuity and our pioneering spirit? We don't know the future, of course, and we can't be sure whether it holds a repetition of the technical and foreign-trade revolutions of the last two hundred years, or the final arrival of Ricardo's stationary state.

The demographers' prediction that human population will stabilize over the next seventy to a hundred years at somewhere between 8 and 30 billion people surely fits at least part of the picture of the stationary state. But a stationary population could coexist with a technologically progressive economy and a rising standard of living, or it could sink back into the Malthusian equilibrium at a bare subsistence level. Looking at the world right now, one can see signs consistent with either path.

Ricardo's Views on Machinery

In revising his *Principles* for a later edition, Ricardo had some second thoughts about the impact of machinery on the well-being of the different classes of society. He wrote up these considerations as a new chapter, "On Machinery."

Ricardo asks himself whether the invention and adoption of machinery benefits each of the classes of society. The immediate effect of machinery is to increase the productivity of labor, which makes commodities cheaper in real terms, according to the labor theory of value. This clearly benefits the landowning class, since they can buy luxury goods more cheaply. It equally benefits capitalists, who find that both their consumption goods and the goods necessary to set their factories in motion become cheaper.

What about workers? Originally, Ricardo tells us, he believed that workers as a class must also benefit from the adoption of machinery, and the consequent cheapening of wage goods, but he realized that this depends on a crucial assumption—that the total amount of capital devoted to the wage fund that supports workers remains at the same size. If this assumption holds, then employment will not fall, and workers will find their means of subsistence becoming cheaper with the adoption of mechanized techniques.

But the mechanized techniques are expensive for capitalists to put in place. Ricardo's second thought concerns the possibility that in order to buy expensive machines, capitalists will reduce the wage fund itself, thus reducing employment of the working class and impoverishing marginal workers.[2] If this is the path that mechanization takes, marginal workers will be unemployed without the creation of other jobs to absorb them, wages will be forced down by competition among workers, and the Malthusian mechanisms of population decline will come into play.

It is difficult for Ricardo to come to a firm conclusion regarding the impact of mechanization, because the cheapening of commodities that benefits the capitalists may lead them to accumulate more, and thus to increase the total capital fast enough to offset the relative decline in the wage fund. Therefore, the actual course of employment depends on the exact balance between the forces of accumulation on the one hand, which tend to increase the wage fund and increase the demand for labor, and technological unemployment on the other, which tends to eliminate jobs and make workers redundant.

Ricardo argues that there is indeed a powerful motive at work to

---

2. Ricardo refers to this in rather obscure language as a *reduction in gross product while net product remains constant*. Here he uses "net product" to refer to the surplus product shared by capitalists and landowners, and "gross product" to refer to the whole output of the society.

encourage capitalists to mechanize. The first capitalists to adopt machine techniques find that their costs of production fall very rapidly. As long as most capitalists in their area lag in mechanization, the price of the output will be determined by the backward techniques, and the innovating capitalists will be in a position to make "super-profits" because their costs are so low. Of course, as the other capitalists come to adopt the same technology, the prices of output will fall and these super-profits will decline. Still, the lure of the super-profits is a powerful motive for capitalists to mechanize.

Ricardo also notes that rising wages themselves will tend to push capitalists to adopt labor-saving techniques of production in order to prevent their costs from rising. As we have seen, one of the effects of diminishing returns in agriculture in Ricardo's model is to raise agricultural prices and money wages. This brings into play the counter-force of technological change as capitalists seek to avoid the rise in costs and fall in the rate of profit that would otherwise ensue.

Ricardo's theory of mechanization raises many of the issues that preoccupy political economists today: trade-offs between job security and productivity, the importance of property rights in innovations to creating incentives for technical change, and the possibility of stubborn periods of mass unemployment. Marx took this analysis as the basis of his theory of technical change in capitalist society.

Adam's Fallacy and the Political Economy of Poverty

Malthus's and Ricardo's attitudes toward poverty and charity show the extremes that Adam's Fallacy can reach. From Malthus's perspective, providing charity to the poor was self-defeating or, even worse, exacerbated the problem of poverty: in his view, charity or the dole allows workers to reproduce even when they have no employment. Thus subsidizing the poor pushes down the wage and the standard of living at which population stabilizes, making the problem of poverty worse at the social level.

This kind of reasoning is characteristic of Adam's Fallacy. Its method lies in contrasting the immediate effects of action (charity relieving the sufferings of the poor) with indirect, systemic effects (charity expanding the population and lowering the standard of living of the poor). Its burden is the necessity of resisting beneficent and moral impulses—do not give to the poor lest you actually create poverty.

Behind this type of reasoning lies the unpleasant truth about capitalist social relations. The organization of the social division of labor through commodity exchange and wage labor systematically inverts the ordinary logic of human relationships. The logic of the commodity system assumes the universal assertion of self-interest in opposition to others. When everyone follows this logic, the system works to produce wealth. But any attempt to circumvent this strange moral logic and help others directly tends to be defeated by the laws of the market. The investor who refuses to profit by investing in slave-trading, for example, actually winds up raising the rate of profit in slave-trading, and subsidizing those who do not have moral scruples in that direction. Sending food to famine-stricken areas depresses food prices, ruins local farmers, and can make hunger worse. The logic of commodity exchange is opposed to moral logic in both its principles and its conclusions. But more important, the reality of commodity exchange and its laws tends to defeat moral action. Thus Adam's Fallacy becomes a real and inescapable part of the experience of life.

3/The Severest Critic

Karl Marx was a student during the waning days of the *ancien régime* in Germany, in the late 1830s and 1840s. Britain, France, and to some degree Spain had consolidated themselves as modern nation-states by the early nineteenth century, but Germany remained divided politically into small kingdoms and principalities. Germany was experiencing the pressures of economic development and the industrial revolution, and there was widespread recognition that the massive political and social changes initiated by the French Revolution were far from complete. Revolution broke out in Germany and Austria in 1848, but the revolutionary movement divided and was unable to unify Germany. Instead the Prussian autocratic state eventually created a German Empire by joining together the non-Austrian German-speaking peoples, thereby setting the stage for the cataclysmic upheavals of twentieth-century history.

The realization that Germany was in the process of epochal social transformation prompted a vigorous debate over the direction and shape of that transformation. The field of this debate in Marx's student days was largely philosophy, and in particular the philosophy of Georg Wilhelm Friedrich Hegel. Hegel struggled with the problem of adapting the theological philosophy of the Western tradition to the emerging secular capitalist society. Hegel's work and that of his successors put religion, history, and social institutions under a searching critical examination, centered around questions like: "Where is history heading?" "What principles guide the evolution of social and political institutions?" "What makes political power legitimate?" "How can the disruptive forces of industrial capitalism be reconciled with traditional religious morality?"

Marx was at the center of this radical questioning of received values, and he developed a theory, historical materialism, to address these fundamental questions. He made a lifelong friend of Friedrich Engels, the scion of a well-to-do German manufacturing family, who had spent several years in the family business in Manchester and had written an extraordinary portrait of the social dislocation and conflict engendered by the industrial revolution, *The Condition of the Working Class in England*. Engels saw Marx's theory of historical materialism as a version of his own views, and he became Marx's collaborator as well as his intellectual and financial supporter for the rest of Marx's life. During this period Marx wrote the philosophical papers now known as the *1844 Manuscripts*.

Marx got involved in the radical wing of German politics and edited a newspaper during the revolution of 1848 that supported the most extreme democratic measures, the political organization of German industrial workers, and the destruction of all feudal property rights. Marx and Engels wrote *The Communist Manifesto* at this time to show the connection of the contemporary upheavals of German and European politics with the underlying forces of social change as analyzed by historical materialism. With the failure of the revolution, Marx was forced to leave Germany and spent the rest of his life in exile, first in France and Belgium, and eventually in London, where he supported himself by writing for newspapers and with the subsidies Engels provided.

Working frequently in the British Museum Reading Room, Marx undertook a massive systematic study of political economy. The early drafts of this work are now known as the *Grundrisse;* Marx supervised the publication of revisions as Volume I of *Das Kapital (Capital),* and Engels prepared much of the rest of the material for publication after Marx's death in Volumes II and III of *Capital* and *Theories of Surplus Value.* Though Marx was an ardent advocate of worldwide proletarian revolution to establish a socialist society, most of his theoretical work in economics concerns the capitalist system, and it is primarily as a theorist of capitalism that Marx's work in political economy remains important today.

Marx worked actively to promote the political organization of workers as a revolutionary force in Britain, France, and Germany. His intellectual genius, brilliant polemical writing, and evident loyalty to the idea of proletarian revolution made him an influential leader of a disorganized, fragmented, but emotionally and politically potent movement. Marx's relations with his political rivals within the workers' socialist movement often took the form of acrimonious and uncompromising conflict. The strain of immense intellectual labor, unrelenting political struggles, and material poverty and deprivation eventually ruined Marx's health, and he was unable to advance his projects much in the final decade and a half of his life. His last major foray into political economy took the form of detailed comments on a draft manifesto of a German Workers' Party *(The Critique of the Gotha Programme).*

Marx's political radicalism coexisted with a conventional Victorian life-style in his marriage to Jenny von Westphalen, the daughter of a prosperous family who devoted her life to Marx and their daughters. Engels, an unrelenting critic of Victorian hypocrisy in sexual matters, lived in a long-term relationship with a woman whom he did not marry, and became one of the intellectual founders of modern feminism through his work on the origins of the family and the state.

Marx was a master of the German critical method and made his contributions in the form of a critique of existing ideas and writing. Marx takes a concept, such as the commodity, as he finds it in Smith or Ricardo, for example, and transforms it by questioning its historical origins and limitations, placing it in relation to a broader range of theories, and forcing it to confront its own social manifestations. By the time Marx is finished, the concept, without losing any of its original significance, functions in a new way in a new context. This "dialectical" theoretical method is a powerful way of developing new insights and questions, though it cannot by itself produce new knowledge of reality without the empirical test of observation or experiment. Marx understood this, and in his writing he argues in parallel at a highly abstract level and at a very concrete historical level, using statistics, government reports, and newspaper reports to explain the immediate significance of his theoretical discoveries.

Marx was a critical genius, and his penetrating transformation of classical political economy into a doctrine of social revolution was a major intellectual landmark of nineteenth-century political economic thought. Marx's intellectual prestige became a much-fought-over legacy in the various political movements that were founded on Marxist ideas, including the Social Democrats who are still a major force in European politics, the Bolshevik Communist parties that ruled Russia and Eastern Europe for much of the twentieth century, and the Asian Communist parties that are even now guiding the modernization and industrialization of China and Indochina. I think it is important to keep in mind that Marx died before these various movements developed, and that, as with other important thinkers, he should not be held responsible for all the good and evil done after his lifetime in the name of his thought. There is much to learn from, and much to criticize in, Marx's work.

Historical Materialism and the Capitalist Mode of Production

Marx's conception of historical materialism addresses the curious problem of the continual change in the *form* of the division of labor in human societies. Other species that adopt a division of labor, such as bees and ants, always organize the hive or hill in the same way. The division of labor appears to be programmed into these species at a genetic level. Human history, on the other hand, exhibits massive, fundamental, structural differences in the division of labor. The size of the human population, its distribution between large and small settlements, the technologies employed, the institutions organizing production, and the political institutions supporting social production all differ greatly over time and space.

On the whole, the nineteenth century believed that human history was a record of progress, of an increase in our collective power to control our conditions of existence. There are various philosophical (or, as Marx would come to call them, ideological) interpretations of human history. Some ancient philosophers, such as Plato, viewed the laws of social and political organization as unchanging over time, and reflecting eternal, ideal principles of justice. Christian theologians explained history as the working out of a divine plan for humankind. Hegel saw history as the progressive realization of the abstract idea, which he associated with God.

Marx's position was that the human social world was part of the physical world, and had a material reality independent of the consciousness of the human beings who lived through it. In this sense Marx was a materialist. (This is not materialism in the sense of an obsessive concern with material wealth, comfort, or consumption, as the word is often used now.)

Marx thought that the laws of social reality were as external and unyielding for any individual living through it as the laws of physics were, but he argued that social reality is constructed from the collective results of individual action through processes beyond any particular individual's control. On the one hand, individuals are always born into an ongoing society with accumulated resources, institutions, beliefs, and knowledge that constrain each generation's choices and action. On the other hand, it is impossible for an individual to act socially except through the web of existing social institutions and relationships, and equally impossible for her to predict the full social ramifications of her choices, because they depend on the actions and choices of other people. "Humanity makes its own history, but not in circumstances of its own choosing," argues Marx in a famous summary of this point of view.

Because social reality is determined by human action, it is subject to historical change in a way that physical laws and biological laws are not, according to Marx's thinking. Over time, the collective actions and decisions of millions of people can fundamentally alter the resources and institutions of society, though not necessarily as the result of their conscious intentions. It is in this sense that Marx's materialism is historical. Social reality is external to the individual and manifests laws that are as objective and unchangeable from the individual's point of view as physical and biological laws. But social reality is the collective creation of the people making up society, so that collectively people can change social laws in a way that they can never hope to change physical or biological laws. Not only *can* people change society, but inevitably they *do*, and this continual process of change is what Marx sees as history. An immediate corollary of historical materialism is that no human social institution lasts forever: in fact, all human social institutions are in a constant process of change and transformation. To put it even more precisely, human social institutions reproduce themselves through changing and transforming themselves. Marx criticizes Smith, Malthus, and Ricardo for talking as if there were universal principles of social and economic organization that could be discovered once and for all and would be valid for all human societies at all times and places.

The task of social science, from this historical materialist perspective, is to study the way in which particular historical social systems reproduce themselves, their laws of motion, and the contradictions through which they undergo transformation into something else. The procedure Marx adopts is to break down the complexity of social reality into its abstract components by the application of the critical method. Once we understand these abstract components, we can reconstruct the complexity of social reality synthetically as their resultant. The image is something like one of those books that show the systems of the human body on different sheets of transparent plastic. As you lay one sheet over another, you see the image of the actual body reproduced as the sum of its component parts.

Surplus Product, Exploitation, and Class

In applying historical materialism to the understanding of human history as he knew it, Marx argued that all past civilized societies had a social class structure, founded economically on class control of the surplus product. (One important critique of Marx's ideas rests on the fact that we know more about the details of history today than he did, and we no longer believe some of the generalizations he took for granted.) Civilized societies, in this view, are all based on their technological ability to produce a surplus product above the immediate needs of the physical reproduction of their workers. Marx argued that in all the societies of which we have a record, this social surplus product was appropriated by a small minority of the population, thereby dividing the society into a class of producers and a class of appropriators of the social product.

Marx believed, for example, that the ancient Greek and Roman societies generated most of their surplus product from slave labor. In this situation the slaves are the direct producers, and the slaveowners the appropriators, of the surplus product. Marx also believed that the surplus product of feudal European society stemmed from the labor of serfs who were bound to the land of their feudal lord. The serfs worked a certain number of days a week to cultivate the lord's land, thereby creating the surplus product that allowed the feudal lord to maintain soldiers and fortifications.

In Marx's language, the appropriation of the surplus product by a narrow class is exploitation of the producing class. A class society is one in which a social surplus product is appropriated by one class through the exploitation of another.

Forces and Social Relations of Production

There are two aspects (or, as Hegelian language has it, "moments") of exploitation. In the first place, the resources of the society must be advanced enough to make the production of a surplus above the reproductive needs of the producers possible. Marx calls the productive resources of a society "forces of production." They include the population, its accumulated means of production, and its knowledge and technology. This concept is very broad and embraces any relevant factor contributing to productivity. For example, knowledge about organizing the division of labor, even though it may not be embodied in any particular machine, is part of the forces of production.

But the technological possibility of producing a surplus does not guarantee that a surplus will actually be produced, nor that it can be appropriated by a particular class. Thus exploitation also involves particular social institutions governing the control over technology, resources, and labor, which Marx calls the "social relations of production." In feudal society, for example, the military power of the feudal lords gave them control over the land and the labor of the serfs. This control was deeply ingrained in the social institutions of the time in the form of feudal privileges and duties. By enforcing these customs, laws, and contracts, feudal lords could get the weekly labor from the serfs required to cultivate their own lands and harvest the surplus product. The serfs would provide for their own subsistence by working on the land made available to them. Furthermore, the surplus product would be available to the lords and under their control as a result of the social relations under which it was produced. The surplus product, in turn, fed the soldiers and knights maintained by the feudal lord to enforce his rights and defend his domain from external threats. Similarly, under slavery the entire product of the slave belongs to the slaveowner. The slaveowner is directly responsible for the slave's subsistence and must provide minimal levels of food, housing, and clothing to the slaves. But whatever the slaves produce in excess of this subsistence minimum is immediately the legal property of the slaveowner, who thus appropriates the surplus product.

One can also think of the surplus product and exploitation in terms of the total labor time of the society's producers. Some part of the labor of a society has to be devoted to producing the goods necessary to allow the producers to reproduce themselves. Marx calls this the necessary labor time. But in any even slightly developed human society, the task of producing the workers' subsistence does not take the whole available labor time. If workers are induced to work longer than is necessary to reproduce themselves, the remaining labor time is surplus labor time. In an abstract sense, what the exploiting class appropriates when it gets the surplus product is the surplus labor time of society.

Marx believed that each historical class society had its own characteristic combination of forces of production and social relations of production, the combination of which he called the "mode of production." Thus the ancient slave mode of production is the combination of the social relation of slavery with the technology of dispersed agricultural production on large estates. The feudal mode of production is the combination of serfdom, feudal privileges and duties, and agricultural production on small, divided strips of land in a communal setting.

Marx argues that the interaction of the forces and mode of production determines the path of technical change in the society. Some modes of production, in his view, tend to stifle technical change and progress because they threaten the stability of the social relations of production. Conversely, the gradual development of forces of production through technology and changes in the organization of labor can undermine and eventually overthrow the social relations of production. In the study of these dynamic interactions of the forces and relations of production lies the secret of historical change. Marx saw the process of historical change as at its root a series of class conflicts, in which the contesting needs and interests of the classes arising from the mode of production are fought out in political, cultural, and military terms. Revolutions like the French Revolution were, in Marx's view, the most dramatic expression of class conflict.

Base and Superstructure

The mode of production, in turn, is only a part of the whole complex of institutions and practices that make up a human society. In Marx's language, it constitutes the "material base" which supports other aspects of society, such as government and laws, religion, education, and culture, including the sciences and arts, which Marx called the "superstructure" of society. Marx argues that there is a complex interaction between base and superstructure in the reproduction of social institutions, but that when push comes to shove, the needs of the base, and particularly of the social relations of the base, determine the outcome. On the other hand, elements of the superstructure often make a critical contribution to the reproduction of the social relations of production.

For example, Marx argues that feudal Christianity played a powerful role in resigning the mass of the serfs to their subordinate social position in feudal society, fostering a psychological obsession with sin and the afterlife that distracted people from the immediate reality of their lives. Similarly, Marx believes that "bourgeois economics," the wing of classical political economy that emphasized the necessity of inequalities in the distribution of property and wealth in capitalist societies, is an apology to defend capitalist social relations of production. It thus plays an important role in persuading capitalist workers of the inevitability of the institutions under which they live.

Marx interpreted societal laws as reflections of the underlying class structure. The first acts of the French Revolutionary Assemblies, for example, abolished the feudal privileges and practices that secured the surplus labor of the serfs for their lords. In Marx's view, this was an expression of the capitalist character of the French Revolution, which sought to free labor from serfdom to participate in the capitalist wage-labor market. Furthermore, Marx argued that the ruling philosophical and religious ideas of a society generally echo the beliefs of the appropriating classes. Medieval theology and philosophy are largely devoted to justifying the privileged class position of the feudal elite, while the literature of emergent industrial capitalism introduces themes of self-reliance and social mobility that are congenial to the "self-made" capitalist.

The Transformation of Modes of Production

In Marx's early work in collaboration with Engels, including *The Communist Manifesto,* he made an attempt to apply the general point of view of historical materialism to constructing an interpretation of world, or at least European, history. This interpretation is organized around the idea of a succession of modes of production, each giving way to the next as the result of its own internal contradictions.

This sketch begins with the notion that Stone Age peoples lived in a type of primitive communism—small communities that shared their very small wealth according to traditional rules. In this mode of production, the forces of production were very little developed; these peoples depended largely on hunting and gathering for their subsistence. As a result of the low level of development of productive forces, there was no surplus to speak of, and hence no class division of society.

The establishment of property relations, particularly property in women and children, destroyed this primitive communism and its mode of production. The establishment of property in women and children made possible the beginnings of settled agriculture, with an attendant increase in potential surplus production. This surplus production was appropriated by priests and kings, thus creating the class structures of the early empires. These empires saw the emergence of gigantic disparities in wealth and power based on the mobilization of agricultural surpluses from wide geographic regions through taxes and tribute enforced by military power.

Under the Roman empire, slave labor in large-scale agriculture became a powerful engine of surplus production, and the method of exploitation shifted from a largely military imposition of tribute to the extraction of surplus labor from slaves through legal institutions. This ancient slave mode of production degenerated through the breakup of the Roman empire, and its military and political institutions, into feudal fragments. The slave populations reproduced by imperial conquests became serf populations bound to the land of a particular local lord, owing their surplus labor to the lord on the ideological pretext that he compensated them by providing military protection.

Feudal society gradually organized itself into nations, fostering the growth of cities, which were freed from feudal subordination. In these cities a nascent capitalism based on trade and small manufactures took hold. Slave and serf modes of production are inherently technically regressive: slaveowners are reluctant to invest in labor-saving devices that may be sabotaged by slaves; feudal lords have an interest in maximizing the labor they control, because of its usefulness as an army in times of crisis. The capitalist, on the other hand, has a strong incentive to transform production through technical change, and to increase the rate of exploitation of wage labor. This leads to the rapid growth of capitalist wealth, and its conflict with the feudal aristocracy, which culminated in the revolutionary turmoil of the early modern period in Europe.

Marx and Engels argue that, just as the contradictions of feudal society led to its transformation into capitalism, the contradictions of capitalist society will culminate in a transformation into socialism. But whereas past transitions from one mode of production to another have always produced a new class society based on new relations of exploitation, socialist society will abolish class distinctions by creating institutions for the social control of the surplus production. Just as capitalism unleashes a huge increase in productive forces through technology, socialism will build cooperatively on these forces of production to create a society in which the satisfaction of human needs rather than the pursuit of surplus product is the ruling motivation. Eventually the superstructure of class society, including the state, will become obsolete, according to Marx and Engels, and the "true history" of humanity can begin.

This brilliant and in many ways insightful sketch of an interpretation of history has been remarkably influential in shaping twentieth-century politics and modern historical research, but it has some important limitations. Marx and Engels simply did not know enough about the detailed social history of non-European nations to make accurate generalizations about their modes of production. As a result, it is difficult to fit non-European cultures and civilizations into this scheme. They also tended to ignore awkward facts that contradicted their interpretation. Feudal European society was in fact very complex, with tremendous variation in the social relations of production between different regions and periods, for example. And the relative importance of slavery as a source of surplus production in the Roman empire remains highly controversial among economic historians.

From a political point of view, a simplistic reading of Marx and Engels' interpretation created the unfortunate impression of a mechanical movement of history which is actually foreign to the critical spirit of the historical materialist method. Some socialist and communist political movements began to view their eventual victories as foreordained by the "laws of history," and as a result came to lose contact with the political and social reality of their time. Marx's discussion of the transition from capitalism to socialism introduces completely different concepts and principles from his analysis of previous modes of production. Whereas previous transformations involved the gradual growth of new class relations within an existing mode of production, Marx seems to envision socialism as the wholesale conversion of the capitalist mode of production to entirely new principles of operation. The prophecy of an end to class relations and class struggle and the beginning of a new epoch of human relations carries a utopian and unhistorical flavor that sits uneasily with the general point of view of historical materialism.

It is necessary to separate the general principles of historical materialism, as a methodological approach to understanding human society and historical change, from the specific interpretation that Marx and Engels put forward in their initial application of these ideas. Despite the limitations and inaccuracies of their scheme of the succession of modes of production, the general point of view of historical materialism raises questions that need to be answered, and directs our attention to important and relevant aspects of human society.

The Commodity and the Theory of Value

Marx had already developed the philosophy of historical materialism before he began the extensive investigation of classical political economy that led to *Capital*. Marx believed that capitalism, though it was not founded on forms of unfree labor like slavery and serfdom, was nonetheless a class society resting on the appropriation of surplus labor time. He looked to the existing political economy to find the "secret" of the ability of capitalists as a class to appropriate surplus labor time in a system that appears to guarantee equal legal and civil rights to workers and capitalists.

What he found in the classical political economists, particularly Ricardo, was a theory that paralleled historical materialism to an astonishing degree. Ricardo also sees capitalist society in terms of class; furthermore, Ricardo's interpretation of the labor theory of value implies that labor creates the whole value of commodities, but receives only a part of their value in the form of wages. Ricardo's labor theory of value, or some close variant of it, thus promised to disclose the secret of exploitation in capitalist society.

The Circuit of Capital

Marx first began to think about capitalist production in "phenomenological" terms (to use Hegel's language), that is, how it appears to us directly. What does capital look like? Basically it is a process in which the capitalist lays out money to buy commodities, which might include the labor-power of workers, and later sells them, or some other commodities produced from them, for more money than he started out with. The problem is to understand where this surplus value comes from.

The circuit of capital very closely parallels the income account of a capitalist firm. In simplified terms, the income account shows the gross profit of the firm on sales as the difference between sales revenue and the cost of the goods sold. In the terms of Marx's circuit of capital, the cost of goods sold is the money the capitalist initially lays out to buy commodities to start production, the capital outlay; sales revenue is the larger sum of money the capitalist ends up with; and the gross profit is Marx's surplus value.

Marx contrasts the circuit of capital with the circuit of commodity exchange, in which someone sells a product in order to buy another product that better satisfies her needs. In the commodity circuit, a commodity is sold for money, which in turn is spent to buy another, qualitatively different commodity. The motive of the capitalist engaging in the circuit of capital is the increase of wealth represented by the surplus value. The motive of the consumer entering the commodity circuit is to consume products of higher use-value, given her needs, than those she can produce herself.

In his earlier work on political economy, Marx started his analysis of capitalist production and society with the circuit of capital. He realized, however, that the circuit of capital already presupposed a complex set of social concepts and institutions: the exchange of products on markets, private property in labor-power and other inputs to production, and money. In a bid for the respect of the German philosophical community, Marx began Volume I of *Capital* with three chapters in which he presented an analysis of these institutions that underlie the circuit of capital. These chapters are both too long and too short. They are a notoriously confusing and abstract introduction to the critique of political economy, and in that sense too long. But at the same time they raise a host of important and complicated issues, many of which they do not resolve completely, and in that sense are too short.

Use-Value and Exchange-Value

Marx observes that all human societies expend labor to produce useful products that meet human needs. (These needs may be biologically determined, like the needs for food and shelter, or socially determined, like the needs for musical instruments, sculpture, and religious ritual objects.) In many human societies products are used by the people who produce them directly, or are distributed among a small group through family or kin ties according to custom. The purpose of production is transparent in these cases, since the product is the direct means to the end of satisfying the need.

But in some human societies, of which capitalist societies are an important subcategory, many products are made to be exchanged for other products. (This is the same idea as Adam Smith's division of labor, viewed from the perspective of the products of labor.) Exchange complicates the relationship between production and need. The producer no longer produces to meet her own need directly (or the needs of her family or tribe), but to meet the need of some other person who will be the ultimate user of the product. She plans to meet her own need by exchanging the product of her labor for the products she herself will use. Marx calls products that are exchanged "commodities." Borrowing potentially confusing terms from Adam Smith, Marx analyzes the commodity in social terms as the combination of "use-value," that is, its ability to meet the human need of the ultimate consumer, and "exchange-value," that is, its ability to meet the human need of the producer indirectly through its power to exchange for other products. In Marx's view, the dual nature of commodities is at the root of the contradictions of modern society.

The Commodity Frontier

People tend to have an ambivalent feeling toward the commodity form of production. On the one hand, it makes possible a division of labor, and provides us with a range of products and standard of living that we could never provide for ourselves directly. On the other hand, commodity production alienates us both from our own labor, which goes to meet someone else's need, and from those who provide us with our needs, since we interact with them only through the impersonal and antagonistic relations of the market.

One of the pervasive effects of economic development is the extension of the commodity form of production to embrace more and more aspects of human life. Self-subsistent farmers exchange only a small part of their product in excess of their immediate needs for a small range of manufactured tools and artifacts, and thus largely meet their own needs by their own direct production. With the development of the division of labor, farmers find it more efficient to concentrate on a single cash crop and to use the money from its sale to meet their own direct needs. But as this happens, people grieve over the loss of the direct, personal, human relationships that mediated the simpler, more self-subsistent system. The commodity form constantly encroaches. House and car repairs, once performed largely by individuals for their own use (and hence not commodities, in Marx's sense), become services offered on the market (and hence commodities). The parent (often a woman) who once spent hours preparing meals for her family (producing a use-value, but not a commodity) eventually finds herself working in a fast-food restaurant to make the money required for her family to eat out several times a week (thus transforming food preparation into a commodity).

Our ambivalence about the commodity form of production lies at the root of the fierce public debates about issues like the financing of medical care (increasingly a commodity, but one that people feel particularly uncomfortable in trading purely according to the laws of the marketplace), the legalization of surrogate parenting for money, the sale of body parts, and the acceptability of creating a market for adopted children.

The boundary between commodities and production for use is

constantly shifting, and thus constantly creating new dilemmas and conflicts between the logic of the market and the logic of the direct human relations that mediate direct production.

Exchange-Value and Money

Marx argues that money in the broadest sense is an outgrowth of the exchange-value aspect of the commodity. The commodity's exchange-value is its power to exchange for other commodities. Money, whatever its particular institutional form, is the crystallization of pure exchange-value, attempting to separate itself completely from any concrete use-value.

This is a plausible conception, but it leads to a number of theoretical complications. In Marx's time money was gold or silver, which are commodities in their own right, and have use-value as well as exchange-value. For example, gold was used in jewelry and dentistry because of its ability to meet human needs directly, as well as serving as an abstract repository of exchange-value. In fact, the only reason gold can function as money is that it has exchange-value itself.

Marx addresses the theory of money through a rather elaborate series of concepts. He points out that in any exchange of products, the quantity of each product represents the exchange-value of the other product or, in his terms, becomes the "equivalent" for the exchange-value of the first commodity. When we consider the exchange of commodities in the abstract, each is simultaneously the equivalent of the other. But people typically pick out one commodity to take on the general role of expressing the exchange-value of the others—to function as the "general equivalent." Marx argues that as commodity production takes hold in a society, one commodity typically emerges as the "socially accepted general equivalent," like gold. In this role the money commodity becomes the measure of value. The state can specify the "standard of price," the units in which gold is measured (the dollar, pound, franc, mark, or yen), but the underlying laws of exchange and production determine the actual relative prices of gold and other commodities.

Once a commodity like gold emerges as the general equivalent, it tends to become the medium of circulation, passing from hand to hand to facilitate the exchange of commodities, and also the means of payment, the ultimate method of settling debts. Because a gold currency is expensive and difficult to maintain (coins are always wearing out and being "clipped"), there is a strong incentive to replace gold in the circulation process with cheaper substitutes, such as silver or copper coins, paper notes, or bank deposits, as long as these substitutes can reliably be turned into gold on demand.

The price theory of the quantity of money   Marx analyzes the quantity of gold necessary to circulate the commodities in an economy on the basis of a completely different principle from his analysis of the value of gold. The gold prices of commodities and the volume of commodities being circulated in a year determine the value of total circulation in a year, just as in Ricardo's analysis (see pp. 66–68 in Chapter 2, and p. 241 in the Appendix). The stock of gold money necessary to accomplish this circulation depends on the number of times each piece of gold can participate in a transaction in a year— the velocity of money.

The stock of gold required to circulate commodities depends directly on the value of total circulation and inversely on the velocity of money. In Marx's theory, in contrast to Ricardo's, the equation of exchange determines the quantity of gold circulating in the economy on the basis of the gold prices of commodities, the quantity of commodities circulated, and the velocity of money. Thus Marx's interpretation of the equation of exchange is exactly opposite to Ricardo's. For Marx, changes in the gold prices of commodities drive the quantity of gold money in circulation, not the other way around.

Since the total circulation is always changing as a result of the growth in the volume of commodities circulated, changes in average prices, and changes in financial practices that alter the velocity of money, the stock of gold required for circulation is always changing as well. In Marx's theory, hoards or reserves of gold held outside of circulation provide the reservoir that allows for the constant adjustment of the circulating stock of money to the total circulation of commodities.

Marx's theory of money is an aspect of his general theory of the commodity. His unification of the theory of the commodity and the theory of money is one of the deepest and most original of Marx's contributions to political economy.

Marx's Labor Theory of Value

Marx adopts Ricardo's interpretation of the labor theory of value, with some important clarifications. First, Marx recognizes that human labor is not the only source of use-value. To produce useful products, human beings always require some previously acquired means of production (even if it is only a stick used to knock down nuts from the higher branches of a tree), and the natural resource base of the earth (the tree itself). The labor theory of value, for Marx, is a theory of the source of exchange-value, and thus a theory limited to production for exchange, that is, commodity production. It might be more accurate to say that labor *becomes* the source of value in conditions of commodity production.

Marx's basic picture is that the expenditure of labor on commodities produces (or adds) value, which is embodied in the commodity and manifests itself as exchange-value in the form of money. Marx warns us, however, that not all labor creates value, but only *necessary, simple, social,* and *abstract* labor as opposed to *wasted, complex, private,* and *concrete* labor. Each of these qualifications points to an important aspect of his theory of the commodity.

To begin with abstract labor, the most difficult of these concepts, Marx notes that when we see labor expended it is always some particular type of labor engaged in some particular productive task: metalworking, computer programming, sewing, weaving, spinning, or whatever. Marx uses the term "concrete" for this aspect of labor. Concrete labor is linked to the particular use-value being produced (steel, computer programs, textiles). Thus in the concrete aspect all labor is differentiated into distinguishable types. But in a commodity-producing society, all labor devoted to commodity production has another, common aspect, the production of exchange-value. In this respect all labor is qualitatively the same, since exchange-value appears as a uniform phenomenon without particular qualities. Marx uses the term "abstract" for the exchange-value-producing aspect of labor. At one level, this is merely a definition. But Marx points out that with the widespread development of commodity production under capitalism, abstract labor becomes a real phenomenon—in statistics, in the market, and in the planning of capitalist producers.

Labor is differentiated not only by its concrete qualitative type, but by its levels of skill, experience, and productivity. If we are to regard exchange-value as being produced by labor, we must make an appropriate adjustment for these differences. Marx follows, and slightly expands upon, Ricardo in arguing that it is possible to reduce more skilled and more productive, that is, "complex," labor to a single common denominator, which he calls "simple" labor. Thus an hour's labor time of a highly experienced and skilled metalworker may count as the equivalent of two or three hours of simple labor, and may add two or three times as much value to the commodity being produced.

The theory of the commodity alerts us to the fact that labor can be expended outside the exchange system altogether, on private production, such as house or car repair, child care, or meal preparation. This labor surely produces use-values—in fact, use-values that may substitute for the consumption of commodities—but it does not produce exchange-value because the products never enter the market and thus do not become part of the social division of labor. Marx calls labor expended on commodities that are exchanged "social" labor. Clearly, private labor by definition does not produce exchange-value.

Finally, Marx points out that the mere wasteful expenditure of labor in and of itself does not increase the exchange-value of the product. A capitalist producer who lavishes unnecessary labor on a product cannot sell it for any higher price than his competitor who achieves the same quality with a smaller expenditure of labor. The exchange-value of commodities, in Marx's view, is regulated by the amount of labor "necessary" to produce the commodity using current good-practice technology and methods. Labor expended in excess of this standard produces no exchange-value and thus is simply wasted.

The labor theory of value tells us that the simple, social, necessary labor time expended in an economy over a year, if we can measure it, is expressed in the money value added to the mass of commodities produced. In terms of the income statement of a capitalist firm, the money value added is just the sales revenue less the cost of raw materials and means of production purchased from other firms, and thus equals wages plus gross profits. (The money value added for a whole economy is closely approximated by its Gross Domestic Product.) The ratio of the money value added to the labor time expended is the quantitative measure of the amount of exchange-value that labor creates in the economy in a given period.

To give an example, the GDP of the U.S. economy in 2005 was about 12 trillion dollars, and the employed labor force of about 150 million persons worked an average of 1600 hours per year. The total labor time (making no correction for complex labor) comes to about 240 billion hours; thus each hour of labor produced on average about $50. Marx constantly uses this method of translating from labor time to its money equivalent throughout *Capital*. This "monetary expression of labor time" has the same units as a wage, dollars per hour, but it is not the same as the wage. The monetary expression of labor time tells us the whole money value added per hour of labor, but workers, as Marx's theory will emphasize later, get only a part of this back in the form of wages. The average wage is typically only a fraction of the monetary expression of labor time.

Price and Value

This macroeconomic approach to the labor theory of value establishes an equivalence between money value and labor time at the level of the economy as a whole. What about the relation at the microeconomic level, in terms of individual commodities? If the prices of commodities were always proportional to the labor embodied in them, then each commodity would be a scale model of the whole economy, and its value added would be proportional to the labor expended in its production. But as we have seen in the discussion of Ricardo (Chapter 2), prices are generally not proportional to embodied labor times for individual commodities.

Marx recognized this point and commented on it in notes that he wrote before publishing Volume I of *Capital*, although these notes were published only after his death in Volume III of *Capital*. In this discussion Marx argues that the deviation of prices from embodied labor times only redistributes the value added among the various commodities produced, without changing the ratio of the money value added to the labor time over the whole economy. This represents Marx's approach to the problem that Ricardo tried to solve through the concept of the invariable standard of value. In essence, Marx takes the whole net product of the society as the standard of value, and argues that its value (which is the value added) must express the labor time expended.[1]

The Fetishism of Commodities

One of Marx's preoccupations throughout his intellectual life was to understand and explain the psychological malaise of modern society. In his youth Marx developed the theory of alienation to address this question. He addresses it again in the first chapters of *Capital* as the "fetishism of commodities."

In his early writings Marx argued that people in capitalist societies suffer because they have lost control of their creative productivity. They labor, indeed, to meet their own and other people's needs, but without the mediation of any personal relationship. Work, which Marx viewed as the highest and most satisfying achievement of human life, becomes merely a means to an end when the worker sells her labor or its fruits on the market for money to buy her own subsistence or even pleasure. Instead of garnering the real human satisfaction of meeting another's need, and having the other meet her need directly and personally, thus cementing her ties to the rest of the society, the worker experiences the division of labor as social isolation and competitive antagonism. Marx attributes the pervasive psychological crisis of contemporary society, its failure to provide a positive, unified spiritual and social context for human life, to alienation. Marx's concept of alienation embraces both the social act of giving up the fruits of one's creative potential to others, thus alienat-

---

1. There is an enormous literature on the theoretical problem (often called the "transformation problem") of the relationship between embodied labor times and prices, and some scholars reject the reading of Marx summarized here. This macroeconomic interpretation of the labor theory of value, however, makes sense of a great deal of Marx's analysis, and provides at least a helpful first step toward understanding Marx's theory.

ing one's labor, and the state of mind of that results, a feeling of apartness, distance, and loneliness in the midst of social life.

In *Capital* Marx returns to this theme as part of the discussion of the theory of the commodity, with a somewhat different emphasis. Here he argues that the commodity system (the whole division of labor with its attendant specialization) is in reality the collective product of the actions and choices of all of us as productive members of society. The division of labor in fact involves each of us in an enormous web of practical reciprocal dependence on other people to meet our needs for subsistence and production. But we perceive this system, which is at heart nothing but our own collective activity, as having an independent existence as an uncontrollable external phenomenon. The system of the market, money, and commodities thus becomes a "fetish"—something that appears to intimidate and control humanity as an external force.

Marx saw this fetishism as being at the root of the most troubling aspects of modern society. The market and the capitalist system, for example, appear to demand never-ending accumulation and the extension of the commodity form, no matter how much damage the process may do to existing human relations and institutions. We are unable to create social institutions to alleviate poverty and meet basic human needs, despite our immensely expanded powers of production, because the pressure of market competition makes us believe we are too poor. Parents wind up overworking themselves to make money to give their children a better life, all the while depriving the children of the direct comfort and love they crave and substituting alienating gifts of money and commodities for direct human company.

In Marx's view, then, all these deeply experienced and deeply resented wounds to modern humanity are at their root self-inflicted, like the catastrophes that befell the heroes of ancient Greek tragedy. The positive side of this vision is that commodity fetishism, like other damaging but self-imposed human illusions, can be dispelled by confronting it consciously and courageously. Like the terrifying nocturnal ghost conjured up by a fevered imagination, commodity fetishism will vanish into thin air in the daylight of critical awareness and analysis. Marx sees this as the revolutionary task of his age.

Today we tend to interpret commodity fetishism in terms of an excessive value put on material consumption—the worship of money and the things it can buy to the exclusion of the self-development that is our birthright. This is surely part of Marx's idea: more precisely, materialism and consumerism are symptomatic psychological side effects of the fetishism of commodities. But Marx urges us to go further, to look past the whole system of commodity relationships to a world of real human interaction that lies beyond it.

The theory of commodity fetishism is a brilliant example of one of Marx's characteristic intellectual maneuvers. He continually looks for ways to turn an existing system of ideas and conceptions upside down (or inside out) to reveal an entirely other and surprising vision hidden within it. In the case of the fetishism of commodities, the raw material is Adam Smith's already powerful vision of the virtuous circle of the division of labor fueling labor productivity and the widening of the market. Marx rewrites the same material to show us a very different psychological reading of the cycle of accumulation and specialization, and a very different dénouement of its drama.

Marx thus takes on Adam's Fallacy directly in elaborating the theory of commodity fetishism. The pursuit of self-interest, even in the context of private property relations regulated by law, is no path to the good life. On the contrary, it blinds the individual to the true conditions of his own existence (ironically, precisely the division of labor that Adam Smith so clearly describes), and prevents humanity as a whole from confronting both its real conditions and the real possibilities for social change that technology and the division of labor make possible. Here we also see Marx taking up and renewing

Godwin's perfectibilism in a strikingly more concrete form. The task of transforming the capitalist division of labor from an imprisoning fetish to a liberating social force in Marx's thought has a historical specificity and psychological urgency which transcends Godwin's idealism.

Capitalist Exploitation and Accumulation

Marx turns in Part II of Volume I of *Capital* to the problem that originally motivated him: the explanation of capitalism as a class society in the historical materialist sense. He bases his explanation on his critical analysis of the theory of the commodity and the labor theory of value.

As we have seen, capitalism is the use of money to make money, which Marx describes in the circuit of capital: the capitalist uses a sum of money as capital to purchase the means of production and labor-power; these combine in the production process to form a new commodity, which is sold (or "realized") for more money than the capitalist laid out. The difference between the money returned to the capitalist in selling the commodity and the money he spends to produce it is surplus value. For the capitalist, surplus value is the objective of the circuit of capital. The explanation of the source of surplus value in terms of the labor theory of value is Marx's immediate analytical project.

In order to motivate our interest in this question, Marx poses it in the form of an intellectual puzzle. The problem is that the exchange of commodities cannot create any new value according to the labor theory of value. When someone pays more money for a commodity than the equivalent of the labor that the commodity contains, value may be transferred from the buyer to the seller, but the seller's gain is just the buyer's loss. Across the whole commodity system, these gains and losses from unequal exchange must cancel out. But we observe surplus value (the profits of capitalist firms) across the whole system. Where does this surplus value come from?

Some economists have tried to argue that profits are disguised wages that compensate capitalists for their actual contribution to production. Marx contends that the magnitude of surplus value is much too large to be explained in this fashion, and that, in any case, money-lending capitalists—banks and bondholders—contribute nothing whatever to the process of production yet still receive surplus value.

Another attempt to explain profits maintains that profit is a compensation for the risk that capitalists run in investing their money in production. This theory is based on the correct observation that riskier investments usually have higher than average returns. Marx argues, however, that what the risk theory actually explains is the distribution of surplus value among capitalists who take varying degrees of risk, not the existence of surplus value at the social level. One can point again to the example of bondholders, who take very low risk but typically earn a positive, if relatively low, rate of return.

If we accept, provisionally, the labor theory of value, with all of Ricardo's logic and prestige behind it, how can we explain the emergence of a surplus value in capitalist production? This is the conundrum that Marx poses for himself to solve.

Surplus Value, Wage Labor, and Exploitation

Marx argues that the only logical solution to this problem is to find among the commodities the capitalist purchases with his capital one which has the special property that it creates exchange-value as the capitalist uses it up in the production process. As the capitalist uses this special commodity, the exchange-value created gets added to the value of the commodity being produced. If this special commodity costs the capitalist less than the value it has the power of creating, the capitalist is in a position to appropriate the excess as the surplus value, or profit.

The labor theory of value tells us that it is the expenditure of labor that creates value, so the special value-creating commodity must be the "labor-power" of workers, their ability to do useful work in the production process. Marx regarded the distinction between labor, the actual expenditure of human effort in production, and labor-power, the capacity or potential of workers to do useful work, as his major original contribution to political economy. Smith and Ricardo use the same term, labor, both for the input that capitalists purchase on the market and for the activity that adds value to commodities, thus confusing what Marx viewed as the key distinction on which the profitability of capitalist production actually rests. What the capitalist purchases is not labor, according to Marx, but labor-power, which has two important consequences. On the one hand, if the value of labor-power is smaller than the value that labor produces, the capitalist will reap a surplus value from production, which explains the origin of profit. On the other hand, the mere purchase of labor-power does not guarantee that the workers hired will actually expend useful, value-creating labor, which explains the emergence of structures of labor discipline and incentives in capitalist production.[2]

From this point of view it becomes critical to understand what determines the value of labor-power. Marx gives several different answers to this question in different discussions in *Capital*. In Part II of Volume I of *Capital* he follows the reasoning of Ricardo and Malthus rather closely, arguing that what proximately determines the value of labor-power is the subsistence cost of reproduction. In order for

---

2. The value of labor-power is the labor time equivalent of the wage. For example, if the monetary expression of labor time is $40/hour, and the average wage is $20/hour, the labor time equivalent of the wage is 1/2 hour: in other words, the labor-power that can expend an hour of useful value-creating labor costs the capitalist the equivalent of 1/2 hour of labor. The difference is the source of surplus value, or profit, according to Marx's interpretation of the labor theory of value.

workers to survive, regenerate their own capacity to labor, and reproduce, they require a certain amount of food, shelter, clothing, and so
forth, which they must, according to Marx, on the whole purchase as
commodities. The wage must adjust to allow workers to purchase
these commodities (which is in essence Ricardo's and Malthus's theory of wages), and this socially and historically determined standard
of living controls the value of labor-power.

Marx points out that in order for labor-power to appear as a commodity widely available in the market, workers have to be free in a
dual sense. In the first place, workers have to be legally free to sell
their labor-power, which is inconsistent with serfdom and slavery.
Thus capitalism is, according to this analysis, structurally hostile to
forms of bound labor like slavery and serfdom, and it struggles to
abolish bound labor, in political contexts like the French Revolution
and the American Civil War. In the second place, however, workers
will not sell their labor-power on the market if they have their own
access to the means of production—the tools and raw materials necessary to carry on productive activity. Workers who own their own
means of production will prefer to work for themselves and will not
become wage-laborers who sell their labor-power as a commodity.
Workers thus have to be freed historically from access to the means
of production, which Marx views as the explanation for the movement to create private property in land in the early modern period in
Europe through the enclosure of common grazing and forest land,
which was traditionally used by peasant families.

The analysis of wage labor as the sale of the commodity labor-
power is Marx's way of viewing capitalist society as a class society in
the terms of historical materialism. The point is that the value of labor-power is normally less than unity in a functioning capitalist society with positive profits. This means that the labor time equivalent
of workers' wages is only a fraction of the labor they actually perform. The capitalist appropriates the excess as profit, or surplus
value. Even though the worker bargains as the legal equal of the cap-

italist employer, the capitalists as a class, through their ownership of the means of production, appropriate the surplus labor time of the society in money terms as profit, and this is the mechanism of the capitalist exploitation of workers. Marx shows that while the mechanism of capitalist exploitation is different from the mechanism of feudal or slave exploitation, the effect in class terms is the same: the appropriation of a social surplus product by a particular class.

The Components of the Value of Commodities

The labor theory of value, supplemented by the theory of wage labor, implies that at the level of the capitalist system as a whole there is a critical difference between the money capitalists lay out as wages to purchase labor-power and the money they lay out to buy other inputs to production (tools and raw materials). From the point of view of the labor theory of value, the money laid out for raw materials and other non-labor inputs simply returns to the capitalist unchanged when he sells the produced commodity. As a result, Marx calls the non-labor component of capital outlays "constant capital" (though a better term would have been "nonexpanding capital"). The money that capitalists lay out as wages, on the other hand, returns to them with the surplus value representing the labor expended by workers for which they have received no equivalent in the form of wages. Marx calls the wage component of capital outlays "variable capital" (although a more descriptive term would be "expanding capital"). The sum of constant and variable capital is the cost of the commodity. The sales price of the commodity includes the surplus value, so that the whole value of the average commodity is the sum of constant capital, variable capital, and surplus value. The value added is just the sum of variable capital and surplus value, the living labor expended to produce the commodity. (In the Appendix, pp. 244–246, various ratios of these components are defined and analyzed.)

The capitalist, not perceiving that the social source of surplus value is the expenditure of labor alone, attributes the profit to the whole capital stock. This makes sense because of the tendency for competition among capitalist firms to equalize profit rates in different sectors of the economy, which makes it appear that profit arises from capital, not from labor. From a social point of view, Marx argues, the central ratio is the ratio of surplus value to the flow of variable capital, because that represents the division of the living labor time between the reproduction of the workers and the surplus value appropriated by the capitalists. He calls this the "rate of surplus value," or the "rate of exploitation."

The Working Day

Marx uses the metaphor of the "social working day" to explore the issues raised by his class analysis of capitalist society. He asks us to imagine the whole labor time of a society as a single grand working day. (Of course, we could just as well think of a working year or any other particular unit of time.) The labor theory of value postulates that this working day is proportional to the value that labor adds to commodities. It is important to see that Marx implicitly assumes here that all production is exchanged through the market and takes the form of commodities.

From the point of view of social reproduction, the working day is divided into the labor time necessary to produce the subsistence goods workers require to reproduce themselves (necessary labor time), on the one hand, and the labor time devoted to the production of surplus (surplus labor time), on the other. From the point of view of the labor theory of value, the necessary labor time corresponds to the wage portion of the value added, and surplus labor time corresponds to the surplus-value part of value added.[3]

---

3. If the social working day is 8 hours, the monetary expression of labor time is $40/hour, and the average wage is $20/hour, the necessary labor time will be 4 hours, and the surplus labor time 4 hours. Total value added is $480 per worker, of which $240 goes to wages.

In class terms, Marx calls the part of the working day that corresponds to wages "paid" labor time, and the part that corresponds to surplus value "unpaid" labor time. He does not mean, of course, that workers get paid wages for only the first 4 hours of their working day; they receive wages for all 8 hours. But the labor time represented by the wage is only a fraction of the labor that the workers actually perform.

The image of the working day represents the distribution of waged labor time, the labor performed in society as the result of the sale of labor-power as a commodity. In reality, however, social labor time includes non-waged labor time, such as housework and child care. Thus the whole social labor time is larger than the value added or the waged labor time, and the necessary labor time to reproduce society is bigger than the paid labor time of waged workers.

As commodity production spreads through the society, more and more necessary social labor becomes waged labor, extending the waged working day. (See the graphic presentation on pp. 246–249.)

Absolute Surplus Value

Marx argues that the root of surplus value is the extension of the working day beyond necessary labor time. In historical terms, capitalism arises in societies with relatively primitive technologies, in which people, left to themselves and with access to the means of production, will work only the minimum time necessary to produce their subsistence. In order for capitalist production to become profitable, the capitalists have to find ways to induce workers to work longer than the necessary social labor time. Marx calls the extension of the working day "absolute surplus value."

The length of the working day became a major issue in the political class conflicts of developing capitalism. Labor unions and left-wing political groups found strong working-class support for legal measures to limit the working day. Important elements of capital, particularly large enterprises with the most advanced technologies, also supported limits on the working day on the ground that they could absorb the increased costs much more easily than their backward competitors. "Wages and hours" legislation became a centerpiece of labor policy in most industrial capitalist countries. In the United States, for example, the limitation on the working day takes the form of a fine employers must pay to workers for overtime, usually a premium of 50% on the regular wage ("time and a half for overtime").

As we have seen, the necessary labor time is actually the time required to reproduce not just the individual worker but also the worker's family. In this perspective the working day is not only the individual worker's waged labor time, but the labor time contributed by the whole family as the reproductive unit of the working class. Thus the labor of workers' spouses and children contributes to absolute surplus value as well. One aspect of attempts to control exploitation by limiting the working day was the banning or regulation of child labor and the establishment of legal restrictions on the employment of women. The gender bias inherent in this policy contributed to the marginalization of women in the capitalist labor market. An important goal of feminism has been the abolition of these restrictions on the right of women to sell their labor-power on equal terms with men.

Relative Surplus Value

There are inherent limits to absolute surplus value. Long working days or working weeks sap workers' energies and lead to lower productivity as a result of fatigue, inattention, and accident. As these limits become apparent, capitalists turn to other methods of increasing surplus value. If the upper limit of the working day is fixed, the only way to increase surplus value is to lower the value of labor-power, that is, to reduce necessary labor time. Marx calls this movement "relative surplus value."

While capitalists always have an interest in depressing the value of labor-power by lowering the actual consumption of workers, workers have an equally strong interest in resisting. Reductions in the standard of living of parts of the working class have been an important factor in increasing the rate of surplus value in a few periods of capitalism, for example, in the early years of the industrial revolution in Britain and after 1970 in the United States. But the more common pattern has been for workers' standards of living to rise with capitalist development, at the same time that the rate of surplus value increases. This is only possible if the productivity of labor is rising so that the labor value of the commodities workers consume is falling. Under these circumstances a constant level of workers' standard of living can be produced with a smaller proportion of the working day, so that surplus value can increase. The rate of surplus value will tend to increase even if workers' standards of living rise, as long as the rise is smaller than the increase in labor productivity.

Capitalist Competition and Innovation

The phenomenon of relative surplus value is social: it is the result of general and gradual cheapening of the wage goods that workers consume. No individual capitalist, no matter how large his capital, can have much direct effect on the value of labor-power. The competition among capitalists, however, manages to direct their efforts toward finding technical innovations that lower the costs and prices of all commodities, and thereby indirectly lower the value of labor-power.

If a particular capitalist is lucky enough to find a technical or organizational innovation that lowers his own costs of production, he is in a position to appropriate "super-profits" above the average profit rate because prices of his commodity will be determined by his competitors' higher costs. These super-profits can be very large, as the experience of innovators in the computer industry has shown. The advantage of each innovation, however, wears off over time as competitors discover the same or equivalent cost-reducing methods and adopt them. As all the capitalists in an industry cut cost, competition forces the price of the output commodity down, gradually eliminating the super-profit. After a time the capitalist finds himself back where he started, with the average rate of profit, and has to search for a new innovation to start the cycle again.

While this process brings capitalists back to their initial competitive position, it has lasting effects for the society in lowering the costs and prices of commodities. Generalized over the whole spectrum of capitalist production, the search for super-profits through innovation is a powerful engine of technical change.

Marx sees the technical progressiveness of capitalism as its deepest inner nature. His analysis of technical change grows out of Adam Smith's discussion of the widening division of labor. Marx is at pains to show that the process is not a general ahistorical feature of human society, but rather is specific to the competitive mechanisms and social relations of capitalism. While Marx will have none of Adam's Fallacy, his vision of the actual dynamics guiding capitalist production is Smithian.

The cheapening of commodities tends to lower the value of labor-power, but the political and social aspirations of the working class constitute an important counter-tendency. As workers seek a higher standard of living and more room for their self-development, they tend to raise the real wage and the value of labor-power. Marx puts much less emphasis on this aspect of capitalist development, because his political rhetoric was based on the claim that workers had nothing to gain from the continuation of capitalist development. But history indicates that the evolution of the value of labor-power and the rate of surplus value is the result of the interplay of technical change and the social struggle of workers for higher wages.

Accumulation, Technical Change, and the Falling Rate of Profit

The circuit of capital ends with the capitalist in possession of more money value than he started with. Since the possibility of recommitting this money to the circuit of capital and having it expand once again is always present, Marx argues that the typical pattern of capitalist production is one of expansion, or "accumulation." But the process of accumulation is not a purely quantitative expansion of capital because with each round of the circuit of capital, new technologies and organizational forms appear and are incorporated into production. Accumulation is Marx's version of Smith's virtuous circle of positive feedback between the extent of the market and the division of labor. Marx's contention is that Smith neglects to explain that the whole process is based on the exploitation of labor through historically specific social relations of production.

Both Smith and Ricardo believe that the profit rate tends to fall with the accumulation of capital, and Ricardo gives a rigorous explanation of this tendency on the basis of diminishing returns due to limited land and the growth of rent. Marx also believes that the rate of profit tends to fall as capital accumulates but cannot accept Ricardo's model of diminishing returns because Marx, like Smith, believes that it is the inner nature of capital to overcome diminishing returns through technical innovations. He also believes that the rate of surplus value—the ratio of surplus value to variable capital, or of profits to wages—tends to rise with capitalist development because of absolute and relative surplus value.

The rate of profit is the ratio of surplus value to the total capital invested in production. We can also think of this as the ratio of the surplus value per worker to the capital invested per worker. Ricardo's theory assumes that the surplus value per worker in industry is determined on the marginal land in agriculture, and that it falls over time because of diminishing returns to investment in agriculture. It is not hard to see that a fall in the surplus value per worker will, other things being equal, tend to lower the rate of profit. Marx, on the other hand, argues that the broad tendency of capitalist production is to *raise* surplus value per worker by lowering the labor value of commodities faster than the workers' standard of living rises. The rate of profit can fall with a rising surplus value per worker only if the capital invested per worker rises fast enough to offset the increase in the surplus value per worker.

In Marx's view, this is what tends to happen over the whole sweep of capitalist development. Capitalism starts its historical career by taking over backward and primitive techniques developed in other modes of production. These techniques—handicraft methods using primitive and cheap tools—are productive enough to provide only a small surplus product above the workers' needs of reproduction. Thus surplus value per worker is of necessity very low initially. On the other hand, the means of production required by these primitive methods are small in quantity and cheap to purchase, and therefore the early capitalists don't have to invest very much money to get production started. Capital invested per worker is thus also quite low, and the profit rate, even with the very low level of surplus value per worker, is high.

As capitalism takes over the production process, it begins to mold and shape it through technical innovation. Relative surplus value tends to raise the level of surplus value per worker, but the capitalists as a class find that their more advanced methods of production require much larger investments of capital in factories, heavy machinery, and large quantities of raw materials to be worked up into finished products. Capital invested per worker rises, and, in Marx's view, tends to rise enough to force the rate of profit down over time.[4]

---

4. Historical statistics tend to show that Marx's account is correct for some, but not all, periods of capitalist development. In the United States, for example, Marx's pattern of rising surplus value per worker, rising capital invested per worker, and falling profit rate appears from 1869 to around 1910 and again from 1950 to 1990. But the intervening period, 1910–1950, shows a different pattern in which labor and capital productivity grew equally rapidly, capital invested per worker did not rise, and the profit rate recovered dramatically.

Marx's conception of capital accumulation unifies relative surplus value and the process of technical change that lies behind his account of the falling rate of profit. The theory of accumulation is Marx's synthesis and extension of Smith's vision of the virtuous cycle of widening division of labor and extension of the market. From one point of view accumulation is a quantitative increase in the value of capital, an aspect that Marx discusses as "expanded reproduction." Expanded reproduction envisions an economic system increasing in scale without qualitative change, so that the techniques in use, the division of value added between wages and surplus value, and the value of capital invested per worker are constant, and only the scale of the system changes. But when real-world capitalists accumulate, they seek out new techniques of production, reorganize firms through mergers and acquisitions, and find new sources of labor-power, thus introducing qualitative changes into the system. Adam Smith sees one aspect of these qualitative changes in the widening division of labor. For Marx, they are all aspects of a single unified process of capital accumulation.

The Reserve Army of Labor

One aspect of the qualitative changes that accompany the accumulation of capital is fluctuations in the demand for labor-power. Periods when the demand for labor-power rises rapidly as a result of the quantitative increase in capital alternate with periods when rapid increases in labor productivity reduce the number of jobs and employed workers. In Marx's vision these fluctuations in employed labor are accommodated by fluctuations in the "reserve armies of labor," pools of potential labor-power that absorb unemployed workers in periods of slack and provide supplies of labor in periods of high demand.

The reserve army of labor thus plays a role in regulating the level of wages and the rate of profit. When rapid accumulation raises the demand for labor-power and competition among capitalists threatens to raise wages, competition from the unemployed will tend to reduce the pressure on wages. When rapid technical change disemploys large numbers of workers and threatens to create a glut of labor-power, in-flows from the reserve armies of labor diminish or even reverse, reducing the downward pressure on wages.

Marx distinguishes three categories of the reserve army of labor. The "floating" reserve army is closest to what modern economists call unemployment: the pool of workers temporarily displaced and actively seeking new jobs. The floating reserve army consists of people who are proletarianized, that is, dependent on wage labor for their reproduction and survival, even though they are not actually employed.

Some part of the floating reserve army never finds work, and falls into the "stagnant" reserve army of labor—proletarians who fail to find industrial employment and fall into lives of crime and dependency. Only extreme ups and downs of the labor market affect the stagnant reserve army.

Most important to the long-term development of capitalism is the "latent reserve army," the huge mass of potential proletarians that exist at the margins of the capitalist system in traditional agricultural societies and groups of people who don't participate in the labor market within capitalist society. In nineteenth-century British capitalism, for example, the latent reserve army consisted in the first place of British landless agricultural workers who were displaced from the rural agrarian economy by the enclosure of common lands and the rationalization of agricultural production, and in the second place of landless Irish agricultural workers. The phenomenon of the latent reserve army continues to be important in the development of world capitalism. During the European "economic miracle" recovery after World War II, European countries depended on flows of migrants from southern Europe, northern Africa, and Turkey to meet rapidly growing demand for labor-power. The U.S. economy has drawn on migrations from Europe, the Caribbean and Mexico, Central America, and Asia at various points in its growth. Marx's analysis suggests that these flows of migration play an important role in regulating the fluctuation of wage levels in growing capitalist economies. In many developing economies, a crucial role is played by the flow of labor from traditional villages to urban industrial employment. Often these flows start with a migration of young men and women who enter the urban labor force temporarily, hoping to amass enough wealth to return to their villages to marry, buy land, and start families. Over time these temporary migrations become more and more permanent as people stay in the cities to marry or because they prefer to live there.[5]

It is not hard to see that the great economic drama on the world scene of the next twenty-five to fifty years is going to be the mobilization of the latent reserve armies of labor in Asia, Africa, and Latin America through the accumulation of capital in the advanced capitalist countries. How this process will take place, what institutions will evolve to shape it, and what transformations it holds in store for the economies involved are fascinating unresolved questions.

----

5. In the last forty years women have constituted an important part of the latent reserve army of labor for advanced capitalist economies, as labor force participation rates for women have risen and women have increasingly become waged workers. Current research in economic history suggests that women typically played an important economic role in traditional agricultural societies, and that the period from around 1920 to 1960 in the United States, when many women spent most of their lives in non-wage labor in the household, was an anomaly.

Primitive Accumulation

Marx concludes the first volume of *Capital* with a discussion of the historical origins of capitalism, the process he calls "primitive accumulation." From Marx's historical materialist point of view, the interesting question is how the means of production of pre-capitalist societies, which did not have the form of transferable private property, were converted into private property that could serve as capital. In Marx's view, only a small part of the initial capital of the system was accumulated from the profits of merchants and small early-capitalist enterprises. The great mass of the initial stake, he argued, had to come from the forcible conversion of already-created means of production into capital.

Thus primitive accumulation is a powerful lens through which Marx views the history of early modern Europe. As he describes it, the conversion of means of production accumulated under pre-capitalist modes of production to capital was largely the result of violence: wars, revolutions, massacres, expropriations, and religious upheavals. Traditional history reads these events in terms of the consciousness of the individual participants and their ideologies, but Marx sees deeper historical forces knitting them together in a unified pattern.

Many of the processes of primitive accumulation continue to play an important role in the world as the capitalist form of production spreads across the globe. For example, the "green revolution" in traditional agriculture, which introduced new seeds, pesticides, and methods of cultivation into traditional agricultural societies, has also had powerful effects on property rights and property distribution. The exploitation of the fertility of the new agricultural methods often requires considerable investment of resources, so that the richest farmers in a village benefit the most economically from the transformation; they wind up owning an even larger part of the land, and indirectly controlling a larger part of the village's productive resources through loans. The spread of commodities produced by advanced capitalist technology also tends to displace traditional products and producers, and to convert their means of production into capital. From a Marxist point of view, primitive accumulation is an ongoing aspect of capitalist accumulation, not just a historical hypothesis about early modern Europe.

The Transition to Socialism

Toward the end of his life, Marx was asked for his comments on a program drafted in the town of Gotha at a conference aimed at forming a unified German Socialist Workers Party from the various fragmented groupings created by the quarrels of charismatic socialist leaders (including Marx). This program is a classic committee production: every other word is a compromise, as the drafters tried to find a way to integrate the contradictory slogans of the warring factions. Marx has a good time skewering these various evasions in his comments, which are the only reason anyone even looks at the Gotha program itself anymore.

The divisions between Marx and the other socialists, however, are not just intraparty political quibbles, but raise some fundamental issues of political economy. There was (and remains) a strong tendency on the left to see the problem of exploitation under capitalism purely in terms of wages being only a part of the whole value produced. From this point of view, the project of socialist transformation ought to be achievable by eliminating what Marx calls surplus value (gross profit) altogether, and making sure that the whole value added gets into the hands of the workers. Marx always opposed this way of looking at matters, from his earliest polemics directed at other left-wing politicians. Curiously, in this context Marx plays the role of the conservative economist who reminds his fellow-socialists of the reality of budget and resource constraints.

Marx begins his criticisms by reviewing some basic results of his critique of political economy. He reminds us that labor alone cannot produce use-values, that is, concrete products, but requires the services of means of production (tools and equipment) and the natural productive powers of the earth. The key point for Marx is that under capitalist relations of production, private ownership has transformed the means of production, including land, into capital which can appropriate surplus value. For Marx, the socialist project is to change the form the surplus product takes: to abolish surplus value by socializing the surplus product so that it will no longer be appropriated by any particular class.

The Gotha program's somewhat blurry language seems to envision a society in which products still take the form of commodities, but in which workers (the "direct producers") receive the whole value created (the "undiminished proceeds of labor"). Marx argues that this is naive and dangerous thinking because it is unworkable. Such a society would have no surplus product at all, and would be incapable of reproducing itself or advancing. He puts forward an alternative model in which the workers receive only a fraction of the total product, just as in exploitative modes of production like capitalism, but where the surplus value is controlled socially, not privately.

Marx's model has two major features. First, there is some mechanism for securing social control of the surplus product before any output is distributed to workers. Marx refers to the surplus product as "deductions" from the total product, and makes a list of the purposes to which these resources will be devoted: replacing worn-out productive facilities, providing for the expansion of the means of production, creating reserves against natural catastrophes and other social risks, supporting those "unable to work" for one reason or another, and funding education, health, and other social consumption needs. Under capitalist relations of production, these social functions are financed privately: capitalists undertake gross investment and provide insurance reserves, and the taxing of surplus value is the source of whatever spending the capitalist state may make on education, health, welfare, and poor relief.

Whatever is left over after these deductions is to be distributed among the workers. In discussing the principles on which this distribution might take place, Marx produces one of the most fascinating passages in all his many pages of writing. He begins from the premise of the Gotha program that the principle of distribution should be participation in social labor. Presumably the idea is that workers would earn a claim on the social product proportional to the number of hours of social labor they perform. This harkens back to the earlier ideas of "Ricardian socialists" who proposed a "labor money" system in which labor certificates earned by work would circulate as money. This principle appears to be one "equal right," since every worker would participate in the distribution in proportion to her or his participation in the social labor time. Marx, however, points out the contradiction inherent in this way of thinking about distribution:

> This equal right is an unequal right for unequal labor. It recognizes no class differences, because everyone is only a worker like everyone else; but it tacitly recognizes unequal individual endowment, and thus productive capacity, as a natural privilege. It is, therefore, a right of inequality, in its content, like every right. Right, by its very nature, can consist only in the application of an equal standard; but unequal individuals (and they would not be different individuals if they were not unequal) are measurable only by an equal standard insofar as they are brought under an

equal point of view, are taken from one definite side only—for instance, in the present case, are regarded only as workers and nothing more is seen in them, everything else being ignored. Further, one worker is married, another is not; one has more children than another, and so on and so forth. Thus, with an equal performance of labor, and hence an equal [share] in the social consumption fund, one will in fact receive more than another, one will be richer than another, and so on. To avoid all these defects, right, instead of being equal, would have to be unequal.[6]

This passage is an important antidote to the uncritical assumption that Marx was a "leveler," interested only in equality of distribution. In fact, he is a sharp critic of simple-minded egalitarianism.

In an effort to explain the tentative nature of his adoption of the Gotha program's principle of distribution, Marx invokes an even more radical vision of social transformation, a society of productive abundance in which there would be no systematic rules of distribution at all. His summary of this vision, "from each according to his ability, to each according to his need," has become famous. For believers in socialism it is a ringing affirmation of the goals of communism, while to skeptics it epitomizes the naive denial of the fundamentals of human nature.

Marx then returns to a theme which runs through all his work, that patterns of economic distribution are only a reflection of the organization of production. The unequal distribution of wealth and income in capitalist society, he believed, stemmed directly from the fact that capitalist production is organized as wage labor under the control of the capitalist. The Gotha program's apparent implicit ac-

---

6. Karl Marx, "Marginal Notes to the Programme of the German Workers' Party" (1875), in Karl Marx and Friedrich Engels, *Selected Works* (New York: International, 1977), p. 324.

ceptance of the commodity form of production and the wage-labor form of production (but with a higher wage) seemed to Marx to be hopelessly contradictory.

Marx's comments on the Gotha program also give us some insight into his ideas concerning the actual political process that might achieve the transition to the radical socialist vision he put forward. Marx here refers to the "revolutionary dictatorship of the proletariat" as the transitional form of political power. It is very difficult for us, after the upheavals of the twentieth century, to put this phrase in anything like the context of the late nineteenth century, but it is important to try. The phrase "revolutionary dictatorship" is a reference to the "terror" phase of the French Revolution, in which the revolutionary government gave unlimited police powers to a small "Committee of Public Safety," which used them to destroy the resistance of the feudal aristocracy (and anyone else who happened to get in their way) through a quasi-judicial campaign of legalized murder featuring the guillotine. On the whole, European public opinion in the later nineteenth century grudgingly approved of this phase of the French Revolution as an unpleasant but necessary episode in the democratization of European society.

In using the phrase "revolutionary dictatorship of the proletariat," Marx thus links the project of revolutionary socialism with the broader movement of democratic revolution that constituted (and still constitutes) the core of the modern vision of political evolution. As Marx saw it, the historical impulse to democracy could not in the long run stop with the realization of limited political democracy and citizens' rights while economic inequality continued to worsen under capitalist social relations of production. Marx therefore added "of the proletariat" to this phrase to specify the content of the revolutionary dictatorship. In his view, the transition from the private control of surplus through the exploitation of labor to a socialization of surplus product would require the use of the most extreme measures of political struggle that Europe had ever witnessed. This is a chilling and fateful foreshadowing of the travails of the twentieth century.

The general outlines of Marx's vision of socialism are clear enough. He distinguishes the concept of surplus product from surplus value, and distinguishes the solvable problem of getting rid of surplus value and the exploitation of workers from the impossible problem of doing without a surplus product. He argues persuasively for the necessity of a thoroughgoing transformation of the organization of production to support a change in the control of the social surplus. In the background of Marx's vision is the desirability of maintaining high levels of labor productivity on the basis of advanced technology. His insistence on the need for a social surplus product under social control is realistic, and is probably the main reason why only Marx's ideas, out of all the nineteenth-century socialists, posed a credible threat to capitalist society. Other socialists envisioned the direct distribution of the whole social product to workers in one form or another, and these ideas could not be taken seriously as proposals for organizing modern industrial societies.

If we step back a bit from Marx's rhetoric, however, we can see that his vision of socialism bears a very strong resemblance to capitalist society. Workers do not receive the whole value created directly, just as they do not in capitalist society. Marx's socialist society has a surplus product which is (or at least could be) invested to expand the means of production, just as most of the surplus value in capitalist society is devoted to capital accumulation. From the point of view of, say, non-European traditional societies, Marx's form of socialism might be almost indistinguishable from capitalism in its broad outlines.

The Gotha program also reveals devastating gaps in Marx's argument, gaps that grew into some of the worst features of the revolutionary socialist project in the twentieth century. Marx seems completely unaware of the problems of institutional power that are inherent in his brief phrases describing the social control of the surplus product. Who will actually decide how much of the product has to go to gross investment, to poor relief, to education, and so on? What institutional mechanism will secure the necessary resources and make sure that they are used productively and not squandered in corruption or waste? Who will police the mechanisms of distribution, either the labor-based distribution of the Gotha program's socialist phase or the needs-based distribution that Marx imagines in a distant communist paradise? Given the need to transform the organization of production to correspond to new social principles of distribution, who will actually run the factories? Who will decide what and how to produce once society has dispensed with capitalists and their managers? Either Marx had no answers to these questions, or he thought they were trivial and secondary administrative problems that would be solved in the actual evolution of socialism. The experience of twentieth-century socialism, however, underlines the critical importance of these questions for the socialist project, and the terrible inadequacy of Marx's analysis to suggest viable answers to them.

Marx and Proletarian Revolution

The most important issues involved in understanding the interplay between Marx's work in political economy and his politics, especially his revolutionary politics, are technical progress and the growth of labor productivity on the one hand, and the determination of the real wage on the other. As we have seen, surplus value, the difference between what labor produces and what workers consume as wages, is the form the surplus product takes in capitalist society. Marx saw the key to understanding the dynamics of capitalist society as understanding the basic forces determining the size of the value added and its division into wages and surplus value. In particular, Marx analyzed this division in the form of the rate of surplus value or rate of exploitation, which is the ratio of surplus value to wages. Marx's thinking on the implications of classical political economy for the possible revolutionary transformation of European society has at least two major phases. In the earlier phase Marx put the emphasis on the tendency for the rate of exploitation and surplus value creation to increase unstably and unsustainably in capitalist development, a law of increasing exploitation.[7] As he learned more about political economy and watched the evolution of European capitalism, he began to put more emphasis on the law of the falling rate of profit.

Classical political economy expresses two polar visions of the determination of the size and distribution of surplus value. Adam Smith in *The Wealth of Nations* puts the main emphasis on the technological dynamism of capitalism as a mode of production, envisioning essentially unlimited growth in labor productivity sustained by an ever-widening division of labor. Smith is coy about his views on the evolution of real wages, but seems to think that they may rise substantially in rapidly growing capitalist economies. Ricardo, in contrast, sees labor productivity as always ultimately limited by diminishing returns due to the exhaustion of resources and land, and along with Malthus, he accepts the idea that population growth resulting from rising fertility when workers' standards of living increased would prevent the real wage from rising very much above subsistence.

Marx's innovation in this classical political economy line of think-

---

7. This point of view underlies Marx's pamphlets *Wage Labor and Capital* and *Wages, Price, and Profit* (sometimes entitled *Value, Price, and Profit*). In the latter text we find, for example, the remark, "The general tendency of capitalist production is not to raise, but to sink the average standard of wages."

ing, at least in his early writings on political economy, was to combine Smith's vision of an unlimited increase in the productivity of labor as a result of capital accumulation, with Ricardo's and Malthus's theory of a subsistence wage.[8] In fact, in some of his writing Marx projected the catastrophic effect of capitalist development on traditional modes of production, and the resulting decline in standards of living, as a progressive fall in subsistence wages and "immiserization" of the producing class. History since Marx's youth has largely borne out Smith's and Marx's position that the technological dynamism of capitalist production will overcome resource and land limits and thus will defeat Ricardo's diminishing returns. In the first half of the nineteenth century there were few signs in the actual experience of industrial capitalism that the subsistence wage theory was wrong, though it turned out to be dramatically off the mark in the longer sweep of the history of capitalist development.

The critical implication of Marx's novel combination of ever-increasing labor productivity with a stagnant subsistence wage is an unlimited but self-contradictory rise in the rate of surplus value. To put this another way, if labor productivity rises without limit and real wages stagnate, wages become a vanishingly small component of value added. This pattern of distribution would have deeply destabilizing effects on capitalist society. Marx's early discussion of the long-run tendencies of capital accumulation, class relations, the stability of capitalist economies, the political economy of capitalism, and proletarian revolution as a vehicle for the transformation of the capitalist mode of production centers on this vision.

---

8. Marx criticized Malthus's derivation of the subsistence wage as a demographic equilibrium, and substituted the theory of reserve armies of labor to underpin it.

The Contradictions of an Ever-Rising Rate of Exploitation

How does a capitalist society experiencing an unlimited rise in the rate of exploitation look and feel? It is not hard to see (and many other social observers in the first half of the nineteenth century, including both realistic conservatives like Disraeli and radicals like Carlyle, shared Marx's vision in this respect) that such a society faces numerous unmanageable economic and social contradictions.

One immediate economic problem is how to sustain aggregate demand with an unstably increasing rate of surplus value. Workers' spending would become a vanishingly small part of the flow of spending required to realize an immense social product. Capitalist spending on investment could soak up quite a large part of the difference, but from Marx's point of view this could only make matters worse over time, since investment would widen the division of labor and accelerate the rise in labor productivity. If capitalist consumption were to fill the gap, it would mean an ever-increasing and socially explosive gulf between a lavish and wasteful capitalist life-style and a stagnant or declining standard of living of workers. In any case crises of demand (over-production) would become increasingly frequent, severe, and intractable.

But Marx saw this predictable economic dysfunction of the capitalist system with unlimited rises in the rate of exploitation as a superficial expression of a much deeper and more important political contradiction, which he thought would have major historical consequences. As the rate of exploitation rises, workers would be confronted with an ever-growing contrast between their immense and growing powers of production and their shrinking control over the fruits of those powers. This is the setting for a politics of resentment and class confrontation purely on a distributional level. The higher the rate of exploitation, the more severe would be this perceptual and politically explosive stress on class relations.

But even growing resentment over distributional inequality was not the deepest implication of this contradictory situation, in Marx's view. Resentment can be managed, repressed, and co-opted in a variety of ways. Indeed, a sufficiently vigilant and resourceful ruling class can contain class struggle for a long time. But there would be another factor in this type of capitalist society that it would be reasonable to suppose would eventually become decisive. As the surplus of the society continued to grow without bounds, the project of socializing the surplus would appear realistic and desirable to more and more people of all classes. Even if a socialist system were to be much less efficient productively than the capitalism it replaced, the existence of an enormous surplus product largely being wasted on capitalist consumption would represent a huge cushion. Thus one inescapable effect of a constantly rising rate of exploitation would be the growing *practicality* of the socialist project.

Marx saw clearly and shrewdly what this scenario would imply for a practical politics. The ruling class would be faced with constantly increasing problems of managing economic instability and class tension. In the long run, every measure they might take to manage these problems would make them worse. The real political struggle, in Marx's mind, was to make the working class into a responsible and credible agent for the management of the economy, but at the same time to combat reform-oriented working-class politics. This is the foundation of Marx's two-sided politics. On the one hand, he constantly excoriated those who argued for ameliorating conditions under capitalism as reformists doomed to long-run irrelevance by the growing contradictions of capitalism. This amounted to an argument that nothing should be done to improve the lot of the working class under capitalism on the grounds that nothing *could* be done until the socialist revolution had put the working class in the driver's seat. On the other hand, Marx vigorously opposed opportunistic and idealistic tendencies among the working classes that peddled nostrums like labor-money or redistributive schemes which failed to address what he regarded as the fundamental contradictions of capitalism.

There are some serious problems with Marx's political program. It would require an almost superhuman restraint to keep working-class political movements from supporting tempting reforms of capitalism such as wages and hours legislation, but this was the logical implication of Marx's principled revolutionary position. Marx's analysis of the contradictions of capitalism, despite its brilliance, is understandable only at an extremely abstract level in which immediate experience often has to be overlooked. The dynamics of capitalist social relations at the class level, for example, are quite different from the experience individual workers have with individual employers. The logic of Marx's abstract analysis often leads to political action that is at variance with the perceived advantage of individual workers. Thus the difficulty of maintaining consistent and principled adherence to the abstract analysis led to a revolutionary politics that tended to become anti-democratic and manipulative. Furthermore, as we have seen, Marx refused to confront the practical problems of organizing production in a socialist economy, or to address the serious questions of the political organization of a socialist society. Instead of considering the long-term problems of reproducing revolutionary democracy, he focused, perhaps "realistically," on the need for iron discipline and even revolutionary terror in order to secure revolutionary power (that is, the dictatorship of the proletariat). If indeed revolutionary socialism had come to power in societies with gigantic social surpluses, it is not completely unreasonable to suppose that its leadership would have had a long time, decades if not centuries, to work out these details, and might be in a better position to address these questions than Marx himself. Nonetheless, there was a connection between the abstract character of Marx's analysis and the alienating and polarizing political practice which it often led to in real revolutionary political movements.

What Happened to Real Wages

If wages had indeed continued to stagnate at subsistence levels in industrial capitalist economies, Marx's program might have had a good chance of success. In fact, many of the components of his analysis were confirmed by historical experience. Crises of demand did become more frequent, more severe, and more socially disruptive through the nineteenth and early twentieth centuries in the advanced capitalist economies. Class struggle did become the central political preoccupation of European capitalist society. The politics of class resentment and social revolution gained the allegiance of an important part of the working classes, especially in Europe. Revolutionary crises did occur in which working-class parties led by Marxist socialist revolutionaries played a leading role. It is not hard to imagine a social revolution led by advanced working-class elements in European societies in which wages continually failed to rise in step with labor productivity.

In the 1850s, when Marx was beginning his intensive study of the classical political economists, an improvement in British industrial working-class standards of living started to become apparent. By 1868, when Marx published the first volume of *Capital,* the notion that industrial capitalism would always tend to depress the wages of workers to the subsistence level had become highly doubtful.

While statistics on income distribution in the nineteenth century are spotty, we know a great deal more about the share of wages in the twentieth century. The wage share in national income (or net domestic product, which, with small adjustments, is equal to national income) is a good operational equivalent of what Marx calls the value of labor-power. If we take the productivity of labor (in terms of what economists call "real" output) as given, then the (real) wage and the value of labor-power move together: a higher real wage implies a higher value of labor-power, and vice versa. But when the productivity of labor is rising, as is typically the case for industrial capitalist economies, a constant real wage implies a falling value of labor-power (or wage share), and a constant value of labor-power implies a real wage rising at the same rate as labor productivity.

The observation that the wage share varies rather little over long periods of capital accumulation in industrial capitalist economies has become one of the "stylized facts" on which modern theories of economic growth are based. Although wage shares in modern capitalist economies are not completely fixed, and small variations in the wage share have large implications for the profitability and viability of capitalist production, by and large real wages have grown at about the same rate as labor productivity over long periods of capitalist development. Thus neither the stagnation predicted by Ricardo and Malthus due to diminishing returns, nor the unstable explosion of exploitation, on which Marx based his initial analysis of capitalist development, have come to pass.

Just why wages have tended to rise with labor productivity in capitalist economies is a rather deep puzzle. Many people assume that it is "natural" for wages to rise when productivity rises, but Marx's analysis of the wage contract and wage labor makes it clear that this is not true. The wage is not a share of the value added, but a fixed contractual payment from the capitalist employer to the worker. If productivity rises, the capitalist reaps the whole benefit as profit, and has no interest in raising workers' wages because of this change alone. If wages rise at roughly the same rate as labor productivity, this must be a result of other factors.

There are three broad types of explanation for the relative stability of the wage share. First, there is a tendency for workers' subsistence levels to increase with their productivity. It is hard to imagine the ill-housed, ill-fed, ill-clothed workers of the early industrial revolution operating the sophisticated technologies of modern production. But this type of explanation can go only a limited way toward explaining wage share stability. For example, workers living at standards of living that differ by orders of magnitude in different countries in the modern capitalist world operate essentially the same technologies.

Second, the class struggle that Marx identified as the expression of capitalist social relations of production produces political pressure for policies that lead to higher wages at the level of the capitalist system as a whole. What Marx called "defensive" class struggle (the formation of unions, strikes, labor solidarity, and the like) also can enforce higher wages outside the competitive bargaining process between individual capitalist and worker. But these institutions are weak in some capitalist economies which have a stable wage share.

Third, there could be systematic stabilizing feedback effects involving the rate of technical progress in capitalist economies, the size of the reserve army of labor, and the wage. High wages are an important incentive for capitalists to discover and implement labor-saving technological changes. These changes in turn diminish the demand for labor at any level of capital accumulation. If capital accumulation is very rapid, as it is when wages are low and profit rates are high as in economies at early stages of capitalist development, the growth in the demand for labor tends to exhaust the easily available reserves of labor, and wages (and the wage share) tend to rise. This increases the incentives for labor-saving technological change, which in turn lowers the rate of growth of the demand for labor and puts downward pressure on the wage and wage share. This feedback system could also be an important element in the stabilization of the wage share.

Whatever the reasons may be, the stabilization of the wage share in capitalist development has far-reaching implications for the political economy of modern capitalism. As Marx became aware of the phenomenon of rising wages in the 1860s, he made efforts to adapt his analysis of capitalism and its long-run tendencies to accommodate it. From an analytical point of view, Marx shifted his attention from the assumption of a subsistence real wage to the assumption of a constant (or slowly falling) value of labor-power. When labor productivity is not increasing, these assumptions amount to the same thing, but when labor productivity *is* increasing, they have quite different implications for the behavior of real wages. Marx also shifted his attention from the tendency for the rate of exploitation to rise to the tendency for the rate of profit to fall with capitalist development. From a polemical point of view, Marx shifted his rhetoric from the "absolute" to the "relative" immiserization of workers as the consequence of capitalist development. The relative immiserization of workers refers to a slowly rising rate of exploitation and fall in the value of labor-power which is compatible with rising worker standards of living.

While these theoretical innovations in Marx's thought provide important and lasting insights into the dynamics of capitalist economies, it seems to me that they are very inadequate substitutes for the theory of the unstably rising rate of surplus value as a motivation for social revolution. The falling profit rate is indeed a chronic complaint of mature capitalist economies, and constant political efforts are required to offset and control this phenomenon. It could indeed, if it were allowed to play itself out, threaten the viability of capitalist accumulation (though the effect would be more similar to Ricardo's stationary state than to the world-historical transformation of the mode of production that Marx originally hoped for). But in the end, the falling rate of profit suggests that capitalism's difficulty is *too little* surplus value. This is a much less dialectically powerful observation than the claim that capitalism suffers from *too much* surplus value, which was the implication of the model of the subsistence wage and rising labor productivity. For one thing, there is no particularly plausible reason to think that socialist organization of production will actually realize a larger surplus product than capitalism. In fact, there are strong reasons to think that socialist organization of production will result in weaker labor discipline and poorer social coordination of the division of labor, so that the surplus product would be smaller. Marx's shift from the law of rising rate of exploitation to the law of the falling rate of profit transforms the project of socialist revolution from a pragmatic, commonsense response to a social dilemma into an exercise in speculative and utopian social engineering.

Marxist Theory and Social Change in the Twentieth Century

In the twentieth century Marx's ideas of class, exploitation, and revolutionary social change played an important historical and ideological role, but not one centered on actual proletarian revolution. The historical destiny of Marxism turned out instead to be twofold: to mitigate instability in the core capitalist economies through the institutionalization and regulation of exploitation; and to spread capitalism in the periphery as a powerful agent of modernization.

One of the consequences of the success of capitalism in industrial capitalist countries was the projection of the contradictions of capitalism over the rest of the world. The resulting social and cultural crisis created a terrible dilemma for the non-capitalist societies that confronted it. In many countries, the strategy of cooperating with and trying to absorb alien and often incomprehensible capitalist institutions and values in a spirit of resignation to the inevitable led to a stagnant dependency. Marxism, on the other hand, provided an alternative which promised a route to modernization, that is, the destruction of traditional cultures and social relations, without surrender to the hegemonic claims of world capitalism. Outside Europe and North America, Marx's unflinching economic realism instilled the key capitalist values of accumulation and commodification in modernizing nationalist elites.[9]

The Revolutions That Did Happen

In Russia the modernizing moment of Marxism first reached the world stage, finding a direct expression in Menshevism and an indirect expression in Bolshevism. The Mensheviks understood that Russia's basic problem was to transform its sprawling, unsystematic, traditional political and economic system into some version of modern capitalism, as a stage of social development which was a necessary preliminary to socialism. They argued with persuasive logic that the most efficient role for Marxist socialists would be to support and accelerate the development of capitalism in Russia. (This support by socialists would be particularly helpful in light of the disorganized incompetence of Russia's own nascent bourgeoisie.) The Bolsheviks, perhaps fundamentally through their lack of confidence in the ability of the Russian bourgeoisie to accomplish anything even in alliance with the Mensheviks, decided to take the responsibility for the modernization of Russian society into their own hands. After a flirtation with a version of the Menshevik model in the New Economic Policy of the 1920s, the Stalinist wing of Bolshevism transformed Marx's theories of primitive accumulation, commodification, proletarianization, and capital accumulation into a caricature of capitalist economic development. This system, based on a politi-

---

9. In Japan, a traditional but extremely pragmatic samurai ideology performed some of these functions. The dominant warrior values of this movement, however, forced Japanese capitalism into an unstable political path culminating in the catastrophe of the Second World War, reminiscent of the suicidal dénouements of samurai legends. Only under the succeeding tutelage of a different (American) strain of pragmatic warriors could Japan find a more or less stable integration with the world capitalist system.

cally enforced and highly efficient system of exploitation of labor, had remarkable success for several decades. We can see now that from a historical point of view Russian Communism held onto the Stalinist system too long and too inflexibly, stubbornly refusing to recognize its own historical mission to develop a Russian version of capitalism.

The history of China in the twentieth century offers an even clearer instance of the modernizing face of Marxism as a path to capitalism. The choice between allowing capitalism to destroy and reshape the institutions of a defeated traditional society and using Marxist ideology to maintain national independence while transforming those institutions also shaped Chinese political history in the twentieth century. Whether the Chinese Communist regime, in contrast to Russian Communism, will find a way to transform itself into a viable political base for an independent capitalist economy remains to be seen. Marxism has played a similar role as an agent of modernization that facilitates the establishment of capitalist institutions in many other countries, including India, Indonesia, Vietnam, and South Africa.

Thus Marxism has been a powerful agent of social change in that part of the world facing the crisis of confrontation with a highly developed and aggressive European capitalism. In these cases, Marxism has been more successful in securing national independence through the stresses of the emergence of capitalist institutions and the transformation and destruction of traditional social forms than in securing socialism through proletarian revolution.

The Revolutions That Didn't Happen

In the industrialized capitalist countries, twentieth-century Marxism has also played a central role in social change while shedding the revolutionary guise that Marx tailored. "Revisionist" Marxism turned Marx's analysis of the contradictions of capitalist social relations into a powerful political and social tool for managing capitalist societies. In Europe, the combination of Social Democratic political parties and strong unions stabilized class relations. Exploitation, which in Marx's time roused an instinctive negative moral reaction in most people, has become the accepted institutionalized pattern of social organization. Workers have come to understand the functionality of surplus value as the form of social surplus in capitalist society. As the power of capitalists to dispose of this surplus value by themselves has gradually been contained and shared with other classes through political institutions and appeals to public opinion, the exploitation of labor has become a cliché rather than an offense to moral sensibilities. Class divisions retain some power to outrage public opinion, but they more often play a functional political role. The importance of Marx's analysis of capitalism in this process should not be underestimated. Where Marx's analysis of capitalism is still a part of the education of the public, citizens have to come to some kind of terms with the reality of exploitation as the kernel of economic activity in capitalist societies. The view that exploitation is a necessary evil, to be condemned when it goes too far and harnessed to ideologically acceptable ends, is a natural equilibrium under these circumstances.[10]

The Socialist Idea

Both the social democratic and communist strains of twentieth-century Marxism have experimented extensively with socialism through the political control of economic enterprises. Despite the high hopes and noble aspirations of the advocates of these systems, they have turned out on the whole to be failures or disappointments. The col-

---

10. Here the United States, where no version of Marxism has played much of a role in shaping ideology or politics, is an important exceptional case.

lapse of the Soviet Union was not the direct result of the failure of its centralized economic institutions, which continued to function in their own way right up to the political crisis that overthrew the Soviet system. But the Soviet economy did have major problems in the areas of fostering innovation, ensuring quality of commodities, maintaining work discipline, and moving from a labor-surplus to a labor-constrained investment policy that put tremendous cumulative strains on its political system. The Chinese have consciously embarked on a policy of dismantling and neglecting the state sector in favor of the private sector, which in recent years has been responsible for the majority of gains in jobs and output. Cuba's periods of rigorous socialism, to which the regime has retreated in periods of external political pressure, have also resulted in inferior economic performance in terms of increases in output and improvements in the standard of living.

Likewise, the attempts of Social Democratic parties in Europe after the Second World War to socialize major economic sectors in the framework of bourgeois political institutions were not convincing successes. The infusion of capital from the state treasuries did improve the performance of these sectors by insulating them from financial instability, but these gains were largely offset by mediocre management and the burdens of political patronage. It would be wrong to accept the dogmatic conclusion of liberalizing privatizers that state organization of productive enterprises is invariably inferior to private management, but there is little evidence of the claimed superiority of the socialist model either. The historical obsolescence of the state socialist model is the proximate cause of the current ideological crisis of socialist politics, since it has forced socialists from their natural radical role as social innovators into an unnatural conservative posture of preserving existing state institutions.

It would be a mistake to see the political collapse of the state socialist project as the end of Marxist politics. Marx, after all, was after bigger fish than just the constitution of corporate boards of governors; and the issues of exploitation, imperialism, and class divisions are far from being resolved by neo-liberal policies.

Revolution and the Mode of Production

Given Marx's stunning success in identifying both the general pattern and particular contradictions of industrial capitalist development, what accounts for the failure of his theory of proletarian social revolution?

Proletarian social revolution is not the only pathway to social change in capitalism that Marx considered. He was acutely aware of the tendency for capitalist institutions to adapt and evolve in response to historical and social pressures. For example, Marx regards the phenomenon of the corporate or joint-stock form of capitalist enterprise as a kind of imperfect "socialization" of capital which prefigures socialism. The actual policy proposals that conclude the *Communist Manifesto* were achieved as reforms not many years later in most advanced capitalist countries. But Marx did bet on proletarian social revolution in industrialized capitalist societies in a big way, and this bet seems farther than ever from paying off.

One puzzling issue in this area is that Marx took the transformation of the slave-based mode of production of the ancient world to feudalism, and that of the serf-based feudal mode of production to capitalism itself, as his main historical examples of social change arising from contradictions in the social relations of production. Yet neither of these historical analogies support key elements in Marx's vision of proletarian social revolution.

In the transition from feudalism to capitalism, for example, it was not the exploited class, the serfs, who overthrew the old mode of production. A third social element, the nascent bourgeoisie, were the active political agent of the destruction of feudalism. In the course of creating political and social conditions favorable to the development of capitalism, the bourgeoisie transformed labor from serfdom to wage labor, and created a different exploited class altogether. The contrast with the theory of proletarian socialist revolution, in which the capitalist working class, formed within bourgeois institutions and starting from bourgeois ideology, somehow takes on the world-historical role of establishing socialism, is striking.

This problem is connected with Marx's insistence on the economic realism of the content of socialism. In the *Critique of the Gotha Programme*, for example, Marx reiterates the necessity for a viable socialist society to mobilize a social surplus, like class societies. What distinguishes the appropriation of this surplus from class exploitation is supposed to be the social character of the process, and thus what Marx envisioned could be described as the self-exploitation of the producing classes. (This was in fact the big bone of contention between Marx and Proudhon, Lassalle, and the Ricardian socialists, who all proposed in one way or another the return of the complete "fruits of labor" directly to workers.) In essence, the socialist regime would be operating a kind of collective capitalism. But the bourgeois revolutions were not aimed at allowing serfs to take over the land and manage their own manors. Despite his vigorous critique of the commodity form of production, Marx's concrete vision of socialism carries with it a lot of capitalist baggage.

Another puzzling feature of the analogy between the emergence of the capitalist mode of production from feudalism and the emergence of socialism from capitalism has to do with the inherently decentralized and cellular character of capitalist social relations. Capitalism does not require political control of the state to exist, though it always seeks political control of the state in order to flourish. The basic metabolism of capitalist production, based in decentralized production for exchange, is resilient and robust. If it is for some reason checked or destroyed in one part of the world, it can regenerate itself, like a biological organism that can grow back from a severed part.

Therefore, capitalism was able to exist and grow stronger as a tendency toward a new way of life subsisting in the interstices of feudal society. There appears to be no way, however, for socialism to develop in the interstices of capitalist society as a real social practice. It is true that socialism flourishes in capitalist society as an ideological tendency, but that is a far cry from people actually being able to live out, even partially, the experience of an alternative mode of production.

Where Has the Revolution Gone?

The twentieth century was not friendly to Marx's vision of proletarian revolution. There is still, however, tremendous force in his historical materialist critique of capitalism as a historically contingent, limited, and contradictory mode of production.

Capitalism has not shed its fundamentally contradictory character. The enormous differences in wealth and power that we confront on a global scale today dwarf even the stark social polarities of industrial England and Europe in the nineteenth century. Capitalist economic development continues to be a vehicle for the development of forces of production, as Marx and Engels saw in the *Communist Manifesto*. But this process continues to bring with it massive destruction of traditional societies and the perpetuation of extreme poles of wealth and poverty both within developing capitalist societies and between them. In light of these realities, Marx's dream of a revolutionary transformation of social relations to realize the potential benefits for human development in capitalist technology and organization remains potent and compelling.

The twenty-first century will in all likelihood see an epochal change in the demographic context of world capital accumulation. The world population seems destined to stabilize, but in a highly uneven and polarized fashion, with a majority of the world's people in relatively poor societies with a younger population confronting a minority of rich societies with an older population. Since the process of capitalist development has always in the past rested on the availability of labor reserves to keep wages from rising, and on a widening division of labor to permit steady increases in labor productivity, this demographic transformation poses a fundamental challenge to historical patterns of capital accumulation. If capital accumulation is to continue in something like its historical pattern, technical change will have to separate itself from the division of labor, so that increases in labor productivity in themselves can constantly replenish labor reserves.

This question seems inextricably bound up with the problem of the division of labor. One of the most uncompromising and difficult of Marx's positions was his insistence that the contradictions of capitalism have their roots in the commodity form of production itself. Thus Marx seems to imply that there are only two possibilities: either humanity has to give up the division of labor along with the commodity form of production that has historically organized it, or it has to find alternative institutions to support a complex division of labor. It is difficult to imagine either of these worlds concretely. Friedrich Hayek argues that the real barrier to socialism is not so much the weak material incentives that socialist producers would face as their inability to figure out what and how to produce in the absence of markets and market signals. How would even the most idealistically and altruistically motivated socialist personality know reliably whether a particular use of her or his resources was a net benefit to society? This is an issue that contemporary adherents of socialist revolution cannot escape easily. It is bound up with the difficult issues of political control of production in a socialist society, and the whole question of political rights and liberties outside the context of bourgeois society.

The forces Marx saw as leading to revolutionary social change in capitalist societies remain potent and present. The contradictions of capitalist society, projected now on a world scale, continue to spur passionate critical thought and action. The moment in which these forces might have concentrated in decisive centralized revolutionary change, however, has most likely passed. We live in an epoch in which these potential agents of change are dispersed into thousands of particular, often apparently unconnected, struggles over income distribution, social justice, environmental protection, and personal security and freedom. It remains to be seen whether these moments of social transformation will coalesce to transform capitalist society.

4/On the Margins

One of the most curious turns of events in the history of ideas is the displacement of Ricardian economics by "marginalist," or, as it has come to be called, "neoclassical" economics. The battlefield on which these doctrines contend is the theory of value (or price), but much more turns out to be at stake. Where classical political economy tends to be historical and inductive, generalizing from real historical experience, marginalism tends to be mathematical and deductive, striving to explain experience within the framework of a set of predetermined axioms. Where the great themes of classical political economy are dynamic and developmental, bound up with change and evolution, the great themes of marginalism are static and allocational, bound up with the concept of efficiency. Where classical political economy conceives of equilibrium as the averaging out of ceaseless fluctuations, marginalism sees equilibrium as actually being attained or approximated in reality. Where classical political economy has strong roots in sociology, and accommodates emergent categories like class, marginalist economics roots itself in utilitarian philosophy and admits no social category that transcends individual action, or the simple combination of individual actions. Where classical political economy sees market relationships as expedient means to the end of national wealth and prosperity, marginalism sees market-determined allocation as an end in itself.

This story is all the more curious because marginalist doctrine presents itself as an extension of Ricardo's logical method and of his theory of rent. Marginalism, however, rejects the labor theory of value despite Ricardo's strong adherence to it as the only logical basis for economic reasoning.

The labor theory of value is at its root a cost theory of price, in which relative prices are determined by the relative costs of production of different commodities. As a result of this general "vision" of the economic process, the classical economists were not very concerned about demand as a determinant of price. (Recall that Ricardo explicitly excludes goods, like rare paintings, whose price depends solely on their scarcity from the general principles of value determination through labor time.) The classical economists did recognize that the usefulness or use-value of a commodity is a precondition for its having exchange-value, but they also pointed out that the overall usefulness of commodities had no correlation with their value or price. The most famous expression of this point of view is the "diamond-water" paradox: water is much more useful and necessary to human life than diamonds, but in normal circumstances in temperate climates, water has a much lower exchange value than diamonds.

In the classical economic view, diamonds are costly because it takes a great deal of labor to produce them owing to their low geographic density. Water is cheap (in temperate climates) because it requires relatively little labor to secure a water supply from springs, streams, or wells. Presumably (though as far as I know no classical economist directly addressed this question) the classicals would pre-

dict that water would be expensive in the desert, because it would require a lot of labor to produce or transport water there.

Adam's Fallacy Needs New Shoes

The diamond-water paradox by itself would not have precipitated a
paradigm shift in political economics without the contributing force
of historical and political changes. After the 1860s advanced capitalism in Britain and the United States entered a period of rapid
growth and consolidation into large monopolistic cartels and trusts,
and Ricardo's version of Adam's Fallacy began to wear thin. The important political conflicts in this period pitted capital against labor
over issues like the limitation of work hours, the right to organize
and strike, the level of wages, and the stability of employment.
Ricardo's language and conceptual framework when applied to these
issues look uncomfortably like—well, like Marx.

The situation cried out for a modernized, up-to-date version of
Adam's Fallacy. What better place to look than in mathematical
physics? Or in evolutionary biology? After all, these "hard" sciences
had the assets of immense prestige and considerable scientific successes.

The history of economics in the late nineteenth century oscillates
between these two poles. At the mathematical physics end of the
spectrum, William Stanley Jevons, Carl Menger, Vilfredo Pareto,
John Bates Clark, Irving Fisher, and Léon Walras, among others, la-
bored to create an axiomatized, mathematical political economy that
could endow the social relations of capitalism with the aura of "natural laws" that guaranteed the stability and rationality of economic
life. At the biological end, economic historians and economic sociol-
ogists like Thorstein Veblen worked to situate contemporary capitalism as the outcome of a historical evolutionary process, marked

as such by the paradox and irony it exhibited. Alfred Marshall, perhaps the most influential figure for the emergence of twentieth-century economics, internalized this oscillation, adopting the evolutionary rhetoric of biology while taking care to state his economic principles as reflections of mathematics (which he made sure to relegate to obscure appendices in his textbook).

In different ways, the mathematical and biological versions of political economy both address the need to refurbish Adam's Fallacy. The mathematical version tries to remove the question of morality altogether from economic life, which it represents as governed by objective laws which we have no choice but to follow exactly in our "freedom of choice." The biological version is more critical and less celebratory of the social relations of capitalism; it sees capitalism as the result of, and a stage in, an ongoing evolutionary process. But evolution is a process without, as Hegel would say, a subject. Mammals do not organize revolutionary takeovers, and dinosaurs do not make suicide pacts. The morality of capitalist social relations here is submerged in the inexorable flow of evolutionary selection, survival of the fittest, and adaptation.

Marginalism

Jevons and Marginal Utility

The marginalist "revolution" begins with the claim to offer a more adequate theory of the role of demand in the determination of market price than the classicals put forward. Jevons's breakthrough was his realization that "marginal utility," that is, the usefulness of an increment of the commodity over the amount an individual is already consuming, is very different from the total utility the individual gains from the consumption of the commodity. Thus relative prices may be quite disproportionate to ratios of total utilities, but still proportionate to ratios of marginal utilities.

According to Jevons's reasoning, a rational utility-maximizing individual apportioning a fixed quantity of a resource among competing uses will begin by assigning the resource to the highest utility use, and will continue until marginal utility in that use falls to the level of marginal utility in the next best use. Then the agent must apportion the resource between the two uses to keep their marginal utilities equal (but presumably falling as more of the resource is applied to each) until the marginal utility of the third-best use is reached, and so on until the resource is exhausted.

A good example is individual allocation of time. Everyone has an absolutely limited amount of time in a day, and has to allocate this limited resource among various uses: sleep, eating, study or work, exercise, quarreling, romance, and so on. From the marginalist perspective, each individual starts by allocating time to the most vital use, say, by sleeping. At the point where eight, or seven, or six hours or less are devoted to sleeping, the individual may feel that the marginal utility of an extra ten minutes of sleep is no longer higher than the marginal utility, say, of eating. The first ten or twenty minutes devoted to eating may lower the marginal utility of that activity to the next most pressing use, say, studying for a test in a course. (The individual may also have to sleep a few more minutes to drive the marginal utility of sleep minutes down to that of test-preparation minutes.) A similar story can be told about the allocation of money income or wealth.

Throughout this process of allocation, the marginal utility of the scarce resource in all the uses to which it is being put must be equal (though all marginal utilities are falling as more of the resource is allocated), or else the agent could increase her total utility by reallocating the scarce resource from a low to a high marginal utility activity.

Thus Jevons arrives at his law of equalization of the "final degree" of utility.

This way of looking at human affairs lends itself easily to the employment of calculus, which here enters into an intimate relation with economic theory. One can write the allocation problem as a constrained maximization problem that can be solved by calculus methods.

Jevons shows that this mathematical approach can be applied to the case of allocating a limited money income among several competing uses. The mathematical conditions for maximization require that the marginal utilities of a dollar spent on each use be equal. Thus Jevons argues that exchange on markets, where there is a single price for each commodity, leads to the equality of ratios of marginal utility to ratios of prices. This doesn't prove, of course, that marginal utility ratios *determine* price ratios. In fact, the setting of the argument assumes that market prices are already given.

The vision of the marginalist approach is based on a considerable leap of imagination. The marginalists see actual market prices in real economies as exactly analogous to the ratios of marginal utilities that an individual equalizes in making a rational allocation of resources. The economy as a whole, in this view, can be viewed as one big rational resource allocation process. To carry out this analogy, the quantity of the various commodities available to society has to be taken as given, so that their relative scarcities can determine marginal utilities and hence price.

One difficulty the marginalist point of view encounters in developing this vision is that an economy consists of many competing individual maximizers, who may have different utility functions. The marginalist position, however, is that the economy, despite being made up of many different individuals, acts in essence *as if* it were a single individual maximizing a single consistent utility function by allocating a single pool of scarce resources. The arguments supporting this assertion are the occasion for much of the conceptual and mathematical complexity of marginalist economics. One shortcut, which neoclassical economists frequently take, is to assume that all the individuals in society are exactly alike, so that they can be reduced to a "representative agent," and then to work out how the representative agent would allocate the existing stocks of commodities, and what marginal utilities (whose ratios will be interpreted as market prices) will result. The rational-agent interpretation, however, does not do much to clarify how markets actually work. A society of identical representative agents would not have to exchange commodities on markets, because each agent would be a scale model of the whole economy and could accomplish the allocation alone.

We can see that the marginalists are talking about *market prices,* not *natural prices* in classical terms. We can also see that the most congenial setting for the marginalist theory of price is the short run, in which stocks of commodities are given, rather than the medium or long run, in which the stocks of commodities will change as a result of production and consumption.

We can also see that from the marginalist point of view, all resources are either fully employed or not scarce. As long as a resource can add to utility in some use or other, all of it will be used. Another way to put this is to say that from the marginalist perspective, unemployed resources have to have a zero price. Still another way to put the point is that any resource that has a positive price must be fully employed, unless something is preventing its application to its next best use. Yet another way of stating this implication is that all resources that can pay their own costs of employment will be employed. These are simply consequences of viewing society as one big rational individual who is allocating scarce resources among competing ends. The view that resources must either be scarce, fully employed, and commanding a positive price, or on the other hand abundant, only partially employed, and with a zero price, is deeply tied up with the marginalist vision, but is incompatible with the view, for example, that some workers are involuntarily unemployed in recessions or depressions. It is, however, quite consistent with Say's Law, since it implies that resources like labor that are displaced from one use (say, by foreign competition) will be transferred to their next best use rather than left unemployed.

Menger and Factor Prices

Carl Menger applies the logic of marginalism to the problem of input prices. For Menger, inputs are "higher order goods," which are valued not because of their direct utility to a final consumer, but because of their indirect usefulness in the production of consumable goods. Menger thus sees a chain of valuation leading from final goods, which are valued according to the principle of marginal utility, back up the chain of production.

At the top of the chain the ultimate inputs to production, like land and labor, are valued according to their scarcity. Thus Menger views these highest order goods as fixed in supply, with completely inelastic supply curves, and their prices as being determined essentially like rents in Ricardo's theory.

Menger's argument underlines the basic strategy of the marginalist theory of value, which is to link the price of goods to their absolute scarcity. The marginalist theory therefore requires, logically, that the total available supplies of inputs to production be known before prices can be calculated. (This key postulate of marginalist theory is often left implicit in discussions of the way supply and demand determine equilibrium prices.)

In the case of labor, the marginalist view requires us to think of a fixed maximum labor supply that each individual controls and potentially puts on the market. Since people do not actually sell the maximum possible amount of labor-power, the marginalists regard individuals as effectively "buying back" some of their own labor time (paying the market equilibrium wage rate) to be used as "leisure," that is, non-wage activities. Leisure, as we have seen, includes a number of non-commodity-mediated activities, like bearing and rearing children or household maintenance. The demand curve that determines the wage as a rent includes this theoretical private demand for leisure as one of its components.

At first glance, the idea that there is a fixed amount of every economically relevant good at any moment in time appeals to common sense, but it runs into some perplexing problems when we try to make the marginalist theory operational. For example, exactly how do we determine the total supply of labor in the U.S. economy, which we would need to do in theory to predict the real wage level? Do we include teenagers and retired septuagenarians? We know that higher real wages in the United States will tend to increase documented and undocumented migration. Do we then have to include all the potential labor supply that might move into the U.S. market? In using the marginalist theory, labor economists resolve these questions by one or another set of relatively arbitrary assumptions, because the theory itself cannot give much guidance.

Clark and Distribution

John Bates Clark uses the marginalist approach to factor pricing to discuss what determines the distribution of income between wages, profits, and rents. Clark's aim, as he makes clear, is not just to explain, but also to *justify* the distribution of income that results from the market. This is Clark's version of Adam's Fallacy. He sees profit and wage rates as the outcomes of basic economic laws that are imposed on society by scarcity. In Clark's mind, the rule that each factor receives the value of its marginal product turns into the principle that each factor receives returns in proportion to its contribution to production.

Later neoclassical economists have recognized the fallacy in

Clark's interpretation of marginal products, though their under-standing of this subtle point does not always trickle down to what students are actually taught in microeconomic theory courses. The point is that there is no way to determine the "contribution to pro-duction" of any one input in a complex production process which requires all the inputs. Take away all the labor, or all the capital goods, and you reduce production to zero, so it appears that each factor actually contributes the whole product. Marginal products at best are a way of *imputing* the value of the product among the vari-ous inputs, and there is no particular moral argument that the owner of a factor with a high marginal product *deserves* a higher factor price.

Clark is particularly interested in using marginal productivity the-ory to explain and justify profit flows in capitalist economies as re-flections of the "marginal product of capital." According to Clark's reasoning, an individual small firm (or capitalist) is too small to in-fluence market wages and prices of capital goods. As a result, the firm can price out any technology at current market prices, and choose the lowest-cost technology available. In doing this, it appears to the firm that wages and capital costs are different inputs to pro-duction. The firm may choose a technology that uses more labor, as measured by wage cost, and less capital, measured as the costs of the capital inputs, or it may choose one that uses less labor and more capital. In choosing the lowest-cost technology, the firm can be seen as equating the value of the marginal products of labor and capital to the wage and the average profit rate.

Clark then wants to turn this argument around in the typical marginalist way, and argue that it implies that the wage and profit rate are determined by the scarcities of labor and "capital." He views profits, like wages, as rents in the Ricardian sense. (Neoclassical economists often call profits "quasi-rents," acknowledging that the capital stock changes over time, but is fixed at any moment in time.)

This argument led to a great deal of controversy, which reached a peak in the 1960s and 1970s in what is called the "Cambridge capital controversy": a group of Cambridge, England economists led by Joan Robinson argued with a group of Cambridge, Massachusetts economists led by Paul Samuelson and Robert Solow over whether Clark's theory was consistent in real-world settings where there are many different kinds of capital goods. The problem stems from the fact that in considering the choices of the individual firm, Clark takes the prices of all the various capital goods as given, which seems justifiable, given the assumption that the firm is a relatively small part of the factor markets. This reasoning establishes the equality between the wage and profit rate and the value of marginal products of labor and capital. In this context, the given market wages, prices of capital goods, and average profit rates determine the marginal products of labor and capital as a result of cost minimization. But when Clark tries to turn the equation around, and argue that marginal products of capital and labor determine equilibrium profit and wage rates, he fails to consider the issue of the determination of the prices of the various capital goods. Joan Robinson argued that although these prices are given to the individual firm by the market, they are determined within the system for the whole economy, so they cannot be taken as data in determining wages and profit rates. Furthermore, as the prices of capital goods vary, the same physical collection of capital goods (factories, machines, and so forth) will represent different amounts of "capital" in Clark's sense. Therefore, the Cambridge, England critics established, it is not possible to speak of a given amount of "capital" whose scarcity determines the profit rate as a quasi-rent in a real world economy.

The Cambridge, Massachusetts side of this debate eventually admitted that Robinson was correct in pure theory, but most neoclassically trained economists continue to use the concept of "capital" as a scarce input to production, and most undergraduates are taught to think of the profit rate as being determined by the marginal product of "capital." At the most abstract level, neoclassical general equilibrium theorists attempted to dispense with the concept of "capital" by studying equilibrium with an arbitrary number of specific capital goods, each of which has its own quasi-rent. This leads to a very complex theory which has its own problems, particularly in the treatment of time.

Where Do Prices Come From?

The marginalist approach starts from the situation of an individual household or firm making transactions on well-organized markets where there is a uniform (or close to uniform) set of prices for commodities. This makes sense even within the classical political economy setting. In an economy with a well-developed division of labor, each household or firm will have to exchange its endowment or product on the market to buy the commodities it needs.

But where do the prices at which commodities are exchanged come from? If we start by considering a collection of households and firms *before* market prices are established, what process leads to the formation of market prices? This is the problem of general equilibrium, the most abstract (and some might say ideological) branch of economic theory.

The first thing that occurs to us in contemplating a situation where households and firms have not exchanged commodities on the market is that there are likely to be large opportunities to make gains from exchange. Households that have only labor-power to sell, and no food, are going to be willing to sell labor-power at very low prices, and firms that have produced commodities but not sold them yet will be willing to sell them very cheaply in a pinch. We can measure the willingness of households to buy and sell commodities when the economy as a whole is not in equilibrium as the "reservation prices" of the agents—the maximum (minimum) price at which the agent would be willing to buy (sell) a commodity. There are large economic surpluses latent in this situation, and they can be realized by actually bringing together potential buyers and sellers and exchanging commodities at prices that look advantageous to both sides. This is the process of voluntary market exchange. As market exchanges take place, the reservation prices of households and firms will tend to move closer together. Once a household has sold some of its labor-power and bought food, its need for that particular exchange declines, and the terms on which it will exchange food for labor-power become less extreme.

Vilfredo Pareto contrasts the initial pre-exchange position of the economy—where reservation prices are very far apart, there is no uniform price of commodities, and there is the possibility of large gains from exchange—with the position of the economy after a lot of exchange has taken place. In the limit, he imagines a position where the reservation prices of all the households and firms have become equal, and there are no further possible gains from exchange. At such a position no more voluntary exchange will actually take place, and there will be a uniform set of prices for all commodities, shared by all the households and firms as a result of their previous exchanges. Neoclassical economists call these positions "Pareto-optima." There is actually nothing particularly "optimal" about a Pareto-optimum, since nothing in the process of voluntary exchange guarantees a good distribution of income and economic surplus among the various participants. Some households and firms may come out of the market exchange process with the lion's share of the economic surpluses.

Pareto allocations (to use a more neutral term) can be looked at in two ways. On the one hand, they represent the systematic conclusion of voluntary commodity exchange: at a Pareto allocation, there are no more opportunities to realize economic surpluses through exchange. In this sense the Pareto allocations are the states of equilibrium of the dynamic exchange process. In theory, any voluntary exchange process will lead to a Pareto allocation if it is carried on long enough. From another point of view, the Pareto allocations represent the squeezing out of all the potential economic surplus from the division of labor. At a Pareto allocation, it is impossible to make any household or firm better off (say, by reallocating commodities through legislation) without making some other household or firm worse off. (If legislators could rearrange the commodities to make *all* the households and firms better off, then voluntary exchange could do the same thing.) Thus the Pareto allocations are efficient insofar as all the available economic surplus has been squeezed out of the system.

The second way of thinking about Pareto allocations leads to another version of Adam's Fallacy. Voluntary exchange, which represents participation in capitalist social relations and supports the division of labor, is a good thing (not necessarily a moral good, but at least a utilitarian good) because it squeezes all the potential economic surplus out of the system. Thus it is not just a question, as Smith presents it, of putting up with the social relations of capitalism as a necessary evil, or as means to an end. Once economic efficiency takes hold as a good in itself, it imposes a positive moral duty to pursue self-interest within the framework of commodity exchange.

Legislative interference with free exchange, in this version of Adam's Fallacy, frustrates the spontaneous tendency of the market to realize all of the available economic surplus created by the division of labor. (The fact that legislative interference might also lead to a more equal *distribution* of economic surplus tends to be ignored or down-pedaled in this way of thinking.) This is the root of the presumption in marginalist economics against state intervention. Take, for example, taxes. A tax on a commodity prevents some potentially mutually advantageous exchanges from taking place when the surplus to be gained from them is not large enough to pay the tax. Thus taxes and other government interventions lead to a loss of potential economic surplus—to inefficiency. The only case to be made for taxes and other interventions, in this view, is that they promote some other social good (such as the public services the taxes are used to pay for) which outweighs this loss of economic surplus. This version of Adam's Fallacy has become the staple of economics teaching and the foundation for the overwhelming proportion of modern neo-classical economic research.

Which Pareto Allocation?

There is, however, a major loose end in the general equilibrium argument. There are a whole lot of Pareto allocations, because there are a whole lot of voluntary exchanges that can take place from any pre-exchange starting point. When any two (or more) households and firms come together to exchange commodities, they are likely to find that their reservation prices are quite far apart. This makes it easy to find voluntary exchanges—in fact so easy that there will be a huge number of possibilities, amounting to exchange at any price between the reservation prices. Since the only way to get to a Pareto allocation is to allow a very large number of voluntary exchanges, each of which allows considerable leeway as to the actual price, the system can wind up in a large number of different Pareto allocations. One dimension in which these Pareto allocations will differ is in the distribution of economic surplus among the households and firms. (They may also differ in the final prices of commodities.)

This possibility makes it difficult to persuade people of the neo-classical version of Adam's Fallacy. People are in fact very aware of the possibility that they will be taken advantage of in voluntary ex-change—not in the sense that they can't refuse (under normal circumstances) offers that are disadvantageous to them, but in the sense that they will accept too low a price for what they sell or pay too much for what they buy because of their ignorance of other exchange possibilities. This market-paranoia goes back a long way. We can find it in Aristotle's discussion of fair pricing, in the Judaic Law governing fairness in trading, and in medieval philosophical discussions of the concept of just price.

Marginalist and neoclassical economists know that once a uniform system of prices has been established in the market, the decisions of households and firms are determined, given their income. Thus it is tempting to solve the problem of indeterminacy of equilibrium by supposing that households and firms know the eventual equilibrium prices before they actually exchange commodities. This is the path that Léon Walras followed in developing general equilibrium theory. Walras's idea was that somehow agents could discover the equilibrium prices before any actual exchanges occurred. To accomplish this, at least in theory, Walras invented a fictional auctioneer to "cry out" experimental prices to see if they might be the equilibrium prices. When the auctioneer has somehow found the equilibrium prices (which turns out to be an intractable problem from a mathematical point of view), he announces them to households and firms, who then carry out their transactions at those prices.

Walras's scheme is not convincing because it purports to separate two inextricably linked aspects of market exchange: the transfer of ownership of commodities and the discovery of price. In real life, the only way to find out how much someone is willing to pay for something is to make him an offer and see if he will accept it. There is no alternative to "putting your money where your mouth is" and "putting up or shutting up" when it comes to commodity exchange.

Marginalism and Social Welfare

The marginalist revolution, in addition to its claim to overturn the labor theory of value, and cost-of-production theories of value in general, has also led to a fundamental change in the analysis of economic policy and the relation of the state to the market. This change represents a shift in focus from capital accumulation and growth to utility maximization and production efficiency as the aims of economic policy.

Adam Smith's critique of the mercantilists was that in putting one asset, the national gold stock, at the center of policy, they supported policies that increased the stock of gold but reduced national net worth at market prices. The neoclassical economists turn the tables on Smith by arguing that the real end of economic activity ought to be consumer satisfaction, or utility, not net worth at market prices. Just as there are cases where maximization of the gold stock is opposed to maximization of national net worth, there are situations where maximization of national net worth at market prices may not maximize consumer satisfaction. Neoclassical economists describe these situations as cases where social cost and private cost diverge. A typical example is an unpriced environmental externality, like air pollution. The pursuit of national net worth at market prices often leads to the proliferation of polluting industries. The average consumer may find herself worse off as a result: the increased wage and dividend income from the industrial development may not compensate her for the health and comfort lost to severe environmental degradation.

The idea that the goal of economic activity is the satisfaction of individual consumers is deeply rooted in the structure of marginalist thought, which sees subjective utility evaluation as the regulating factor of price and value. This leads neoclassical economics to quite a different style of analysis of policy problems from the classicals. For example, Ricardo's advocacy of free trade was based on his desire to lower wage costs, raise the profit rate, and promote capital accumulation and growth. Neoclassical economics, on the other hand, advocates free trade as a means to achieve increased efficiency in the allocation of resources, that is, increasing the subjective utility of at least some individuals without reducing the subjective utility of others.

With this foundation, neoclassical analysis is not committed to laissez-faire policy: it supports intervention in cases of monopoly, incomplete information, and externalities. Since it is very hard to think of a real-life economic transaction that meets the stringent requirements of perfect competition, complete information, and full pricing of all consequences, neoclassical economics opens the door to widespread government intervention.

Adam Smith urged thrift on his students as a path to greater national wealth. Neoclassical economics, in contrast, is neutral on the question of individual saving: the individual should make her own choice as to the allocation of income between current and future spending. If private utility-maximizing decisions lead to low saving and low growth, that just represents the efficient allocation of resources from a neoclassical point of view, and there is no reason to intervene to alter the private decisions.

The original utilitarian basis of marginalist economics offered a strong argument for the redistribution of income from the rich to the poor. This argument is based on the idea that economic policy should maximize the sum of all the utilities of the individuals in a society. Most utilitarians believed that the marginal utility of income to the rich, who have a lot of income, is lower than the marginal utility of income to the poor, who don't have very much, so that the total of social utility will be increased by shifting income from the rich to the poor.

Modern neoclassical economists mostly reject this utilitarian analysis of income distribution on the ground that it is impossible to make objective comparisons of utility across individuals. The upshot of this doctrine is that economics can only recommend Pareto-improving changes in allocation, that is, changes that make some individuals better off without making anyone worse off. Unfortunately, very few real-world political economic issues offer clear-cut opportunities for Pareto-improvements, which greatly limits the influence of neoclassical theory on policy.

Marginalism, Classical Political Economy, and Time

While the advocates of neoclassical doctrine argue that marginalism displaced classical political economy simply because the former is a better or truer or more general theory, matters are not actually so simple. There are many phenomena—for example, class conflict, social distribution, population growth, and capital accumulation—that the classical model addresses more directly and with more insight than does the neoclassical point of view. The marginalist notion that prices are always reflections of scarcity appears in some lights to give a more coherent and general theory of price than classical cost-of-production theories, but there are some severe problems with this claim as well.

One problem is that the marginalist point of view has difficulty accommodating time as an element in human affairs. When we think of a real economy, we notice that expectations about the future play a key role in determining the utility and marginal utility of current goods, on which the marginalist theory of price depends. The value of a piece of land, for example, depends not just on what it can produce this year, but what crops might be planted on it in the future, and what technologies might be developed to cultivate it. The valuation of current assets through expectations establishes the budget constraints for individuals, and thus underlies their demands for current goods and services. The apparent advantage of the marginalist theory is that it gives an unambiguous theory of price as determined by relative scarcity, but the demands that represent scarcity are themselves highly dependent on expectations. Without a theory of expectations, the marginalist theory of price is incomplete.

One formal response to this problem, which has been frequently adopted in the neoclassical economics literature, is to imagine that there are markets pricing all potential goods and services for the entire future. The existence of such markets would restore the determinacy of the neoclassical theory, at least at an abstract level. Unfortunately we know that in reality, the spectrum of existing markets falls far short of the range necessary to fill in this gap in the theory. One response to this observation is the assumption of "rational expectations," the postulate that individuals act *as if* they had the knowledge of future prices and contingencies which they would require to make coherent demands in the present. The implausibility of this rational expectations doctrine is one of the weakest points in contemporary neoclassical economics.

Time is clearly an underlying issue in the contrast between neoclassical and classical points of view in another sense as well. The classical economists hoped to deal with time and economic fluctuations through the concept of long-run averages of price (Smith's natural prices). The neoclassical point of view, in contrast, resolutely takes the short run as the focus of its analysis, and tries to explain what the classicals would call market prices. Neither of these analytical strategies seems completely adequate to deal with the complex, time-bound character of human economic life. In the absence of a compelling synthesis of the long-run and short-run perspectives, and a coherent treatment of the problem of expectations, perhaps we had better keep *both* classical and neoclassical analyses in mind, with the idea of choosing the appropriate perspective for whatever particular problem we face.

Veblen and Conspicuous Consumption

In the 1890s when marginalist economics was rapidly developing its doctrines of market equilibrium and efficiency, the University of Chicago's prestigious and widely read *Journal of Political Economy* was edited (and largely written by) Thorstein Veblen, an American original genius. Veblen came from an immigrant family that settled into the hard life of the western prairie. He instinctively took a stand on the margins of American capitalist life, devoting himself to tart, funny, paradoxical observations of its irrationalities and complacency. Veblen's contempt for social conventions and respectability landed him in hot water with his university colleagues and administrators over and over again during his academic career. Nevertheless, he managed to produce a series of books that cut to the heart of what life in advanced capitalism actually feels like. Veblen is the Ecclesiastes of Adam's Fallacy, conveying the human distortion and cost of capitalist social relations in a mordant and stylish prose.

Conspicuous Consumption

Veblen read and wrote penetrating reviews of Marx as well as the emerging neoclassical authors. He thought that they both, in their different ways, missed the point of what was going on. For Veblen, the force driving advanced capitalism was the competition for status and respectability. What those who were lucky enough to achieve substantial (or even modest) wealth and income in capitalist societies actually wound up doing with their money was trying to outspend each other on impressive displays of expensive but useless junk. Veblen's capitalist personalities are paranoid and narcissistic, seeking to find in all these displays of wealth the secret of their own identities.

Veblen's picture of capitalist American society is too close to the mark to be ignored, but it poses very awkward questions for marginalism. If consumption itself is socially determined, what becomes of the idea that production and the market function only to realize economic surpluses inherent in individual tastes? The virtuous spiral of economic development from Veblen's point of view looks more like a riot of self-indulgent display.

What, then, keeps the system ticking? Veblen's version of the distinction between use-value and exchange-value is his opposition of the "pecuniary" and the "workmanlike" in the personality of individuals. The pecuniary impulse seeks to cash out effort and discovery into monetary wealth, while the instinct of workmanship wants to find elegant solutions to real human needs. The pecuniary impulse is heedless of the waste of resources: the more wasteful an activity is, the better, since it more convincingly demonstrates the social superiority of the wasteful spender. The instinct of workmanship is to conserve resources to maximize their usefulness.

Veblen saw these two contradictory aspects of human personality inextricably intertwined in the American capitalist society of his day. For him, the great drama was the predictable submergence of the instinct of workmanship to the imperious demands of conspicuous consumption in encounter after encounter. Philanthropists may build academic buildings with grand porticos and many steps, but the classrooms in these buildings are often badly ventilated and have acoustics that make it impossible to hear an instructor's lecture clearly. (Veblen himself was an inveterate mumbler, who retreated to the corner of the classroom farthest from the students to convey his galvanizing social critique in a dull, low monotone.) Today, Veblen would be the theorist of the tail fin, the trophy house, and body-piercing.

We can see in Veblen a distinctive response to the dilemmas of Adam's Fallacy. For Veblen, the threat capitalism poses to conventional morality is less important than the threat capitalists pose to engineers. The danger is not that the ruthless pursuit of self-interest will destroy interpersonal bonds of obligation and reciprocity; it is that the heedless pursuit of self-aggrandizement will overwhelm the practical good which science and technology can offer humankind. Veblen has no more luck in offering a solution to these dilemmas than the other great thinkers who have confronted Adam's Fallacy. One senses that Veblen feels the instinct of workmanship is just as deeply rooted in human beings as the pecuniary instinct, and thus has just as good a chance in the long run to shape society. But Veblen is not a revolutionary with a program, or even a prophet with a message. He adopts the voice of the dispassionate, scientific observer, no more involved emotionally with the behavior of his subjects than the lepidopterist is with the fate of the butterflies pinned to his specimen board.

The Evolutionary Model

For Veblen, the appropriate methodological model for economic science was evolutionary biology: the springs of consistent human behavior lie in evolutionary history rather than in abstract rationality. For example, the descendants of mountain shepherds will spend immense resources to grow small plots of grass around their houses in arid California deserts. How else to explain this but as the coding of behavior in genes through evolution? How else to explain the emergence of the corporation and systems of regulation except as an incident in evolutionary sociology? It is all very well for economists to assert formal marginal conditions for efficient resource allocation, but the heart of the matter lies in human life, imagination, and aspiration, which social scientists cannot address adequately with their cold equations.

While the evolutionary approach does much to dispel the mathematical aridity of marginalist economics, it does not do a great deal to return human beings and their moral concerns to the center of economic thinking. Evolution, as we observe it in nature, is an impersonal process that follows its own inexorable logic. Despite the ideological tendency to read evolution as having a direction and a goal (complexity, human consciousness, progress of some kind or other), evolutionary theory has nothing to say about the desirability or value of its outcomes. The view that economic relations are shaped purely by evolutionary forces removes the moral question from economic discourse altogether. This is an extreme and unsatisfactory response to Adam's Fallacy. It is true that evolutionary economics is free of the cant of efficiency that dominates neoclassical economics, and it replaces static equilibrium with a vision of dynamic change. These are intellectually refreshing and stimulating perspectives. But how much guidance can we as individuals, enacting the evolutionary process in our day-to-day pursuit of jobs, bargains, and technological innovations, take from this Olympian viewpoint? We still face the problems of how to deal with the marginalized, lost, and imperiled individuals that industrial capitalism and market forces leave in their wake. The evolutionary process, which is ruthless in eliminating the less fit from the future, gives even less moral comfort than Adam's Fallacy to human beings living through the present.

5 / Voices in the Air

ndustrial capitalism ran into heavy weather in the first half of the twentieth century. The failure of the European political system to contain the explosive competitive pressures of imperialist rivalry led to the First World War and changed the face of Western civilization. The financial system which twentieth-century capitalism had inherited proved inadequate to cope with the immense increases in productive power unleashed by advances in technology and business organization, and this precipitated a worldwide depression. These events created a crisis of confidence in capitalist political and economic leadership.

The dilemma underlying Adam's Fallacy took an even more serious form in the twentieth century. For Smith, the question was how to reconcile amoral capitalism with the moral life. For the early neoclassical economists, the issue was how to optimize the generation of economic surplus as a good in itself. For the generations of the twentieth century, the problem was how to live with or even through the chaotic forces unleashed by capitalism on a world scale.

Three visions contended for supremacy in political economy in this period, centered on the thinking of John Maynard Keynes, Joseph Schumpeter, and Friedrich von Hayek. As capitalism reconstituted itself in the aftermath of the Second World War, it was the ideas of these three men which shaped institutions and attitudes. Each in his own way recapitulated Adam's Fallacy, but with differences in nuance and emphasis that have become the political fault lines of modern capitalist society.

John Maynard Keynes

John Maynard Keynes (to distinguish him from his less famous economist father, John Neville Keynes) was born in 1883 (the year Marx died) into a moderately prosperous academic family in Cambridge, England. Keynes was a bright, self-indulgent young man, who entered King's College Cambridge in the first years of the twentieth century at a time of considerable intellectual ferment. He spent a great part of his life involved with King's College in one way or another.

The religious, philosophical, and moral certainties of Victorian society were crumbling under the pressures of Darwinian evolution, the emergence of mass society, and nationalism. Keynes was at the center of a group at Cambridge who were strongly critical of Victorian orthodoxy in their personal and political lives. This group became part of the Bloomsbury circle, whose artistic and literary work, as well as their unconventional sexual and personal behavior, left an indelible mark on twentieth-century sensibility. Keynes was a central member of this group, a close associate of Lytton Strachey, Virginia Woolf and her sister Vanessa Bell, and Duncan Grant. Keynes was an active homosexual as a student and young man; later in life he married a Russian ballet dancer and lived with her quite happily until his death. The Bloomsbury group's strong critical stance against Victorian moral orthodoxy is echoed in Keynes's devastating critique of Victorian financial and economic orthodoxy.

During the First World War Keynes was recruited by the British government to help it manage the immense financial problems the war created, a task in which Keynes showed resourcefulness and creativity amounting to genius. Since his social circle tended to be pacifist and critical of the war, Keynes's deep involvement in the financial management of the war created severe moral conflicts for him. Nevertheless, he clearly liked the influence and power that came with participation in the inner circles of government. After the war Keynes was a key member of the British delegation to the ill-fated peace conference at Versailles. He was convinced that the hard-line policy pushed by the French, of forcing the Germans to pay for the costs of the war through reparations, was infeasible and would lead to a politically and economically unstable future for Europe. After the conference Keynes made himself famous by publishing a brilliant and harsh book, *The Economic Consequences of the Peace,* putting forward these critical prophecies.

After the war Keynes returned to King's College as a don (but never professor), and was at the center of British economic scholarship during the 1920s and 1930s. He invested the endowment of King's College with great success, making it rich, and he also made, lost, and recovered a considerable fortune for himself by speculating in foreign currency markets (especially against the German mark). During the 1920s Keynes wrote a series of books and pamphlets on monetary and macroeconomic issues. The British economy fell into stagnation with chronically high unemployment after 1926 when Winston Churchill, then Chancellor of the Exchequer, decided to return the pound to convertibility to gold at its prewar parity. Keynes was bitterly critical of this decision, which he estimated would require a 20% deflation of money wages and prices in Britain.

In the early 1930s Keynes concentrated his efforts on writing *The*

General Theory of Employment, Interest and Money, the most influential work in economics certainly of the first two-thirds and possibly of the whole of the twentieth century.

Despite declining health due to heart disease, Keynes returned to government service during the Second World War. After negotiating the first postwar loan from the United States to Britain to aid British recovery after the war, he served in a last effort before his death as the British government's representative to the Bretton Woods conferences that established the International Monetary Fund and the World Bank.

World Capitalism in Keynes's Time

Keynes's adult life spanned a period of wrenching crisis for the world capitalist system centered in Europe. Nineteenth-century capitalist expansion led to a fierce competition among the European powers for colonies in Africa and Asia and for control of world markets and resources. This competition set the stage for the catastrophe of the First World War, which destroyed a generation of European youth along with the autocratic monarchies of Russia, Germany, Austria, and the Ottoman Empire. The world financial system changed dramatically during the war, as nations discovered the immense flexibility and power inherent in central banks at the same time as they abandoned the gold standard that had regulated international trade and investment.

Although the major preoccupation of economic policy after the First World War was to restore the prewar gold-standard system and the financial and economic stability it had seemed to confer, world capitalism was tested by one extreme crisis after another. In the early 1920s Germany was racked by unprecedented inflation as a result of speculation (by Keynes, among others) against the German currency and the political inability of the Germans to cope with the crushing burdens of reparation payments. When the German currency was stabilized, Britain's decision in 1926 to return to prewar parity for the pound created labor unrest and long-term stagnation in the British economy. A few years later in 1929 the U.S. economy entered a sharp recession, which developed into a catastrophic depression with huge unemployment, deflation, and financial destruction. Throughout the 1930s world capitalism was struggling to manage the social, political, and economic strains of the depression, which came to an end only with the outbreak of the Second World War and the associated military buildup.

The themes of Keynes's major work were shaped by this distinctive period in capitalist development. In retrospect it appears that the inter-war turmoil was an unusual break in the pattern of capitalist economic development, but at the time people assumed that the problems they were experiencing were inherent in capitalism and would recur. One reason for the moderation of these problems of instability after the Second World War was the presence of institutions and ideas, including not least Keynes's theory, invented to deal with the crises of the inter-war period.

To contemporary observers, laissez-faire policy seemed to be inadequate to cope with the problems of advanced industrial capitalism. Without the anchor of gold, speculation in currencies produced pressures for inflation or deflation in national economies, which destabilized them politically and led to chronic unemployment. The forces leading to classical equilibrium appeared to be weak or inoperative for much of this period. Many people during this crisis argued that socialism, along the lines of the communist model of the Soviet Union, was the only workable alternative. Keynes was a strong critic of central-planning socialism, and aimed rather at reforming capitalism to make it function better through a great expansion of the economic role of national governments and central banks.

Say's Law and Laissez-Faire

Keynes begins *The General Theory* with a critique of Say's Law. Say's Law (which we have already encountered in Chapters 1 and 2) is the principle that in the aggregate, the demand for commodities arises from the willingness of households and firms to supply commodities. If Say's Law holds, government policy can have no influence on aggregate spending or employment, although it can influence the allocation of total spending and employment among different commodities (say, by taxing some more heavily than others). Keynes recognized that the validity of Say's Law was critical to the traditional case for laissez-faire. His rejection of Say's Law has far-reaching implications.

Ricardo, for example, argues that supply—the willingness of the owner of a productive resource like labor, land, or capital to offer the resource for productive employment—creates demand sufficient to take the aggregate product off the market. People have to spend their money one way or another, according to Ricardo's reasoning. If they sell their labor-power or capital services, they will turn around to buy consumption goods. If they choose to save rather than to consume, then they will have to buy capital goods through investment with their incomes. One way or another, the demand will be there to buy back what has been produced.

The marginalists also see market exchange as essentially the bartering of one good or service for another. In this context it is difficult to distinguish between supply and demand. In marginalist terms, labor buys goods, and goods buy labor.

The marginalists and the classical economists always allow for the possibility that supply and demand in particular markets might not balance, because relative prices have not adjusted to their equilibrium levels. But if some market, say, the market for labor, is in excess supply, some other market, say, the market for commodities, must be in excess demand according to this reasoning. There is always some configuration of relative prices that will eliminate these sectoral excess supplies and demands. If we observe a market, say, the labor market, with chronic excess supply manifesting itself as unemployment, the cure must lie in encouraging the price in that market, the real wage, to fall. In this framework the ultimate cause of excess supply is always some factor that prevents prices from adjusting freely, and the ultimate cure for excess supply is the removal of these hindrances to changes in prices. In the labor market, these hindrances are legislation like minimum wages, or elements of monopoly power like trade unions, which prevent the necessary adjustment of wages to clear the labor market.

The reasoning of both the marginalists and the classical economists rests heavily on the assumption that the monetary and financial mechanisms of the economy work extremely efficiently. Ricardo expresses this idea by saying that "money is a veil," so that it makes sense to analyze economic relations as if labor and commodities exchanged directly for each other. In marginalist and neoclassical economics money is of use only because of what it can buy, and the structure of the analysis presupposes that goods and services, including labor, can exchange directly for each other.

Another way of putting this is to say that the classicals and neoclassicals think of a world in which the velocity of money is infinite. Thus the length of time over which any individual holds financial assets between her sale of one good and her purchase of another is vanishingly short. In terms of Marx's circuit of commodity exchange, in which the seller of a commodity for money turns around and spends the money to buy another commodity, the time that value spends in the intermediary form of money vanishes. Believers in Say's Law might further argue that even if the velocity of money is not infinite, their analysis will be a good approximation to reality as long as the gap between sale and purchase is short and highly predictable, that is, the velocity of money is high and stable. Then the real economy will act very much as if labor were exchanging directly for goods and goods for labor, and the implications of Say's Law will be largely valid.

Keynes argues that Say's Law is completely out of date in economies with a highly developed financial system. When there are numerous and varied financial instruments in an economy, the sale of one commodity may be separated by a long and variable period from the purchase of another. If the lag between sale and purchase lengthens, there may be insufficient monetary demand to buy back all the commodities produced and offered for sale on the market. In this case some firms and households are "liquidity-constrained," rationing their purchases of commodities because they simply do not have the financial resources to buy.

Under these circumstances, the decision to spend money has a kind of positive externality for the economic system as a whole. The spender has the private advantage of purchasing the commodity she wants, but she also increases the money balances of another agent, which permits that agent to make a desired purchase that was previously impossible because of financial constraints. Because individual spenders do not take into account the external impact of their decisions, the volume of spending may be too small to employ all the resources of the economy, and there is a case for government intervention to subsidize spending (or to spend itself) to make up the difference.

The rejection of Say's Law, however, has further implications for the general argument of laissez-faire. If the free market is prone to stagnation of demand and unemployment of resources, many policies that make no sense under the assumption of Say's Law can be defended. For example, classical and marginalist economists argue that protectionist tariffs can only divert employment and investment from more profitable to less profitable sectors, and cannot change the total volume of employment of labor or capital. But if Say's Law doesn't hold, then the jobs lost to free trade will not necessarily be offset by other jobs created elsewhere in the economy; a protectionist tariff may increase the wealth of the nation by raising the employment of its labor and capital. Similarly, government spending under Say's Law reasoning can be justified only if the social rate of return to the government investment is higher than the rate of return to private investment. Taxing or borrowing to spend simply in order to create demand can only reduce the welfare of the society by diverting resources from their most profitable uses. But if Say's Law does not hold, government spending may employ resources that otherwise would be idle, and thus can increase the wealth created.

Given the importance of laissez-faire arguments in the political economy of capitalism, and the potential for government intervention in markets, we can see that the ideological stakes riding on the assumption of Say's Law are very high indeed. In fact, most people seem to think about the economy very much as if Say's Law did not hold: they think that jobs lost to international trade are lost completely, and they never connect up the system-wide effects of market equilibrium in their minds. One of the missions of economics is to educate people out of these prejudices. The appearance of Keynes's economics, in which Say's Law, one of the most fundamental principles of economic analysis, is questioned, created a delicate problem for economic theory as a whole.

In the 1940s, when Keynes's ideas were coming to dominate economic theory in the United States and Britain, this problem was addressed by a compromise, enunciated by Paul Samuelson, among others—the "neoclassical synthesis." The neoclassical synthesis held, in agreement with Keynes, that free markets cannot guarantee the full employment of productive resources (or at least not very fast), so that governments and central banks have to adjust fiscal and monetary policy to ensure full or close to full employment. Once full employment demand has been achieved, however, the basic force of the laissez-faire analysis comes back into play, and markets should be largely free to allocate resources without further government intervention. Ingenious as it was, this idea of the neoclassical synthesis proved to be unstable ideologically. In the 1970s, economists espousing monetarist and rational expectations theory insisted on the need to return to the full classical and neoclassical orthodoxy, including the assumption of Say's Law, and, to a considerable extent, they captured the high ground in economic theory (if not in economic policy).

Say's Law is an important pillar supporting Adam's Fallacy. If Say's Law is wrong, then the purported social advantages of capitalist social relations become contingent and uncertain, and the argument for putting up with the moral disadvantages of capitalism is correspondingly weaker.

Labor Markets and Unemployment

A great deal of attention has been given to Keynes's analysis of the labor market, and to the category of "involuntary unemployment" which he defines in *The General Theory*. The problem is that Keynes seems to accept the conceptual apparatus of the marginalist analysis, but the concept of involuntary unemployment appears to be inconsistent with the marginalist definition of equilibrium.

In the marginalist conception of equilibrium in the labor market, firms hire workers up to the point where the wage equals the value of the goods one more worker can produce (the marginal product of labor). Workers in turn supply labor up to the point where the marginal utility of the goods and services which the wage can buy is equal to the negative marginal utility of working an extra hour (the marginal disutility of labor). Equilibrium in the labor market is defined by the equality of the marginal product and the marginal disutility of labor. The marginal product of labor is measured by a demand schedule for labor, which slopes downward because of assumed diminishing returns to the employment of labor with a fixed capital stock.

Keynes explicitly assumes that his labor market equilibrium must lie on the marginalist demand schedule for labor, that is, that the real wage must be equal to the marginal product of labor, and that the marginal product of labor declines as employment expands with a fixed capital stock because of diminishing returns. But Keynes insists that the labor market may come into what he regards as equilibrium in a situation where the real wage exceeds the marginal disutility of labor as measured by the labor supply schedule. The unemployed in this situation are willing to work for the going real wage, and even at a somewhat lower real wage. Keynes defines these workers as "involuntarily unemployed."

Marginalists can conceive of the labor market being in *disequilibrium*. They would not dispute the characterization of the resulting unemployment as involuntary, although they would prefer to speak of an "excess supply" of labor. But they believe that at a disequilibrium, there are forces tending to lower the real wage. Here is the critical disagreement between Keynes and the marginalists, since Keynes insists that involuntary unemployment can coexist with equilibrium of the labor market.

To some degree this must be a semantic disagreement, since the marginalist conception of equilibrium is clearly defined and refers to points at the intersection of the supply and demand schedules for labor. But Keynes argues that there may in fact be no forces tending to lower the real wage even when the real wage is above the supply price of labor. His argument is that the only way workers could respond to the excess supply of labor would be by cutting the *money* wage, since actual wage bargains are made in terms of money, not real goods and services. Keynes agrees that there might be a sharp fall in money wages in the presence of involuntary unemployment, though he does not think this is a good thing for the economy by any means. (In the early 1930s when unemployment was very high, money wages in the United States did drop rapidly.) He argues, however, that cuts in money wages cannot bring about a fall in the real wage, because money wages are such a large part of the costs of production. As money wages fall in the economy, all producers find their costs lowered, and competition will force them to lower the money prices of goods and services in proportion. This, of course, keeps the real wage—which is the ratio of the money wage to the prices of goods workers buy—constant, and leaves the economy with involuntary unemployment.

Keynes argues persuasively that a downward spiral of money wages and money prices is the last thing an economy suffering from substantial unemployment needs. The deflation of money prices and wages increases the real interest rate and the burden of servicing existing debts, and thus may discourage businesses from undertaking new investment, thereby making the liquidity constraints in the economy even more severe. (Of course, the deflation makes the holders of existing debt richer in real terms, and might prompt them to spend more on consumption. But lenders tend to be wealthy households who are unlikely to increase their consumption very much as their real wealth rises.) Keynes noticed that organized labor tended to resist cuts in money wages even during periods of substantial unemployment, and argued that this was a good thing, since it tended to stabilize the price level.

Keynes did acknowledge that a fall in money prices and wages might indirectly help to make the economy more liquid if the central bank maintained the nominal quantity of money, since when prices and wages are lower, the same nominal quantity of money represents more purchasing power, and thus relaxes the liquidity constraint on households and firms. But, he argues, this is a very painful and roundabout way to create more liquidity in the economy, since the central bank could accomplish the same thing simply by increasing the nominal money supply.

Keynes's argument that the mechanisms by which a fall in money wages could bring about a fall in the real wage are weak and indirect is persuasive, but his claim that involuntary unemployment can co-exist with equilibrium in the labor market leaves several loose ends unresolved. For one thing, when there is involuntary unemployment there does seem to be pressure for money wages to fall, and thus involuntary unemployment is not compatible with stability of all the important price variables in the economy. Since involuntary unemployment is clearly not compatible with equilibrium in the marginalist sense, it would have helped if Keynes had explained better what he meant by an equilibrium. What he seems to have had in mind is a position of the economy in which there is no short-run pressure for a change in the volume of employment, even if there is short-run pressure for a change in the money wage.

The problem of involuntary unemployment continues to vex macroeconomic theory to this day. The neoclassical orthodoxy adopts a theory essentially like that of the marginalists, in which in-voluntary unemployment is incompatible with equilibrium. The extreme form of rational expectations theory asserts that the real econ-omy is also always in marginalist equilibrium, so that involuntary unemployment can never be observed. On the one hand, this dis-credits economic theory in the eyes of ordinary educated people, be-cause they feel from their own experience and observation that there are times when they or others would like to work at the going real wage, or even somewhat below the going real wage, and cannot find jobs. On the other hand, it requires the rational expectations theo-rists to find an alternative explanation for the business cycle fluctua-tion in the level of unemployment consistent with the assumption that the labor market is always in equilibrium. One explanation that has been proposed is that actual unemployment is really disguised employment, in that the unemployed are voluntarily staying out of jobs in order to search for better ones. Another argument is that when real wages fall in recessions, employment falls because workers voluntarily withdraw from the job market to wait until the real wage recovers. (There is undoubtedly some truth in this, since labor force participation rates fall in recessions at the same time that unemployment rates rise, but this idea doesn't explain the rise in measured unemployment of individuals who are actively seeking work.)

Expectations and Money

Keynes sees a close relation between the monetary character of the industrial capitalist economy and the essential indeterminacy of its future path. The motivation for a firm to undertake production and thus to hire labor and buy inputs depends on its judgment that it will be able to sell the product at a profit. Industrial capitalism requires investors to risk large sums of money on projects whose ultimate profitability will not be known for many years. In Keynes's view the proximate cause of economic activity is *expectation* of profit. But the future for human beings is always uncertain, and therefore undertaking production or long-term investment requires capitalists to confront and evaluate their uncertain prospects.

Neoclassical economics argues that the evaluation and allocation of risk is the function of freely operating asset markets. The paradigmatic case of market allocation of risks for neoclassical economics is insurance. A group of wealth-holders facing risks, like fire, that are statistically predictable but individually random can pool some of their wealth into an insurance fund and compensate the members that actually experience losses. Neoclassical theory views all risk as being of this statistically predictable character, and sees the continuing development of financial markets as the best way for the economy to cope with risk.

Keynes wrote an influential book on probability theory in his youth, and had distinct views on probability and risk management. He emphasized the difference, also noted by other economists such as Frank Knight, between calculable and therefore insurable risks, and unresolvable uncertainties about which we can form no coherent statistical opinion. He argues that while financial assets and markets can allocate insurable risks, the more important economic risks are unresolvable uncertainties which financial markets may in fact make worse. The problem is that macroeconomic uncertainty is largely generated within the economic system, unlike the risk of individual death or fire. The risk that an economy will plunge into recession, for example, does not arise from uncertainty about external factors like weather, but from uncertainty about the interaction of capitalist expectations. If everyone comes to believe that a recession is imminent, they will reduce their investment expenditure and production levels, thereby reducing incomes and making the expectation come true in a self-fulfilling way. Since the recession is the manifestation not of calculable risks, but of essentially incalculable dynamic interactions of human beings, asset markets cannot allocate or hedge this type of risk.

Furthermore, Keynes maintains that there is a considerable danger inherent in entrusting the allocation of investment entirely to financial markets. When financial risk is calculable, there is a statistical basis on which to estimate the fundamental value of an asset. When the risks are incalculable, on the other hand, there is no rational basis on which to value assets, and market valuations can swing wildly as a result of fashion, herd instincts, or panic, destabilizing investment and the real economy in the process. Keynes argues that in this situation the financial markets are like a type of beauty contest run by British newspapers in which the aim is not to choose which entrant is the most attractive, but which one will get the most votes from the public. To guard against the instability of financial markets, Keynes recommends a "somewhat comprehensive socialization of investment," assigning to the political process the role of economic balance wheel in relation to financial markets.

In Keynes's view the widespread use of money and the development of sophisticated financial markets and assets are in part a defensive reaction against the "dark forces of time and uncertainty" on the part of wealth-holders. Real investment requires the commitment of the investor to a long-term, illiquid, and risky prospect. Financial assets, on the other hand, represent more liquid wealth than can be sold at any moment, and allow the wealth-holder to defer the decision as to the ultimate use of the funds involved. But Keynes believes that this is exactly why money and financial assets are potentially dangerous. In times of uncertainty, wealth-holders will tend to flee from real investment into financial havens and money, thus lengthening the time lag between sale and purchase of real goods and services, and creating a gap between aggregate supply and aggregate demand. While laissez-faire reasoning argues for making available as wide a spectrum of financial assets as possible, and reducing the costs of transactions as much as possible, in order to increase the liquidity of the economy, Keynes sees a case for *restricting* investors' choices, and forcing them to commit themselves to some form of real investment. He goes so far as to suggest that investment of wealth should be something like marriage: an investor should be forced to choose whichever real investment he or she thought had the best long-term prospects, and stick with it for the life of the project.

Short-Term Expectation

In Keynes's view, producers set production in motion, hiring labor and purchasing inputs to production, because their short-term expectation of demand for the product promises them an acceptable profit. If short-term expectation of demand rises, firms will hire more workers, buy more inputs, and increase production. Keynes refs to the schedule relating employment and the short-term expectation of entrepreneurs as the "aggregate supply price" of output, although the concept involves an aggregate value, not an individual price.

Short-term expectation is rather rapidly confirmed or repudiated by the producers' experience in selling the output on the market. Keynes argues that the aggregate demand actually appearing on the market will itself be a function of employment. Higher wage income relieves the liquidity constraint of workers' households, and they will spend at least a substantial fraction of the increased wages on consumption goods. Because only a fraction of increased wage income is spent on consumption (the "marginal propensity to consume" is less than unity), aggregate demand rises by less than a dollar for each dollar increase in incomes generated by new production, and there must be a point of intersection between aggregate demand and aggregate supply price representing a short-term equilibrium in which the short-term expectation of entrepreneurs is just fulfilled.

In neoclassical theory, a firm in a competitive market is assumed to be able to sell any quantity of output at the going market price: the firm demand schedule is horizontal, or infinitely elastic, at the market price. Under these circumstances, the idea of short-term expectation of a given volume of sales on the part of the individual firm makes no sense. Keynes's point is that in a liquidity-constrained economy the abstraction of perfect competition must break down, and individual firms must see some trade-off between price and sales. Since this is, in fact, what real firms see, Keynes's notion of short-term expectation is more realistic than the neoclassical abstraction of the perfectly competitive market. But Keynes never explains exactly how he thinks individual entrepreneurs form their short-term expectation in relation to aggregate demand. Thus there is a lack of microeconomic foundations in Keynes's equilibrium theory. The problem of linking Keynesian macroeconomics to a coherent and persuasive theory of competition among individual firms remains a central unresolved issue in contemporary economics.

Long-Term Expectation

The incomes of workers represent only a part of the value created in production. The rest takes the form of profit (including rent and interest). A small fraction of wages and a large proportion of profit incomes are saved in the form of money or financial assets. Short-term equilibrium can emerge with a positive level of employment only if there is some level of "autonomous" investment spending to offset saving.

Keynes, having lived through the turmoil of the First World War, the European postwar inflations, and the depression of the 1930s, viewed the willingness of wealth-holders to make long-term real investments as something of a miracle. He argued that what would motivate a wealth-holder to make such an investment was the long-term expectation of profitability. The heart of the capitalist system, in Keynes's vision, is the willingness of wealth-holders to speculate on the profitability of the future by making long-term investments. Keynes worried that this kind of speculation depends on a fragile and unstable psychology of investors, who are prone to a kind of manic-depression syndrome, oscillating between extreme optimism about the future, which leads to high investment and a self-fulfilling boom in aggregate demand and employment, and extreme pessimism, leading to low investment and a self-fulfilling depression of aggregate demand and employment. Keynesians refer to this psychological element in the formation of long-term expectations as the "animal spirits" of capitalists.

For a given state of long-term expectation, however, monetary and interest rate policy can, in Keynes's analysis, have some impact on the actual volume of investment. This is because investors will still measure the prospect of profit from real investment against the interest rate established on safe financial assets like bank deposits and short-term government debt. Keynes believed that the central bank could determine these short-term interest rates by expanding or contracting the reserves of the banking system. The central bank can thus resist a manic phase of animal spirits by raising short-term interest rates to discourage an overly rapid rise in investment spending, and may be able to buoy up a depressive phase of animal spirits by lowering interest rates. Keynes had considerable doubt, however, about how much stimulus central bank policy could provide to a depressed economy by lowering interest rates, in part because nominal interest rates can't fall below zero, and in part because depressed wealth-holders may have too strong an absolute preference for liquidity.

Neoclassical theory argues that capitalists should make an investment only when the present value of the goods and services the investment will produce exceeds the cost of the investment. If markets for future goods and services exist, the equilibrium price established in these markets represents the state of long-term expectation. Furthermore, the same forces that lead to equilibrium in current markets for goods and services will operate in these futures markets. If the demand for factors of production in the present falls short of the supply, according to Say's Law reasoning, it must be because demand for future goods and services (saving) exceeds the supply of future goods and services (investment). A fall in the interest rate (an adjustment of relative prices between the present and the future) should increase investment, reduce saving, and lead to an equilibrium, according to neoclassical theory. The problem is that while futures markets exist for a small range of commodities over a short time horizon, they don't exist for major investment projects over a long time horizon. Thus it is not clear that market mechanisms exist to resolve inconsistencies among the long-term expectations of investors and establish an equilibrium. This is a point of deep and unresolved disagreement between Keynesian and neoclassical economists.

Keynes thought that the solution to the inherent instability of long-term expectation was for the government to adopt fiscal and monetary policies which would stabilize aggregate demand, and to take on a much larger share of the total investment of the economy. This would reduce the anxiety of investors about the possibility of catastrophic depressions. Presumably the market alternative would be to create more markets for future goods and services so that market equilibrium could do a better job of stabilizing investment planning.

In the years since the Second World War, advanced capitalist economies have indeed employed both of these strategies. Government spending and taxation now represent one-third to one-half of GDP in most advanced capitalist countries. As a result the effects of liquidity constraints are sharply reduced, since a fall of output and incomes in recession throws government budgets into deficit, and maintains spending streams. At the same time there has been an explosive growth in financial markets and in the spectrum of available financial instruments, which presumably strengthens the ability of wealth-holders to hedge risks and form a more consistent view of the future path of the economy.

But the economic future is not predetermined nor completely predictable, so it is unlikely that futures markets can completely eliminate the instabilities of expectation that Keynes identified. Governments may be no better than markets at predicting the future, but the collective action of society can stabilize some of the key boundary conditions in which capitalist investment takes place, and thus strengthen the "animal spirits" on which the system rests.

The Fate of Capitalism

Keynes's economic analysis focuses on the short run, and on the problem of the full employment of economic resources. Many of the differences between Keynesian and classical political economic theory are traceable to this difference in perspective. In the middle years of the twentieth century, the stability of capitalist growth and the underemployment of economic resources was the overwhelming economic problem of capitalist societies. Today our attention has swung back, at least partially, to longer-run concerns: economic growth, environmental quality, competitiveness and economic leadership, and distributional equity. To a certain degree we have come to take the Keynesian lessons for granted, and have built them into the structures of public finance. They have worked remarkably well, and freed us to think about longer-run issues.

Keynes himself was usually not much interested in the long run. One of his most quoted aphorisms is "In the long run we are all dead." He also argued that there was no long run, only a constant succession of short runs—an observation that raises some very deep questions about the operation of complex systems like economies. It may be true that short-run forces determine the actual paths of economies from moment to moment, but it may also be true that there are pervasive corrective forces that tend to nudge the short-run outcomes into averaging out to a long-run equilibrium. Many economists believe this in some way or other, but it has turned out to be very difficult to demonstrate the existence of these long-run forces, even using very sophisticated econometric techniques for analyzing data.

Keynes did, in his essay *Economic Prospects for Our Grandchildren*, venture some opinions about the long-run fate of capitalism. In his view, short-run instability was the main obstacle to rapid accumulation of capital and a correspondingly rapid rise in labor productivity and standards of living. Keynes believed that if aggregate demand could be stabilized for even two generations, say, fifty or sixty years, the advanced capitalist countries would see a huge rise in standards of living as a result of the rapid accumulation of capital. Keynes thought that the accumulation of capital would proceed to the point where the marginal product of capital approached zero, so that the profit rate and interest rate would also become very low. This would mean the effective disappearance of capitalists as a class without a political revolution—the "euthanasia of the rentier," in Keynes's terms. At very high levels of labor productivity and low profit rates, wages would represent the great bulk of incomes, so that the distribution of income would be much more equal. Keynes believed that future generations would spend this enormous potential wealth less on an increase in material consumption and more on leisure and self-development, ushering in something like Marx's vision of a world in which a person could be a farmer or fisherman in the morning and a poet or scientist in the afternoon.

There are striking echoes of Ricardo's stationary state in Keynes's vision of the fate of capitalism—the decline of the profit rate to zero is a notable example. There are equally striking differences: Keynes seems to have no anxiety about the shortage of natural resources or environmental limits to growth to parallel Ricardo's focus on rent. There are also striking echoes of Marx's vision of socialism founded on huge increases in productivity.

We are collectively the generation of Keynes's grandchildren and great-grandchildren; more than sixty years have passed since the publication of *The General Theory.* Some of Keynes's prophecies have come true. The period after the Second World War was a "Golden Age" of capitalist accumulation, fostered considerably by the stabilizing fiscal and financial policies that Keynes recommended. Labor productivity has increased tremendously, as has the standard of living of the advanced capitalist countries.

But somehow these positive developments have not eliminated the conflicts and anxieties of capitalist economic life to the degree that Keynes hoped. The profit rate has not fallen to zero, nor has the euthanasia of the rentier come to pass. The high levels of productivity we have achieved have brought with them high levels of resource depletion and environmental decay. Distributional inequality shows a tendency to rise, rather than fall, over time with the globalization of capitalism. These difficulties underline the significance of Marx's observation that capital is at its root a social relation.

Complexity vs. Collectivism

Friedrich von Hayek struck out disastrously in an attempt to confront Keynes over the possibility of activist government policy during the Depression of the 1930s, but his influence began to rise in the last quarter of the twentieth century, and now threatens to eclipse that of Keynes. The "Austrian" school of economic theory in which Hayek was educated took upon itself the task of refuting Marx's economic and social ideas. These Austrian economists were staunch defenders of private property and decentralized control of economic resources, and they were sharp critics of collectivist and socialist aspirations. The hostility toward perfectibilism that we saw in Malthus finds an echo among the Austrians.

The Depression-dominated atmosphere of the 1930s posed a frightening threat to these core Austrian economic beliefs. Even normally reliable centrists wavered in their allegiance to laissez-faire economic ideas. The idea that society has some obligation to secure the economic well-being of all its members began to spread widely, opening the door to a host of "collectivist" initiatives, including social welfare legislation, guarantees of labor's right to organize, income redistribution, central planning of industry, state direction of investment, and intentional deficit spending to prop up aggregate demand. While Keynes was a stronger advocate of some of these measures than of others, the thrust of his thinking definitely accepted an activist role for the state to redress major failings of markets, and he contemptuously rejected Victorian laissez-faire theory. At the same time a significant fraction of the European and

American political elite, without actually knowing much about it, saw the Soviet Union as building a credible alternative economic model to capitalism. Much of what the Austrian economists saw as the precious legacy of European liberalism (recognizably a variant of Adam's Fallacy) appeared to be at real risk of submergence in a confused embrace of collectivist and socialist fantasies.

Hayek bravely (and ambitiously) put himself on the front line of these battles. He attempted to head off the growing political pressure for the state to do something about the Depression and high unemployment by developing a compelling Austrian theory of the business cycle which would support the extension of laissez-faire concepts to deficit and interest rate policy. He also detected a fatal flaw in the Austrian position on the possibility of organizing the division of labor through centralized socialist mechanisms, like the central planning bureaucracy evolving in the Soviet Union.

Business Cycle or Capitalist Crisis?

We need not devote too much attention to Hayek's theory of what has come to be called "macroeconomics," the study of economy-wide phenomena such as the level of national income, unemployment, inflation, interest rates, and money. The book he wrote, *Prices and Production,* is very difficult to read and left no discernible mark on later economic discussions of macroeconomic policy.

Hayek's broad case is worth considering as a withered offshoot of Adam's Fallacy. He takes the position that business cycle fluctuations are a rationally explicable feature of industrial capitalism, not a sign of fundamental crisis in the system. The source of these fluctuations, according to Hayek, lies in the incomplete application of liberal principles to the organization and governance of the financial system; this allows and encourages "over-investment" in periods of economic boom and a predictable reaction of "under-investment," leading to unemployment in the succeeding slumps. Any attempt by the government to intervene in these fluctuations, except to extend the general liberal principles of private ownership, commodity logic, and market discipline more consistently to financial markets and institutions, will just make matters worse.

Hayek's attempt to flesh out this general argument in a detailed technical economic analysis ran aground on his failure to set out a consistent, transparent framework of analysis, and, very likely, on some inconsistencies in his own thinking. A devastating review of Hayek's book by Keynes's associate, Piero Sraffa, sank it pretty much without a trace, leaving the field clear for the triumphant advance of Keynes's own quite interventionist ideas for addressing the problems of the Depression.

What Does the Market Do?

On another flank, Austrian economics as the bastion of traditional liberal political economy was engaged in challenging the feasibility of running an economy through socialist central planning institutions. The Austrian economists, in order to be true to their understanding of Adam's Fallacy, were compelled to argue that the concept of socialism was not just bad or inexpedient, but doomed by the existence of economic laws (the laws of the commodity) which have the same force as natural laws. We can no more build a socialist economy than we can repeal the law of gravity, according to this argument.

This is a difficult position to sustain on its face. First of all, capitalism exists and develops in close symbiosis with political and regulatory institutions. The nation-state that emerged in the early modern period in Europe was linked in a host of ways—financial, technological, political, and social—to the emerging capitalist economy. As a result, there are many "models" of capitalism with quite different degrees of government intervention through quite different policies and institutions. Capitalism is also constantly evolving. The capitalism of the twenty-first century has some recognizable links (through bedrock features such as commodity exchange, markets, and international competition) with the nascent industrial capitalism of Adam Smith's day, but it has other features (central banking, powerful governments, regulation of markets, social safety-nets) that are completely foreign to earlier periods. In the face of this historical mutability of capitalist institutions and content, it seems rash to posit the existence of immutable economic laws.

Furthermore, the Soviet Union did indeed manage to organize an impressive spurt of economic development, extension of the division of labor, and growth of productive capacity through its central planning mechanisms for what turned out to be a period of sixty years after the Austrian economists claimed that central planning was impossible. Despite these prima facie weaknesses in the overall Austrian argument against the feasibility of socialism, the debate they ignited greatly increased our understanding of what the capitalist market actually does.

The initial Austrian strategy in this debate started with the observation that the capitalist market, in arriving at an equilibrium price system, effectively computes the solution to an enormous number of mathematical conditions which amount to the equality of the reservation prices at a Pareto allocation. The claim then was that no central planning bureaucracy could feasibly solve this same system because of its mathematical complexity. Since the Austrian economists, as firm believers in Adam's Fallacy, held that the realization of potential economic surpluses was the ultimate purpose of economic life, this seemed to be an unanswerable criticism of socialist central planning.

This argument ran into resistance on two grounds. First, many people were not convinced that the failure to realize every drop of potential economic surplus would necessarily doom a socialist society. There seemed to be a large number of important economic development projects—for example, building industrial factories and the infrastructure to support them—that could be carried on without a completely precise knowledge of a theoretical equilibrium price system. If the central planning mechanism was an effective political and administrative means to mobilize resources for these projects (arguably more effective than depending on unreliable and underperforming Russian capitalists to do the job), why not opt for central planning?

This was a persuasive enough argument for many people in the 1930s, but the defenders of the socialist ideal also managed to turn the Austrian critique of socialism back on itself in an even more devastating maneuver. Drawing on the early observations of Enrico Barone, Oskar Lange and Abba Lerner argued that there was no reason why a socialist economy could not use market methods to find equilibrium prices just as effectively as a capitalist economy. If socialist managers were instructed to compete just as if they were capitalists (even though the state would own the means of production, and no private profit would be at stake), they could reach the same market equilibrium as a capitalist economy with the same resources and technology. This concept of market socialism had an enormous impact on the development of political economy in the 1930s and 1940s.

But this is just another statement of Adam's Fallacy! The market socialists invite us to believe that there is no difference between a socialist and a capitalist organization of the division of labor except for the formal legal mechanisms that support the market, and perhaps the distribution of income. If this is indeed the case, there is little reason to choose one or the other except political expediency or historical accident.

Hayek saw disaster looming for the liberal cause in this episode. He did not believe that socialist managers could ever mimic capitalist entrepreneurs well enough to make socialist markets function.

Thus he was led to shift the focus of this debate in a profound, fateful, and fruitful direction. It is not, according to Hayek, the market form that is critical to organizing the division of labor; it is the content of the market as a clash of personal interests that actually drives things forward. This is Adam's Fallacy pure and unadulterated. The antagonistic relations of the market are no longer a necessary evil to be tolerated for the sake of getting our dinner (and a better one) out of the butcher and the baker, nor even an ingenious game we might play to squeeze out potential economic surpluses. In Hayek's vision the antagonistic relations of the market are the existential core of human existence, the ground from which everything else emerges.

Hayek did not put his point in quite this way. He argued that the real metabolism of the market rests on its ability to force everyone to reveal their private information about needs, technology, and resources, whether they want to or not, and whether they participate in the market enthusiastically, seeking profit, or grudgingly, to defend their conditions of existence. We have seen this aspect of the market already in the idea that it forces people to "put their money where their mouth is" in the actual exchange of commodities to form market prices. Hayek puts this informational aspect of the market in the central position. The capitalist market now appears as a critical component of a complex system of information revelation and exchange. The division of labor itself becomes a by-product and side effect of this play of information. The reason the socialist managers cannot mimic the capitalist market is that they have no direct existential interest to defend and assert in making market exchanges. Socialism imagines that economic life is a means to an end, a method of supplying the material needs without which human life and social life cannot function. The conceit of socialism is that supplying this material basis is just a matter of getting necessary productive work done. In fact, according to Hayek's way of thinking, the central problem is to know *what the necessary productive work actually is.* Even the best-intentioned and most self-disciplined socialist worker-citizens would find themselves helpless to know where to expend their labor effort, or even to know whether what looks like an obvious social need (building a steel mill) may not be doing more harm than good.

In addition to his work in political economy, Hayek was a pioneer in neural science. During the First World War he worked with soldiers who had brain injuries, and later in his life he wrote a major work on brain function. The brain is a paradigmatic example of a complex system, and Hayek's observations on the market lead in the direction of thinking of the capitalist economy as a similarly complex system. The market emerges from individual exchanges just as consciousness emerges from the synaptic interaction of neurons.

The informational vision of the capitalist market undermines the "objective" conception of markets as realizing potential economic surpluses that exist whether the market finds them or not. Hayek's market is decisively *inter-subjective,* a reality that is sustained through and only through the communication of information. Of course, it gives rise to the objective phenomena of production and consumption. It would be a mistake, however, to think that these metabolic social processes could continue without the market's constant elicitation and dissemination of information, any more than the body could continue to respire and digest in the absence of neural function. (The socialist experiment, in Hayek's view, might be likened to a human being in a persistent vegetative state, metabolically functioning but brain-dead.)

The socialist economies, remaining for the most part ignorant of Hayek's discovery of their nonviability, struggled on like doomed dinosaurs for another five decades before their inevitable fate caught up with them. Mainstream economics acknowledged the brilliance of Hayek's insight without actually incorporating it into its fundamental teaching and research program, and the Austrian economists found themselves marginalized as effectively as were the Marxists.

Resurrecting Liberalism

For his part, Hayek turned his attention from doomed experiments in central planning to a much tougher and more powerful opponent, the mixed economy emerging after the Second World War which incorporated so many of what seemed to Hayek the misguided ideas of John Maynard Keynes.

Hayek wrote an intemperate political tract, *The Road to Serfdom,* in which he made the rather implausible claim that government intervention to stabilize and regulate the capitalist economy represented as much a threat to the freedom and dignity of the individual as totalitarian dictatorships did. Keynes's on the whole pragmatic (though inconsistent) program of government stabilization of investment, regulation of financial markets, and provision of a social safety net was in Hayek's eyes a stalking-horse for collectivism. Once people bought the false idea that government could do anything to meet their real needs, they would contaminate and destroy the spontaneous order of the market, and wind up as the dependents of a collective leviathan.

In these views Hayek exaggerates the spontaneity of market organization of the division of labor. Economic history shows how laborious and uncertain the process of establishing and enforcing property rights actually was, and what a crucial role was played by centralized political power. The development of the market is as much a reflection of the development of the underlying division of labor and productive power as the other way around. Market organization without the underlying push of productivity and political organization tends to produce stagnation, not wealth. It is one thing to recognize the power of market forces to elicit and combine private information about productive opportunities, but quite another to deprecate all other forms of social organization of information, from government bureaucracy to legal systems to political life itself.

The positive economic power of collective political action seems to have escaped Hayek's attention. Governments can organize production and create material wealth, and in extreme emergencies like wars and natural disasters, societies look to collective action for rescue. Even in quiet times governments can achieve financial and redistributive ends which private enterprise is helpless to address. The political history of capitalism shows private enterprise appealing to government for regulation again and again.

Despite the extreme and implausible form that Adam's Fallacy took in Hayek's mind, his views have increasingly shaped the ideological debates in political economy since the 1970s. Hayek himself cannily set the stage for these developments, devoting much energy to the elaboration of a viable neo-liberal political program and the nurturing of institutions to disseminate it, including the Mont Pelerin Society and the University of Chicago Economics Department. American political economy debate is awash with versions of Hayek's liberal vision, promulgated by think-tanks funded by enthusiastic capitalist boosters. Hayek emerged from his bruising theoretical defeats at Keynes's hands in the dark days of the Depression to fight again and climb back to occupy the ideological high ground of capitalist society.

The Prophet of Technology

While Keynes and Hayek were struggling over the body and soul of twentieth-century capitalism, Joseph Alois Schumpeter was making his own investigations into its metabolism and anatomy. Schumpeter, born in Austria, but not in spirit an Austrian economist, had served rather unsuccessfully as Austria's Finance Minister in the immediate aftermath of the First World War, and experienced the rough side of Adam's Fallacy. Approaching capitalism with a worldly realism bordering on cynicism, Schumpeter devoted his considerable rhetorical and analytical powers to injecting Marx's theory of technical change into the marginalist framework as a corrective to the equilibrium-fetish of neoclassical economics.

In Schumpeter's view Walras's theory of equilibrium was an outstanding intellectual achievement, but a developmental disaster insofar as real economies ever came close to it. In Walras's equilibrium capital appropriates a uniform normal profit rate, taking account of expectations. While this arrangement succeeds in squeezing out all of the economic surplus available, given tastes and technology, from a developmental point of view it lacks the life of innovation, and hence fails to express the inner spirit of capitalism.

Schumpeter believes that it is the innovative entrepreneur, whose life work is precisely to *disrupt* Walras's equilibrium by introducing new products, new technology, and new forms of productive organization, who does embody this inner spirit. Following Ricardo and Marx, Schumpeter identifies the motive for entrepreneurial restlessness as the super-profits above the normal profit rate which successful innovators carry off. These super-profits are impermanent, though recurring, features of capitalist reality. They are inconsistent with equilibrium because they disrupt Pareto's marginal equalities. Innovation destroys equilibrium and its prices, upsetting the applecart again and again.

The innovative entrepreneur, who combines Veblen's instinct for workmanship with Marx's impulse to change the world, is no less a revolutionary than the Communist commissar. (As we can see more clearly in the aftermath of Soviet Communism, it is even possible for a commissar to evolve into a kind of entrepreneur under specific historical circumstances.) Schumpeter saw entrepreneurs as much more attractive agents of revolutionary change than political commissars, but doubted that society would put up with their disruptive activities indefinitely.

Schumpeter called entrepreneurial innovation "creative destruction," and saw it as the critical moment in the real historical evolution of capitalism. Schumpeter developed his own account of the instability of capitalism, centered on this process of creative destruction, with elements that strongly echo Keynes's and Hayek's conceptions. For Schumpeter the role of banks, and of finance in general, is to bankroll innovation. Expansions of credit unleash a boom founded on the investments of innovating entrepreneurs. Eventually the destructive stage of their innovation comes to predominate, as less innovative capitals fall by the wayside, creating unemployment and financial distress. But this constant pummeling and defeating of expectations is the goose that lays the golden eggs of productivity increase and advances in the material standard of living. Schumpeter returns through Marx's theory of capitalism as a mode of production that systematically generates technical change to the historical bedrock of Adam's Fallacy: the material wealth attainable from the widening division of labor. For a twenty-first century that is overwhelmingly preoccupied by innovation and advances in productivity, Schumpeter is a prophet. His ideas have spawned a major part of the burgeoning technical literature on economic growth.

Schumpeter is pessimistic about the long-run viability of capitalist social institutions. He does not doubt that there is an endless supply of new ideas leading to potentially successful innovations. But he does doubt that Western civilization (still the focus of thinking during Schumpeter's lifetime) will tolerate the suffering in the form of mass unemployment, inequality of wealth, and economic insecurity that the god of capitalism demands as its human sacrifice. Schumpeter addresses the problem of Adam's Fallacy directly in his magnificently conceived (if insufficiently edited) *Capitalism, Social-*

ism, and Democracy. Like Keynes (and Marx in some humors), Schumpeter thinks that capitalism will work itself out of its historical job. As material levels of well-being rise and productive power becomes available to provide a high standard of living to everyone, people will turn away from Adam's Fallacy and institute some type of rational socialism in place of the creative anarchy of the market. Thus Schumpeter saw the ideological tide that horrified Hayek, but saw it as an irresistible historical tendency which would succeed in strangling innovative capitalism.

Veblen could have taught Schumpeter a thing or two, however. The retail mall is a powerful capitalist immune response to collectivism. Schumpeter's prophecy goes far to illuminate the metabolism of twenty-first-century capitalism, especially when it is supplemented by Veblen's social psychology. The glittering prospect of new technological adventures, creating new frontiers of conspicuous consumption, can do a lot to divert people's attention from inequality, poverty, and the social disruption that capitalism wreaks on a world scale. Adam's Fallacy takes a material form in the marriage of high technology and consumer exhibitionism.

6/Grand Illusions

It would be gratifying to end a book of this kind with a convincing synthesis pointing the way to a better future for us all. The reader may also, by this time, perhaps be wondering what I myself think about these weighty issues. But my own personal journey through the thickets of political economy leaves me suspicious of syntheses, and reluctant to pronounce on one side or the other of large issues. All sides in these debates have important lessons to teach about the logic and limited functionality of the social world that capitalism has created.

As Deirdre McCloskey has pointed out, political economy is a kind of rhetoric, which in turn is a kind of persuasion. The great economists all have motives for presenting issues in a way that favors specific beliefs and commitments. The only antidote to this potent rhetoric is an understanding of the arguments being made and their limits, and also an awareness of the many plausible ways to look at the complexity of capitalist social relations and the moral ambiguities they engender. In the end, morality comes down to specific, individual life choices, not systems or institutions. If this book offers the reader some tools and insights in confronting this complex world, I will be content.

Looking in the Mirror

Political economy (and its contemporary descendant, economics) speaks to two types of questions. At one level, political economists offer an account of the logic behind the perplexing phenomena of market capitalism: What are prices? What determines them? Where does wealth come from? What happens to the workers whose jobs are destroyed by technological change or foreign competition? What is money? How does the banking and financial system work? Why is the capitalist system prone to crises and booms? How does the system distribute the wealth it creates? Why is poverty such a stubbornly persistent phenomenon? At another level, however, political economists grapple with the question of how we *feel* about capitalist society: Is capital accumulation a good or a bad thing? Are markets a morally acceptable method of deciding what is produced and who gets access to it? How should we regard the market's verdicts of success and failure on our efforts? How much should we be willing to adapt our ambitions and personalities to the requirements of the system? At this level, political economy addresses the problem of our looking in the mirror to see and judge ourselves.

Economists are aware that the intertwining of these two levels of discussion creates a problem. If some part of Smith's analysis of the workings of capitalism (Say's Law, for instance) is flawed, how much does that impugn his rosy view of the pursuit of self-interest through the market as public benefaction? To what degree does the marginalist economists' fixation on the supposedly "scientific" concept of economic efficiency reflect their anxiety to rationalize the outcomes of market capitalism? Discomfort with this situation has prompted some economists to propose a separation between "positive economics," which purports to contain the generally valid findings of economic analysis, from "normative economics," which explicitly expresses value judgments and goals. Similar distinctions between "value-free" scientific analysis of economic problems (what will happen to the interest rate if the central bank restricts the supply of bank reserves?) and "policy analysis" (just what should monetary policy be doing right at this moment, and how much should it pursue price stability or high employment?) address the same issues.

One conclusion I have drawn from surveying the high peaks of political economy is that this attempt to separate the two levels of political economy is futile. The attitudes promulgated by the great political economists toward capitalism and its social logic cannot plausibly be separated from their analysis of its workings. What Schumpeter called a "vision" of the economy, which must include value judgments, is required for us to think about the economy as a system, and about the regularities of the behavior of individuals operating in that system. It is in the nature of human life that all visions are ambivalent, as well. Each of the visions recapitulated in this book struggles to reconcile positive and negative aspects of capitalist society in some coherent framework.

This effort parallels the great problems of religious theology, which strive to reconcile the bad things that happen in human life with the omnipotence and omniscience of God. At their core, theologies address the problem of evil and why God doesn't do something about it. Political economy grapples with the question of how a social and historical process as creative, fruitful, and intriguing as capitalism can give rise to so many stubborn and ugly problems (and what we might do about these problems, if anything).

Two-Armed Economists

Smith sees human society as a reflection of human character (or *mores*), and he subsumes economic institutions in this general perspective. We create the market as a reflection of our characteristic propensity to "truck and barter." Upper-class prejudices of the eighteenth century viewed commercial employments with suspicion and distaste: the gentlemanly life had its material base in rents, not profits, and its social influence in politics, not entrepreneurship. Smith's economic theology, however, elevates and celebrates commerce and industry; it explicitly endorses the moral views engendered by engagement in commerce and industry. From there, it is only a small step to the view that the material abundance of capitalist society is the direct result of its *mores,* rather than the fruits of ingenuity and hard work.

Adam Smith had the genius to put the positive side of the case for capitalism up front in his account of the virtuous spiral linking the division of labor, labor productivity, and the extent of the market. This vision holds out the promise of a cornucopia of material wealth latent in the antagonisms of the market. So far so good—but, as Smith continues, this bright vision is qualified and complicated. The market rests on property rights, particularly the right to dispose of property freely, which can only be secured by a strong state. Smith, enunciating the classically liberal vision, would like this state to be strong but limited in its power, or at least in its use of its power, so as not to suffocate the spontaneous energies of capital accumulation. But this strong state, in turn, requires a navy (at least if it is located on an island), and the maintenance of that navy requires numerous compromises with the pure principles of laissez-faire and spontaneous accumulation. Smith has artfully presented this picture to his readers to make one moment of the social process he describes (capital accumulation) appear primary, and the other moment (the organization of a strong state) a necessary compromise. But historically, the British state and British capitalism grew up together. In the end, Smith puts almost as much emphasis on the need for external political institutions to channel, shape, and control the potential excesses of capital accumulation as he does on the virtuous spiral itself.

The human degradation that accompanied the early phases of British industrialization and urbanization triggered a powerful backlash among the rapidly expanding middle classes. The figure of the realistic English radical (as often as not female), determined to do something about the suffering of the actual producers of wealth and unwilling to temporize, transformed politics. Malthus, a conservative by temperament, looked for a way of explaining, if not rationalizing, the suffering of the English workers. His theory of population is a striking example of blaming the victim by arguing that the procreative excess of the workers is at the root of the problem of poverty. He sought to reconcile even the most militant of social improvers to the inevitability of suffering. But along with his demographic fatalism, Malthus did argue for specific measures to ameliorate the pressures of capital accumulation on the poor. He was not enthusiastic about the decline of the landed gentry, who in his view provided both employment and a rudimentary social safety net for rural workers. Still, there is nothing in Malthus to suggest that we should actually try to halt or significantly slow industrialization and capital accumulation.

The politics of Ricardo's age confronted a British ruling elite that arose from and represented a traditional landed aristocracy with the unwelcome but unavoidable imperatives of the new capitalist age. These pressures came to an immediate head in the cataclysm of the Napoleonic wars. After the defeat of the Corsican emperor, Britain faced a long and unpleasant agenda of unfinished political business needed to adapt its eighteenth-century system to industrial capitalism: questions of political reform, educational reform, labor standards, and trade and monetary policy. Ricardo masterfully played on the insecurity of the politicians of his time. They had no real interest in modernizing British society, but feared that a failure to accommodate industrial capitalism could put their power and prestige at risk. Ricardo's capitalism is a fragile, self-limiting phenomenon, which needs infusions of technical change and the strong medicine of free trade to prolong its existence. Capital accumulation in Ricardo's vision will do nothing much in the long run for society as a whole, but in the background of his discourse is its indispensable role in providing the material basis for British dominance in world affairs. In the course of building this vision, Ricardo paints as stark a picture of a class-divided society and its antagonisms as one can imagine.

Marx expresses his ambivalence toward capitalism in his account of its history. On the one hand, capitalism is historically limited; whatever is bad about it will eventually be transcended by the emergence of another mode of production. On the other hand, capitalism has a positive historical mission, to develop the forces of production to the point where a civilized and truly human socialism and communism are possible. Thus whatever is bad about capitalism is the price of something good—its opening up of human developmental potential. These dual moral attitudes toward capitalism form the main structure of *The Communist Manifesto,* which presents itself as both a celebration of capitalism (for its role in dooming the feudal remnants of the *ancien régime*) and an indictment of capitalism (for the original sin of class exploitation). Marx's unresolved attitude toward capitalism found its historical expression in the Menshevik argument that socialists should support the development of capitalism in Russia as the quickest route toward communism.

A similar confusing dualism is apparent in Marx's morality. No reader of Marx can come away without an overwhelming sense of the almost Old Testament moral fervor of his writing. His contempt for the bourgeoisie—their hypocrisy, their complacent fattening from the exploitation of workers, their ruthless willingness to commit any crime against the weak in pursuit of wealth, the ultimate emptiness of their culture—burns itself into the reader's mind. But Marx's historical materialism also constitutes a theory of morality as the world-view of the ruling class in any epoch, and therefore morality is subject to complete change with a change in the mode of production. Slavery, which is sanctioned by religion in slave-holding societies, becomes anathema with the emergence of a free capitalist market in labor. Lending at interest, the mortal sin of usury when feudal lords governed Europe, becomes the virtue of financial enterprise with the emergence of industrial capitalism. Rights—such as rights to access common lands for grazing, firewood, and forage—are also subject to complete redefinition when capitalism expresses its need for private ownership of land through enclosures. Where, then, can the firm ground for Marx's moral condemnation of capitalism be found?

I have argued that Marx's ambivalence toward capitalism goes even deeper and infects his very sense of what socialist society might be. The historical materialist theory of class and exploitation projects capitalist social relations historically onto past societies to rediscover the exploitation at the heart of capitalism. Marx's vision of socialism in turn recapitulates the functional form of capitalism. The socialist society must perform all of the economic functions of capitalism, including exploitation (the appropriation of some part of the social product for social ends), accumulation (investment of surplus in expanded production), and distribution according to laws (for example, distribution according to labor effort)—all of which are recognizably capitalist principles. Marx is not the first or last passionate intellect to find the study of capitalist society seducing the imagination into an obsession with capitalist categories of thought.

Marginalist (and neoclassical) economics expresses a deep distaste for the commercial values of bourgeois capitalism, and hopes to find its critical perspective in social engineering. Capitalism is flawed, but it can be fixed, once we understand the inner logic of the market and learn to tinker effectively with it. The extremes of neoclassical attitudes run from the advocates of market socialism like Oskar Lange and Abba Lerner, who propose the wholesale rebuilding of capitalism and markets through conscious state intervention, to the policy skepticism of Milton Friedman, who prefers to let whatever problems capitalism develops work themselves out without recourse to political intervention. Thus we see that from the neoclassical point of view, the politics of regulation and deregulation are in substance the same, centered on the redistribution of economic surplus among sectors of the economy. In its sophisticated form, neoclassical economics finesses the question of morality through a version of pragmatism: capitalist institutions are the ones we have inherited from the past, and we should make the best of them. This is a congenial point of view to a capitalism which itself always outgrows its previous institutional forms. With enough practice, the questions of the ultimate purpose of economic activity and the historical dynamics of capitalist development—its effects on people, communities, and culture—become invisible and incomprehensible. All there is, for the neoclassicists, and all there will ever be, is the reshuffling of economic surpluses, whether through the market or through taxes or regulation.

At first glance, it seems hard to accuse Veblen of much ambivalence about capitalist society: he doesn't like or respect it much. Still, capitalism exists, and the side of Veblen's character that saw himself as a detached scientific observer of the peculiar quirks of human societies is drawn to capitalism as a dynamic evolutionary spectacle. Capitalism is a vehicle for the instinct of workmanship, which Veblen does respect, even if its frivolous aesthetics also include the excesses of conspicuous consumption and pecuniary waste. Veblen is less concerned than most political economists to criticize, change, or cheer on capitalist development. As an evolutionary scientist, he has no real hope of intervening in the process he studies. This ends up as a kind of passive acceptance of the actual course of capitalist development, despite the tart tone of Veblen's sociological critique.

Keynes's ambivalence toward capitalism partakes strongly of the neoclassical tradition. In his view capitalism, especially in its benighted Victorian guise, is hopelessly flawed, and if left to its own devices would perish in the twentieth century from wrong-headed financial and fiscal policies. It needs the discretionary and imaginative intervention of technicians of genius (people like Keynes himself, in fact) to set straight the macroeconomic framework in which capitalism can continue to deliver its material benefits. Keynes's view is a modified and conditional form of Adam's Fallacy, emphasizing the extreme improbability that laissez-faire will find its way to a viable path of development without constant guidance. Keynes also uses the argument of historical boundedness to take some of the curse off the capitalist present when he holds out the prospect of a society of abundance and zero profitability in a few generations.

While there is no doubt about Hayek's unwavering loyalty to the ideology and practice of capitalism, it turns out that his vision also has an element of ambivalence. The problem for Hayek is that actually existing capitalism has always been an imperfect approximation to the ideal process of spontaneous emergence of social order which he so extravagantly admires. In other words, capitalism has never been capitalist enough to realize its existential promise for humanity. As a result, Hayek's capitalism is fragile and permanently besieged by the unenlightened armies of collectivism.

Hayek invokes history, too, in a curious way. The bad times of the 1930s and 1940s which inspired his own seminal work must have degenerated from a more robustly individualist capitalist society of the past. (Nothing is more settled in human thought than the idea that the unhappy present is a degenerated version of a more glorious past.) But when we look closely into the matter, it is very difficult to find just when and for how long an undiluted and pure capitalism actually worked its spontaneous magic. Industrial capitalism had only a dozen decades of life before the 1930s, decades during which its form changed with dizzying rapidity. This ambivalence lends an element of permanent revolutionary dissatisfaction to Hayek's rhetorically conservative economics. No institutional compromise that any society can reach with the forces of the market and capital accumulation will satisfy Hayek. Is the substance of this "conservative" revolution really the restoration of a past golden age of unfettered economic spontaneity, or does it conceal a more restless and ambitious agenda of the constant overturning of all social ties in the name of the market?

Schumpeter's ambivalence is in the ancient European tradition of negative criticism celebrated by Hegel. The only part of capitalism Schumpeter seems to have much enthusiasm for is its restless search for, discovery of, and deployment of new technologies. For Schumpeter the recognition of the immense costs of maintaining this process, in terms of social disruption, loss of community, unemployment, and inequality, is almost a cliché. Schumpeter has the imaginative breadth of vision to see how oppressive capitalism is for those who find themselves at the bottom of the heap, and how helpless capitalism is to avoid empowering precisely those social forces that are its enemies. Schumpeter's vision is darker than Marx's, weighed down by more decades of historical experience.

In reviving the most potent of Marx's themes, Schumpeter escapes some of the pitfalls of Adam's Fallacy. Both Marx and Schumpeter understood the great increases in the productive power of human labor as the result of concrete, cumulative advances and discoveries in technology and science. In the last three hundred years, these advances have taken place in the context of capitalist accumulation, and the mode by which they have spread through society has been the pursuit of profit by individual entrepreneurs and capitalists. But it is a mistake to identify the process of technical innovation and improvement in productivity with the social relations of capitalism and the antagonistic laws of the market. These views lead Schumpeter, wandering near the path that Marx blazed, to see a historical limit to the dominance of capitalism as the mode of organization of production and social life. Schumpeter sees the evolution of a democratically governed, perhaps benign, bureaucratic organization of production—a softer, though no more specific, version of Marx's revolutionary socialist vision.

But Schumpeter cannot (nor can even Marx) completely transcend the presumptions underlying Adam's Fallacy. Schumpeter cannot convincingly imagine an innovative society without the capitalist entrepreneur, any more than Marx can imagine civilization without some form of accumulation.

Escaping Adam's Fallacy

Dispensing with the illusory comforts of Adam's Fallacy lets us see some hard truths about our contemporary globalizing world that are obscured by received economic opinion. This reexamination has to start, however, with a recognition that not everything in the economist's way of thinking is fallacious.

Contemporary industrial capitalism is a successful system for the creation of material wealth. It shows no real signs of running out of cheap labor, natural resources, or new technological ideas. Large areas of the world and their people will very likely follow the path blazed by Western Europe, North America, and Japan, a path of industrialization, urbanization, and movement from low-productivity traditional agricultural employment to higher-productivity industrial and post-industrial production. Industrial capitalism is resilient and adaptive. The population explosion unleashed by improvements in childhood nutrition and basic medical care has been controlled by the forces of the demographic transition. Global industrial capitalism faces serious problems in its use of natural resources and its impact on the environment, but it is already mobilizing to use regulation and its own market logic to mitigate these impacts and avoid an environmental catastrophe.

Adam's Fallacy, however, distorts our understanding of this process in several ways. The most fundamental aspect of the fallacy is to represent capital accumulation, with its accompanying technical and social revolutions, as an autonomous and spontaneous process that is somehow inherent in the expression of "human nature." The history of capitalism and the history of political economy, on the other hand, underline how difficult it is for societies to evolve viable and sustainable institutions of capitalism and how fragile and contingent these institutions are. We have seen that the establishment of viable and stable institutions of capitalist growth requires political initiative, resourcefulness in adapting traditional institutions to the market, patience, persistence, and a fair helping of good luck. Viable capitalist institutions are far from being a spontaneously generated social phenomenon which will reliably take over once the dead hand of political intervention can be removed from markets. "Human nature" seems just as likely to evolve stagnant, predatory power hierarchies as it is to create a progressive capitalism.

Thus we cannot depend on the spread of capitalism by itself to solve the problems of poverty and inequality. Capital accumulation will increase material wealth, but will distribute it unevenly. Indeed, capital accumulation creates new sources of wealth and ways of life by destroying existing sources of wealth and communities. Capital accumulation by itself can continue for the foreseeable future to reproduce the divided, conflictual, poverty-ridden world we live in on a larger scale, with higher levels of technology and material wealth, but no qualitative difference in human relations.

Contrary to the exaggerated claims of Adam's Fallacy, market capitalism is not a stable, self-regulating system. Just as it requires conscious political effort to foster the institutions necessary to make it function at all, it requires continuing political and regulatory intervention to keep the pursuit of self-interest from running off the rails. This is the great theme of Keynes's economic vision, but as we have seen, it runs as a subtext through political economy from Smith to the marginalists. The quality of the debate over the form and content of this regulation can swing wildly from the creative to the banal. On the whole, historically the best results seem to have come from modest and limited efforts to build institutions such as central banks, social security, and antitrust authorities to deal with specific problems. Sweeping revolutionary changes in the system, motivated more by ideological vision than by pragmatic problem-solving, on the whole have had worse outcomes. Capital accumulation on a global scale requires the creation of new institutions of regulation and control of aggregate demand, competition, and environmental impact, as well as the constant adaptation of existing regulatory institutions to new contexts.

As we give up Adam's Fallacy, we can also give up the conceit that there are specific laws of economics parallel to natural laws. Capitalism certainly shapes people's lives and behavior in predictable ways, and gives rise to measurable regularities in economic data. But it is idle fantasy for economists to elevate these statistical phenomena into universal principles. The discoveries of the great thinkers we have surveyed in this book explain remarkably well how the regularities of market capitalism reflect human behavior in specific institutional contexts. There is no equalization of the profit rate in hunter-gatherer societies, nor systematic pursuit of cost-reducing technical innovation in feudal societies. An extended division of labor will, as neoclassical economics never tires of reminding us, both create potential economic surpluses and open up the possibility of market exchange to realize them. These phenomena, however, are not universal and inescapable expressions of "human nature" or human life itself. Human beings created these institutions, as Marx insists, and they can change them if they want to and understand them well enough.

Capital accumulation has its own logic—the discovery and exploitation of opportunities for profit in specific historical and social circumstances. The circumstances themselves are constantly changing, partly as a result of their exploitation for profit. It is only prudent for us, living with capital accumulation, to understand its logic as well as we can. That we understand it as well as we do is largely the fruit of the intellectual labors of these great thinkers and their followers. But understanding the logic of capital accumulation does not require us to surrender our moral judgment to the market, either as individuals or as political actors. The exploitation of any profit opportunity involves a range of consequences, some good and some harmful. There is no escaping the moral relevance of weighing the good and the harm in each case. The fallacy lies in thinking that there are universal principles that short-circuit this process. For example, some countries violate the laws of the market by subsidizing basic necessities like staple grains, cooking oil, and the like, in order to protect the basic standard of living of their poorest members. These subsidies are inefficient; they prevent the realization of economic surpluses and the equalization of profit rates; and they slow down capital accumulation. These side effects of the subsidies are important and have to be taken into account in forming a judgment as to their wisdom and appropriateness, but they are not by themselves enough to settle the case for or against.

Capitalism, given its control over wealth, will never lack advocates for the exploitation of even the most morally dubious of profit opportunities. One of the worst effects of Adam's Fallacy is that it risks endorsing one-sided presentations of complex situations. Whether we call this ideology or theology or just plain opportunism is of less importance than recognizing it when it is happening and resisting it.

Face to Face with Adam's Curse

In the titanic confrontation of Hayek and Keynes in the twentieth century, we come to the heart of the dilemma posed by Adam's Fallacy. Today we depend more and more on commodity production and exchange to supply our material needs; the division of labor has progressed to the point where few people could even survive on their own resources. As commodity logic penetrates more and more areas of human life, its contradictory effects become more pervasive and less escapable. The chronic "crisis" of health care in advanced capitalist societies is Adam's Fallacy in microcosm. As questions of life and death come to carry a bigger and bigger price tag, how do we reconcile our moral sympathy and solidarity with other people's suffering to the implacable logic of money and the commodity? Neither Hayek's revolutionary principled liberalism nor Keynes's expedient pragmatism is likely to provide a final resolution of these dilemmas.

The issues at the heart of Adam's Fallacy are destined to dominate world history for many decades to come. The whirlwind of capitalist economic development is spreading to every corner of the globe in one form or another, bringing its immense opportunities and its equally immense social and moral stresses. Success or failure in connecting to the world capitalist social division of labor will shape the fate of societies and individuals. Although political economy has no magical formula for resolving these issues, I think two lessons can be drawn from the history of political economy for our globalizing era.

First, moral and social conflict are part and parcel of capitalist economic development. Societies that embrace the capitalist project will transform their traditional ways of life, inevitably overturning ancient social, political, and religious compromises. The conceit that coming to terms with global capitalism is only a question of accepting these changes as inevitable is shallow and self-defeating. Societies undergoing these wrenching changes need to have their problems acknowledged and addressed concretely. They do not benefit from vague sermons on the power of capitalist development to raise masses of people from traditional poverty—sermons which at best tell only half the story.

Second, the history of Adam's Fallacy shows clearly the diversity of the actual pathways that developed capitalist economies have taken to reach their current stages of development. There are no unique paths to capitalist development, no magic formulas to hasten the arrival of its uneven prosperity or to alleviate the accompanying social ills. In their dubious efforts to create a "world order" in which capitalism can operate on a global scale, developed capitalist societies often wind up closing off rather than opening up paths for poorer societies. Once we recognize how problematic and traumatic capitalist economic development can be, we would be well-advised to encourage each society to find its own path through the dilemmas of Adam's Fallacy. Every society has made its particular compromises with the supposed laws of the market, and for good reasons. In the end, as I hope this book shows, the material wealth of capitalism arises from human ingenuity, industry, and effort, not magically from a virtuous adherence to the laws of the market.

In confronting these historical challenges, we have as a resource the considerable body of knowledge which the great political economists have created. This knowledge is value-laden, theological as much as scientific, and full of unresolved ambivalence, but it is knowledge. A critical and skeptical understanding of political economy shows us how deeply the intractable problems of modern society are bound up with the promise of material abundance unlocked by industrial capitalism. Political economy seen in this way will not provide easy (or indeed hard) solutions to these difficult problems. It can, however, illuminate the complex issues we need to think about and clear away the cobwebs of uncritically accepted simplifications.

Reading Further

Appendix

Index

Reading Further

I f reading about the great political economists has stirred your curiosity about what they have to say or their lives and characters (or suspicions about the fidelity of my interpretations to their thought), you will want to go on to read their own works, biographies, and works about political economy. While some of the issues they raise have spawned technical and even esoteric literatures of elaboration and critique, much of this writing requires no formal economic or mathematical training.

Adam Smith is easy to read even if hard to make consistent sense of. The standard edition of *The Wealth of Nations* is edited by Edwin Cannan and published by the University of Chicago Press, but there are numerous good alternatives. Bruce Mazlish has edited a useful abridged version, published by Dover, and there are several combined abridged versions with commentaries, such as Laurance Dickey's (published by Hackett). The great weakness in the enormous range of later critical studies of Smith's work is the temptation to read back into Smith later versions of Adam's Fallacy, particularly the formulations of marginalist and neoclassical economics, of which there is no sign that Smith had the slightest inkling.

Thomas Malthus's *Essay on the Principle of Population* is equally famous and equally often republished. It is helpful to have an edition that distinguishes the original pamphlet from its later revision. As the discussion of Malthus in this book indicates, I find it most interesting to read Malthus in the context of the ideological and political debates set off by the French Revolution, as in John Avery's *Progress, Poverty, and Population: Re-Reading Condorcet, Godwin, and Malthus* (Taylor and Francis).

The centerpiece of David Ricardo's work is his *Principles of Political Economy and Taxation,* available in many well-edited and inexpensive editions. Ricardo is a powerful thinker and writer, but not always easy reading because of the abstraction and rigor of his thought.

Biographies of Smith, Malthus, and Ricardo tend to take the form of shorter biographical essays. Robert Heilbroner's *The Worldly Philosophers: The Lives, Times, and Ideas of the Great Economic Thinkers* is an irresistible starting point. Karl Polanyi's *The Great Transformation: The Political and Economic Origins of Our Time* is an excellent summary of the broad historical context in which classical political economy developed.

Karl Marx wrote millions of words, but managed to prepare only a small fraction of his output for publication. *The Communist Manifesto* (available in innumerable editions) retains its power and impact after a century and a half, and uncompromisingly states Marx's basic position. It seems logical to approach Marx by reading *Capital,* of which only Volume I was actually published by Marx himself, the other two volumes being compilations by Friedrich Engels of Marx's unpublished notebooks. (Ben Fowkes's translation, published by Penguin, has become a standard for English-speaking readers.) The first three chapters of Volume I of *Capital* present notoriously difficult problems of interpretation and understanding, and it is not a bad idea to skip them on a first reading to get a sense of Marx's overall vision. Much of the material in the first three chapters of Volume I of *Capital* is explained more completely in *Contribution to the Critique of Political Economy* (International Publishers), edited beautifully by Maurice Dobb. This edition also includes the important methodological Preface that Marx omitted from the original publication. Unfortunately, Marx changed some of the technical terminology between these two versions of his ideas. Behind *Capital* lies the *Grundrisse* (Penguin), extensive notebooks that Marx wrote to clarify his own thinking on political economy. If you have the time and inclination, the *Grundrisse* puts Marx's later thought in a very helpful and useful perspective.

I am reluctant to recommend biographies of Marx. There are plenty of them, and they all tell the same basic outlines of Marx's life. What makes me wary of recommending one is that Marx became even in his own lifetime a powerful political and ideological symbol for both his supporters and his opponents, and biographers have had great difficulty escaping from positive or negative prejudice about Marx to put him and his work in perspective. Marx's language (and in some ways his thought) reflects what now looks like racist and sexist (and European) presumptions of his era, which adds yet another explosive layer of interpretive demands on biography. It might be better to approach Marx through the people around him, such as Engels and Marx's daughter Eleanor. Steven Marcus's *Engels, Manchester, and the Working Class* (Norton) paints a vivid picture of the social upheaval from which Marx and Engels' passionate political economy evolved.

The creators of marginalist and neoclassical economics wrote clearly (many had at least partial training as mathematicians), but it is hard to recommend their work as reading except for those with a professional interest in the history of economics. John Bates Clark's *Distri-*

bution of Wealth: A Theory of Wages, Interest, and Profits (University Press of the Pacific) conveys the flavor of their mixture of analytical logic and dogmatic ideology as well as any of their works. The interesting story behind this movement is its relation to other contemporary social, political, and scientific intellectual developments. Philip Mirowski's controversial More Heat than Light: Economics as Social Physics, Physics as Nature's Economics (Cambridge University Press) opens up these issues brilliantly.

The pleasures of reading Thorstein Veblen have not diminished with the passage of time. His Theory of the Leisure Class (Dover) was the unexpected hit of a first-year seminar I taught a few years ago. Veblen invents a character (himself as a somewhat dyspeptic but "objective" social observer) whose stately scientific prose hits his targets with hilarious precision. Another favorite of my own is The Higher Learning in America: A Memorandum (Kessinger). Veblen's collection of critical essays on economic and sociological research in his life, The Place of Science in Modern Civilization and Other Essays (Transaction), is an invaluable resource to put what later became unquestioned social science doctrine in the perspective of its origins. There are many biographies of Veblen, starting with Joseph Dorfman's Thorstein Veblen and His America (Kelley), which survey Veblen's fascinating and troubled relation to American society and its universities.

John Maynard Keynes's most influential book, The General Theory of Employment, Interest, and Money (Harcourt), despite many brilliant and frequently quoted passages, is hard going. Keynes had his vision straight enough, but he worked in a hurried fashion with a number of assistants to complete the book, which as a consequence has many technical and logical loose ends. It is much easier to approach Keynes's world-view through his essays, particularly Essays in Persuasion (Norton). Keynes's life provides surprising meat for biographers. Donald Moggridge's Maynard Keynes: An Economist's Biog-

raphy (Taylor and Francis) and Robert Skidelsky's three-volume *John Maynard Keynes* (Penguin) are absorbing accounts.

Friedrich von Hayek's works are widely available. I think his thought is best presented in his essays, *Individualism and Economic Order* (University of Chicago Press). The critical and even revolutionary threads of Hayek's thinking can be followed clearly in these writings without too much rhetorical overlay.

Probably the best approach to Joseph Schumpeter's work is *Capitalism, Socialism, and Democracy* (HarperCollins). This massive work is unfortunately uneven and unevenly edited, with passages of insight and brilliance interspersed with repetitive rehearsals of familiar ideas. Schumpeter himself wrote a *History of Economic Analysis* (Oxford University Press) which displays wide reading and deep learning, but in the service of an idiosyncratic interpretation of the development of economics as a science.

Appendix

Demographic Equilibrium

(See pp. 52–53 and 56–59.)

Malthus did not put his argument in terms of graphs (or even, despite its mathematical character, in terms of equations), but it is enlightening for us to do this exercise.

In Figure A1, the horizontal axis measures the "real wage"—basically, the amount of food a worker could put on the table. The vertical axis measures both the fertility rate and the mortality rate (the number of births and deaths per thousand living people). Malthus's proposed laws of population and food supply can be summarized on this graph by a fertility schedule showing the fertility rate associated with each level of the standard of living, and a mortality schedule showing the mortality rate associated with each level of the standard of living.

The fertility schedule in the graph is shown as sloping gradually

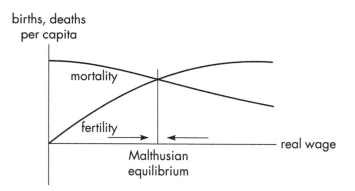

Figure A1. Malthus's model of population links fertility and mortality rates on the vertical axis to the standard of living, measured by the real wage on the horizontal axis. The fertility schedule shows fertility rising slowly with the standard of living. The mortality schedule shows mortality, particularly infant mortality, dropping sharply as the real wage rises. The intersection of the two curves establishes the natural wage rate, at which the population stabilizes. This equilibrium is stable if there are diminishing returns to employment due to limited land resources, because a rise in the real wage will set in motion a population increase that will force real wages back down.

upward, to reflect the impact of higher real wages in earlier marriage and better prenatal maternal nutrition. The mortality schedule starts at a high level, and then declines sharply around the equilibrium level of the real wage. This shape is intended to express Malthus's idea that infant mortality becomes very sensitive to the real wage at some low level. This subsistence real wage is not determined purely biologically, but in part culturally and socially: it represents the level of the standard of living at which normal reproduction starts to decline in a given society and time.

The point at which the fertility schedule intersects the mortality schedule is an equilibrium, where the population will be stationary, with deaths just equaling births. This equilibrium, on Malthus's as-

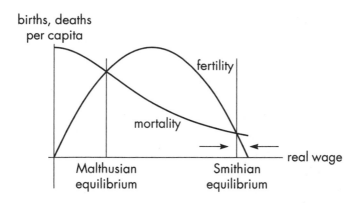

Figure A2. The demographic transition experienced by industrializing economies can be seen in an extension of Malthus's model through a fertility schedule that first rises and then falls as the real wage rises. This reveals two equilibria, one at a low real wage with high mortality and fertility rates, the *Malthusian equilibrium,* and the other at a high real wage with low mortality and fertility rates, the *Smithian equilibrium.* The Smithian equilibrium is stable if there are increasing returns to population due to the division of labor.

sumption of diminishing returns to population given land availability, is stable, because the increase in population that occurs when the death rate falls below the birth rate will tend to raise food prices and lower the real wage. (Over a longer period, the increased population also increases the supply of labor, which will tend to lower the wage rate.) Symmetrically, the rise in infant mortality that occurs as the real wage falls below the equilibrium level will relieve the pressure on food supplies, lower food prices, and allow the real wage to rise.

If we draw the graphs representing Malthus's model on a larger scale, we can see the theoretical significance of the demographic transition, as in Figure A2. This figure shows the possibility that there might be *another* equilibrium in Malthus's model. The first occurs at a low real wage, with high mortality and fertility rates. This is the equilibrium that Malthus described. The Malthusian equilibrium is stable if the wage declines with increasing population due to diminishing returns. But there could be another equilibrium at a high real wage with a low mortality rate matched by a low fertility rate. This Smithian equilibrium is stable if the wage *increases* with increasing population due to the effect of the division of labor. Many economically developed countries in the world give signs of approaching this latter equilibrium.

Theories of Money and Prices

Ricardo's Quantity-of-Money Theory of Prices

(See pp. 66–68.)

The gold prices of commodities, measured by a price index P, and the volume of commodities in a country being sold in a year, measured by a quantity index Q, determine the *value of total circulation* in a year, PQ. The *stock* of gold money necessary to accomplish this circulation, G, depends on the number of times each piece of gold can participate in a transaction in a year, which is called the *velocity of money*, V. In a monetary economy, these two values have to be equal. In modern economics this relation is called the *equation of exchange*, which we can write in the form:

$$P = \frac{GV}{Q}$$

In Ricardo's quantity-of-money theory of prices, the equation of exchange determines the gold prices of commodities, P, on the basis of the quantity of gold circulating in the economy, G, the quantity of commodities circulated, Q, and the velocity of money, V. If the quantity of gold increases, holding velocity and the quantity of commodities circulated constant, gold prices of commodities will rise. Monetarist economists in the twentieth century adopted Ricardo's quantity-of-money theory of prices to argue that price inflation or deflation depends only on the quantity of money in a country, and can always be controlled by controlling the growth of the quantity of money.

Marx's Price Theory of the Quantity of Money

(See pp. 105–106.)

Marx analyzes the *quantity* of gold necessary to circulate the commodities in an economy on the basis of a completely different principle from his analysis of the *value* of gold. The gold prices of commodities, measured by the price index P, and the volume of commodities being circulated in a year, measured by the quantity index Q, determine the *total circulation* in a year, PQ. The *stock* of gold money necessary to accomplish this circulation, G, depends on the number of times each piece of gold can participate in a transaction in a year, the velocity of money, V. Marx's verbal exposition reproduces the equation of exchange, but in the form:

$$G = \frac{PQ}{V}$$

The stock of gold required to circulate commodities depends directly on the total circulation, PQ, and inversely on the velocity of money, V. In Marx's theory the equation of exchange determines the quantity of gold circulating in the economy on the basis of the gold prices of commodities, P, the quantity of commodities circulated, Q, and the velocity of money, V. Thus Marx's interpretation of the equation of exchange is exactly opposite to Ricardo's. For Marx, changes in the gold prices of commodities drive the quantity of gold money in circulation, not the other way around.

Ricardo's Theory of Rent and Accumulation

(See pp. 71–79.)

To help us visualize the whole agricultural economy of a country, Figure A3 arranges standard plots of land, each of which can be cul-

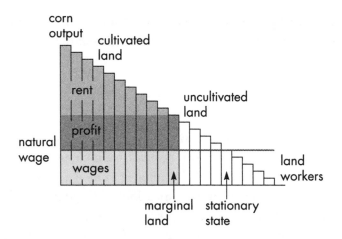

Figure A3. Ricardo's theory of distribution and accumulation. The horizontal axis measures the land in cultivation, ordered by fertility. The unit of land measure is the amount a worker can cultivate in a year, so the horizontal axis also measures agricultural population and total population. The vertical axis measures the fertility of the land. Land is cultivated in order of fertility: the output of marginal land is divided between profit and wages. Land of higher fertility commands a rent. The total rent of the economy is the area of the triangle above the output of the marginal land. Total profit is the rectangle above the natural wage. The stationary state occurs when population is so large that the marginal land in cultivation produces just enough to pay the natural wage.

tivated by one worker, along the horizontal axis in order of their fertility. Any point on the horizontal axis represents a particular small plot of land. Since each plot of land can employ one worker and a fixed "dose" of capital, the distance from the origin to a point along the horizontal axis also measures the number of agricultural workers employed on land up to a given level of fertility and the capital employed in agriculture.

In Ricardo's abstract model, the size of the industrial sector is determined by the amount of agricultural employment, since industrial workers are employed to produce the clothing, tools, furniture, and so on required by the agricultural workers (and themselves). Thus, given the patterns of technology and consumption, and the productivity of labor in the various sectors, there is a one-to-one correspondence between the size of the employed agricultural labor force and the whole population. Under this assumption the horizontal axis can also measure the total population of the country.

The vertical axis in Figure A3 measures the output of corn per plot of land. The marginal product of labor schedule shows the declining output per worker at the margin as less fertile land is brought into cultivation. It is made up of a whole lot of very thin rectangles, each representing one plot of land. The downward slope of the marginal product schedule reflects diminishing returns to labor and capital as a result of the limited availability of fertile land.

The total corn output of the country is measured by the *area* under the marginal product schedule up to the least fertile land actually cultivated (the "marginal land"), since it is just the sum of the outputs of all the land plots cultivated.

Note that this way of drawing the graph implies that output per worker *declines* as total population increases, because workers have to cultivate worse and worse land. The graph exhibits diminishing returns to employment.

In Figure A3, the level of rent on any plot of cultivated land will be the difference between the corn output of that plot and the corn output of the marginal land. The total rent is the area of the triangle formed by the marginal product schedule to the left of the marginal plot.

Ricardo's Theory of Accumulation

The total profits of the society, measured in corn, are represented in Figure A3 by the rectangle lying above the natural wage, and bounded by the extensive margin of land. If all these profits are accumulated, in the next year there will be a larger demand for labor and the population and agricultural labor force will increase, moving the extensive margin to the right in the diagram. This is the basic dynamic of capital accumulation according to Ricardo's thinking.

A little work with the diagram shows that the effect of capital accumulation is to increase the population, food output, and agricultural labor force; to increase total rents; but to lower the rate of profit as the surplus on the marginal land declines as a result of diminishing returns. The total *amount* of profit may increase in the early stages of capital accumulation, because the amount of capital is rising faster than the profit rate is declining, but eventually the amount of profit has to decline as well. If the marginal product of labor and capital—that is, the rectangles representing the fertilities of the plots of land—remains unchanged, the profit rate and the amount of profit have to approach zero.

Eventually, the rate of profit will fall to zero and accumulation will cease. Ricardo called this situation the "stationary state." As the figure shows, at the stationary state the marginal land in cultivation just produces enough corn to pay the real wage.

The reason a capitalist economy facing diminishing returns to limited land reaches a stationary state is clear from Figure A3: eventually the population becomes so large that the marginal land is just fertile enough to pay the natural wage and yields no surplus product at all, and therefore no profit. There is, of course, a very large total surplus of corn, represented by the triangle above the natural wage, but in the stationary state it all takes the form of rent, which, according to Ricardo's assumptions, will be consumed, not accumulated.

The Decomposition of the Value of Commodities

(See pp. 117–118.)
From the point of view of the labor theory of value, the money that capitalists spend for raw materials and other non-labor inputs simply returns to the capitalist unchanged when he sells the pro-

duced commodity. As a result, Marx calls the non-labor component of capital outlays "constant capital" (although a better term would have been "nonexpanding capital"), represented by the mathematical variable c. The money that capitalists lay out as wages, on the other hand, returns to them with the surplus value, represented by the mathematical variable s. Marx calls the wage component of capital outlays "variable capital" (although a more descriptive term would be "expanding capital"), represented by the letter v. $c + v$ represents the total cost of the commodity. The sales price of the commodity includes the surplus value, so that the whole value of the average commodity is $c + v + s$. The value added is just $v + s$, and represents the living labor expended to produce the commodities over a period.

Several ratios of these components play a central role in the Marxist analysis of capitalist production. The markup on costs, q, is the ratio of the surplus value to total cost:

$$q = \frac{s}{c+v}$$

Capitalists are interested in how rapidly their capital investment is expanding, which is the profit rate, r, the ratio of the surplus value, s, to the stock of capital they have invested at any moment, K.

$$r = \frac{s}{K}$$

Total costs measure the *flow* of capital into the production process over a period of time. The ratio of the stock of capital K to the flow of costs $c + v$ is called the *turnover time* of capital, T.

$$T = \frac{K}{c+v}$$

Taking account of the turnover time, we can write the profit rate as:

$$r = \frac{s}{K} = \frac{s}{c+v}\ \frac{c+v}{K} = \frac{q}{T}$$

Explicit consideration of the turnover time complicates the analysis, so that Marx and many economists working in the Marxian tradition tend to assume in examples that $T = 1$, that is, that the whole capital turns over once each production period. In this case the profit rate is just equal to the markup.

Capitalists, not perceiving that the social source of surplus value is the expenditure of labor alone, attribute their profit to their investment of capital. This perception is reinforced by the tendency for competition among capitals to equalize profit rates in different sectors of the economy, which makes it appear that profit arises from capital, not from labor. From a social point of view, Marx argues, the crucial ratio is the ratio of surplus value to the flow of variable capital, because that represents the division of the living labor time between the reproduction of the workers and the surplus value appropriated by the capitalists. He calls this the rate of surplus value, or the rate of exploitation, $e = s/v$. The markup and the profit rate also depend, however, on the proportion of the total costs represented by variable costs, which Marx represents as the ratio of constant capital to variable capital, c/v, and calls the organic composition of capital.

Thus if we want to understand the source of profits correctly from the point of view of the labor theory of value, we must decompose the markup in the following terms:

$$q = \frac{s}{c+v} = \frac{s/v}{(c/v)+1}$$

The rate of profit, in Marx's notation, is given by the expression:

$$r = \frac{q}{T} = \frac{s}{K} = \frac{\dfrac{s}{v}}{\left(\dfrac{c}{v}+1\right)T}$$

The Working Day

(See pp. 118–121.)
Marx's metaphor of the social working day (Figure A4) imagines the whole labor time of a society as a single grand working day. The la-

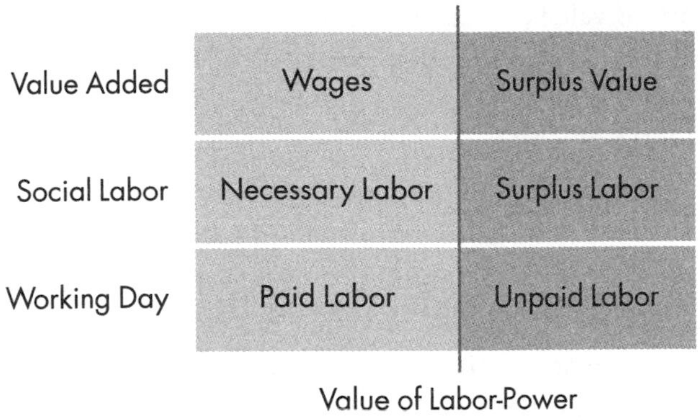

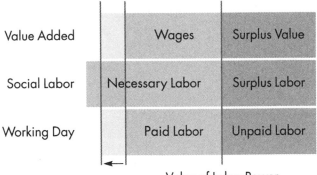

Figure A4. According to the labor theory of value, the value of labor-power divides the value added between wages and surplus value, corresponding to the division of the social labor between necessary and surplus labor and the division of the working day between paid and unpaid labor.

Figure A5. The whole social working day includes necessary labor time expended outside the wage-labor system. The transformation of necessary social labor performed outside the commodity system into wage labor extends the waged working day. This shifts the commodity frontier, and increases social waged labor time.

bor theory of value postulates that this working day is proportional to the value that labor adds to commodities. Marx here implicitly assumes that all production is exchanged through the market and takes the form of commodities.

The image of the working day represents the distribution of waged labor time, the labor performed in society as the result of the sale of labor-power as a commodity. In reality, however, social labor time includes non-waged labor time, such as housework and child care. Thus the whole social labor time is larger than the value added or the waged labor time, and the necessary labor time to reproduce society is bigger than the paid labor time of waged workers. Figure A5 shows the transformation of non-waged necessary labor time into waged necessary labor time through the movement of the commodity frontier.

Absolute and Relative Surplus Value

Marx calls the extension of the working day containing the labor

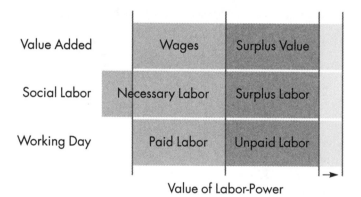

Figure A6. Absolute surplus value is the result of extending the working day without increasing the value of labor-power.

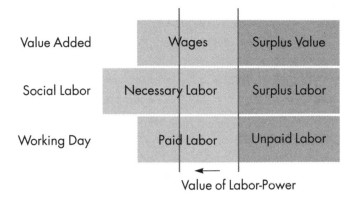

Value Added	Wages	Surplus Value
Social Labor	Necessary Labor	Surplus Labor
Working Day	Paid Labor	Unpaid Labor

Value of Labor-Power

Figure A7. Relative surplus value is the result of reducing the value of labor-power without extending the working day.

time necessary for reproduction of the workers *absolute surplus value,* which is illustrated in Figure A6.

Marx calls the reduction of the labor time necessary for reproduction of the workers through technical change *relative surplus value,* which is illustrated in Figure A7.

Index

collectivism, 208–209, 212, 221
  and complexity, 201–209
colonialism, 182
commodity, 147, 202
  theory of, 100–113
  value of, 115
commodity exchange, 170
commodity fetishism, 110–113
commodity frontier, 102–103, 145, 246–247
  extension of, 111
commodity production, 153
commodity system, moral logic of, 85
Communism, 89, 183
  Chinese, 147
  Russian, 146
communism, 132, 218
  primitive, 97
Communist commissar, 210
Communist Manifesto, The (Karl Marx and Friedrich Engels), 87, 218, 232
community, loss of, 222
comparative advantage, 62
  and quantity of money theory of prices, 66–67
  Ricardo's theory of, 64–66
competition, 19–20
  equalizes profit rates, 22–23
  and labor theory of value, 68–69
  perfect, 195–196
  regulation of, 224
competitive equilibrium, 22–23
complexity, and collectivism, 201–209
complex system, 23, 199, 207
Condition of the Working Class in England, The (Friedrich Engels), 87
conspicuous consumption, 174–177, 220
constant capital, 117, 245
consumer utility, 171
consumption, 184
consumption fund, 29

contraception, 50, 55
contradiction, 92
Contribution to the Critique of Political Economy (Karl Marx), 233
corn, 63
Corn Laws, 80
corn model, 71–79
corporate capitalism, 150
cost:
  of commodity, 117
  of goods sold, 101
  of inputs, 17
  minimization of, 164
  social and private, 171
  theory of price, 156
creative destruction, 211
credit, 41
  in Schumpeter, 211
crisis of over-production, 138
critical method, 89
Critique of the Gotha Programme, The (Karl Marx), 88, 151
Cuba, 149

Darwin, Charles, 54
debasement, 14
deduction, 155
deficit, fiscal, 198, 202
deflation, 183, 190, 241
demand, as determinant of price, 156
demand and supply, 162
demand schedule, of firm, 195
democracy, 133
demographic equilibrium, 52–53, 237–240
  at high standard of living, 58
  Malthusian, 240
  Smithian, 240
  world, 152–153
demographic transition, 56–59, 152–153, 223, 239
dependency, 145

reproduction:
  expanded, 125
  social, 92, 96, 118
reservation price, 166–167, 169
reserve army of labor, 125–127, 153
  floating, 125
  latent, 125
  stagnant, 125
reserves, of gold, 106
resource constraint, 130
resources:
  depletion of, 60, 200
  natural pricing of, 72–75
revisionist Marxism, 147
revolution:
  bourgeois, 151
  motivation for, 144
revolutionary crises, 141
revolutionary dictatorship of the proletariat, 133–140
revolutionary politics, 140
  Marx's, 135–140
revolutionary socialism, 134
revolutions, twentieth-century, 146–148
rhetoric, 213
Ricardian economics, 155
Ricardian socialists, 131, 151
Ricardo, David, 18, 27, 45, 52, 61–62,
  100, 105, 106, 107, 115, 136, 156,
  171, 200, 210, 217
  and falling profit rate, 77–78, 123
  and marginalist economics, 156
  and Say's Law, 67, 184
risk, 26
  neoclassical view of, 192
  and uncertainty, 193
Road to Serfdom, The (Friedrich von
  Hayek), 208
Robinson, Joan, 165
Roman empire, 97
ruling class, 139

Russian bourgeoisie, 146
Russian Revolution, 146

sales price, of commodity, 17, 117, 245
sales revenue, 17, 100–101
Samuelson, Paul, 165, 187
saving, 57, 70, 172, 196
  of capitalists, 76–77
  of landowners, 76–77
  as virtue in Smith, 31–32
  of workers, 76–77
Say's Law, 10–12, 37, 46, 67, 162, 197, 214
  Keynes' critique of, 184–188
scarcity, 63, 162, 173
  determining prices, 160
Schumpeter, Joseph, 180, 209–212,
  215, 222–223
Second World War, 182, 198, 208
self-development, 112
self-exploitation, of working class in
  socialism, 151
self-interest, xii, 2, 32, 43
  pursuit of, 168, 214
self-regulation, 23, 224
  of banking system, 41
self-subsistence, 103
serfs, 93, 96, 116, 150
Shelley, Mary, 47
silver, 104
skills, 64, 107
  and cost of training, 72
slavery, 93, 116
  ancient, 93, 94, 97, 98, 150
  morality of, 219
slave-trading, 85
small country, 36
Smith, Adam, xii–xiv, 1–4, 45, 58, 62,
  73, 75–78, 102, 115, 123, 136, 168,
  171, 179, 215–216
  and falling profit rate, 24–25, 123
  and saving, 30–33, 172